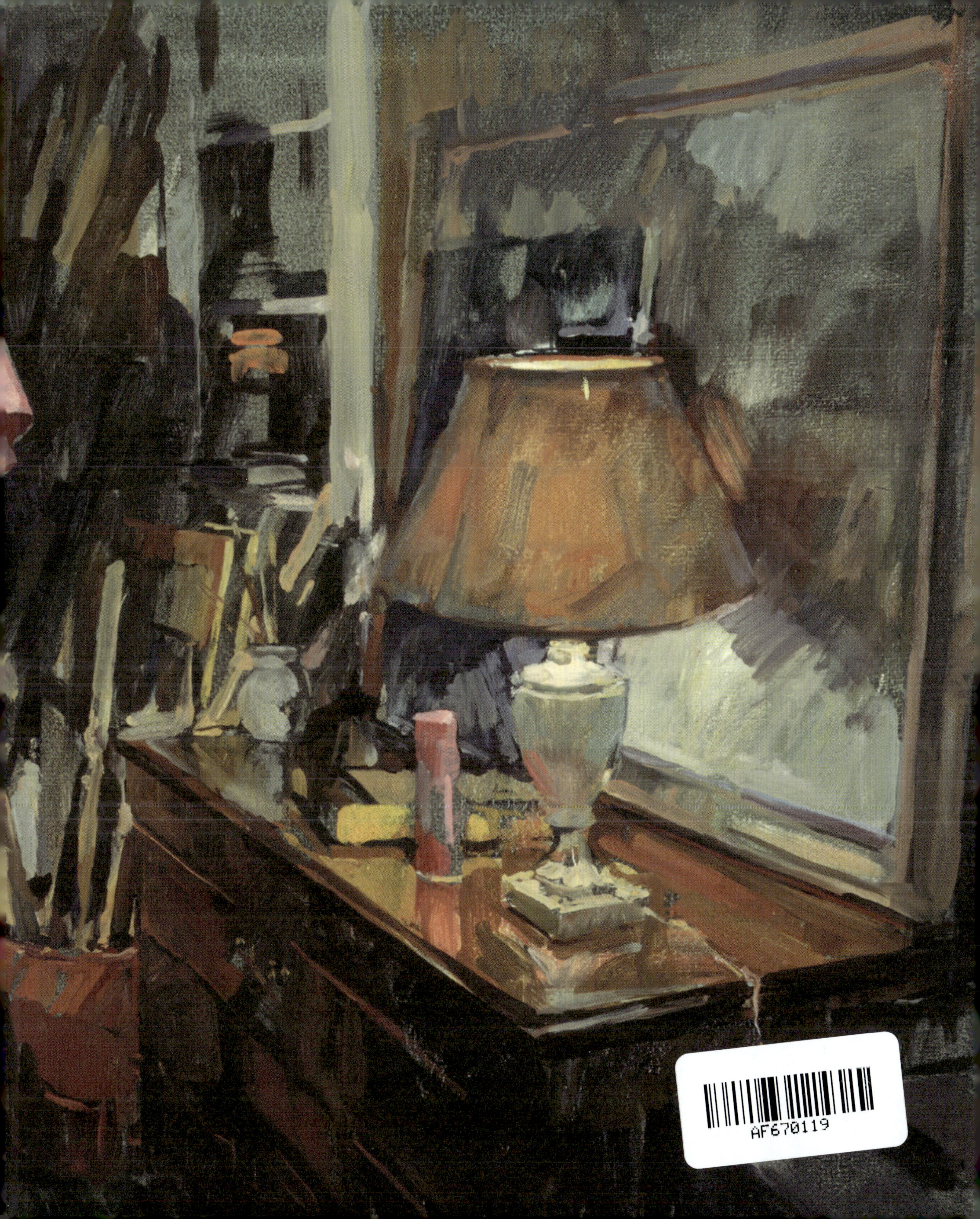

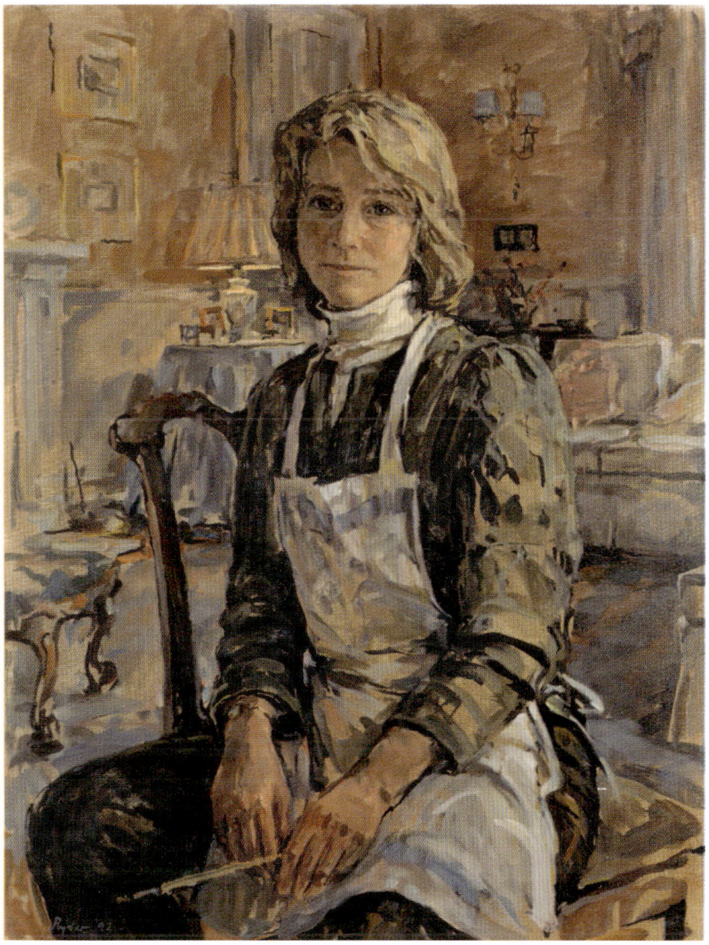

LOOKING THROUGH

THE LIFE AND WORK OF

SUSAN RYDER

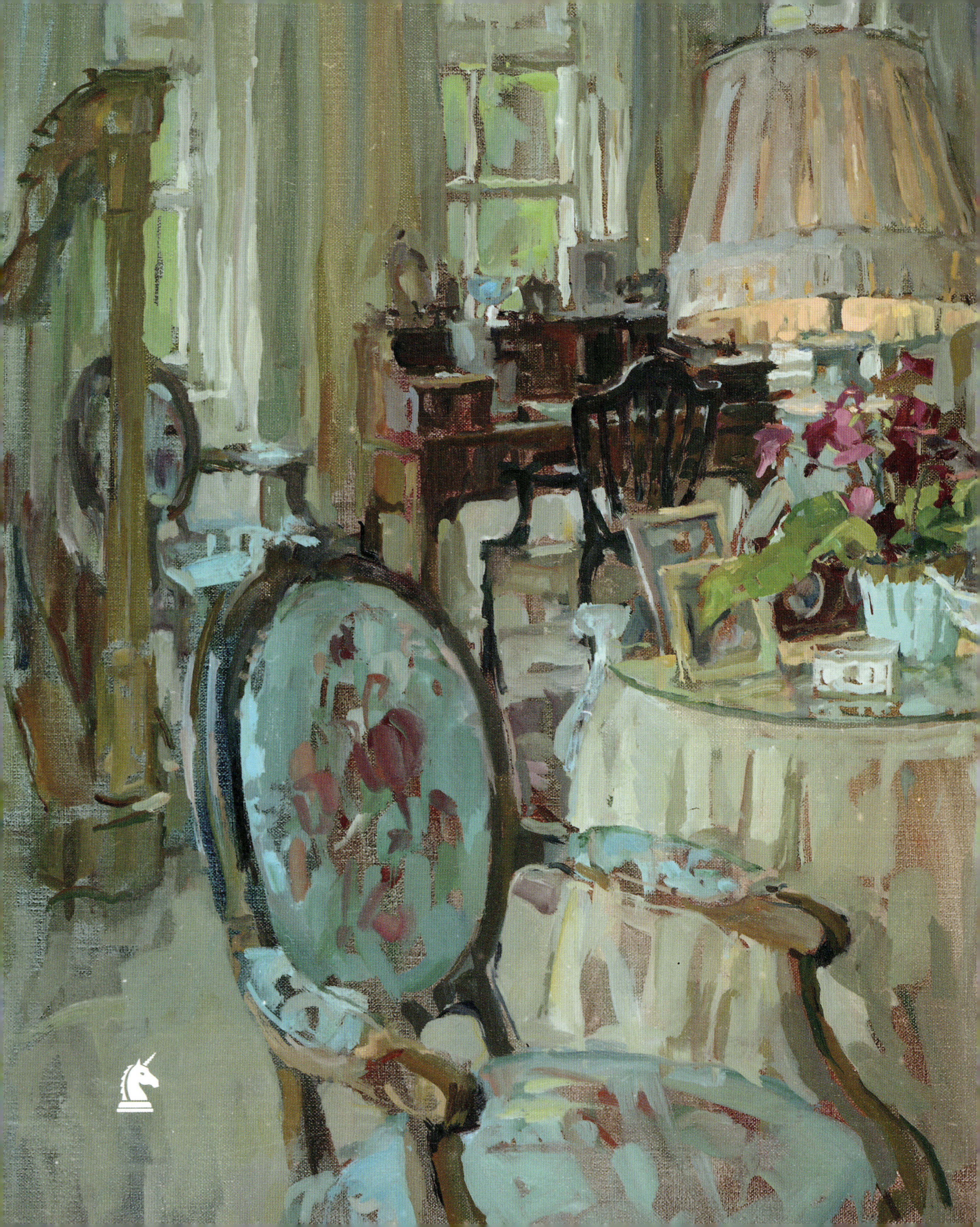

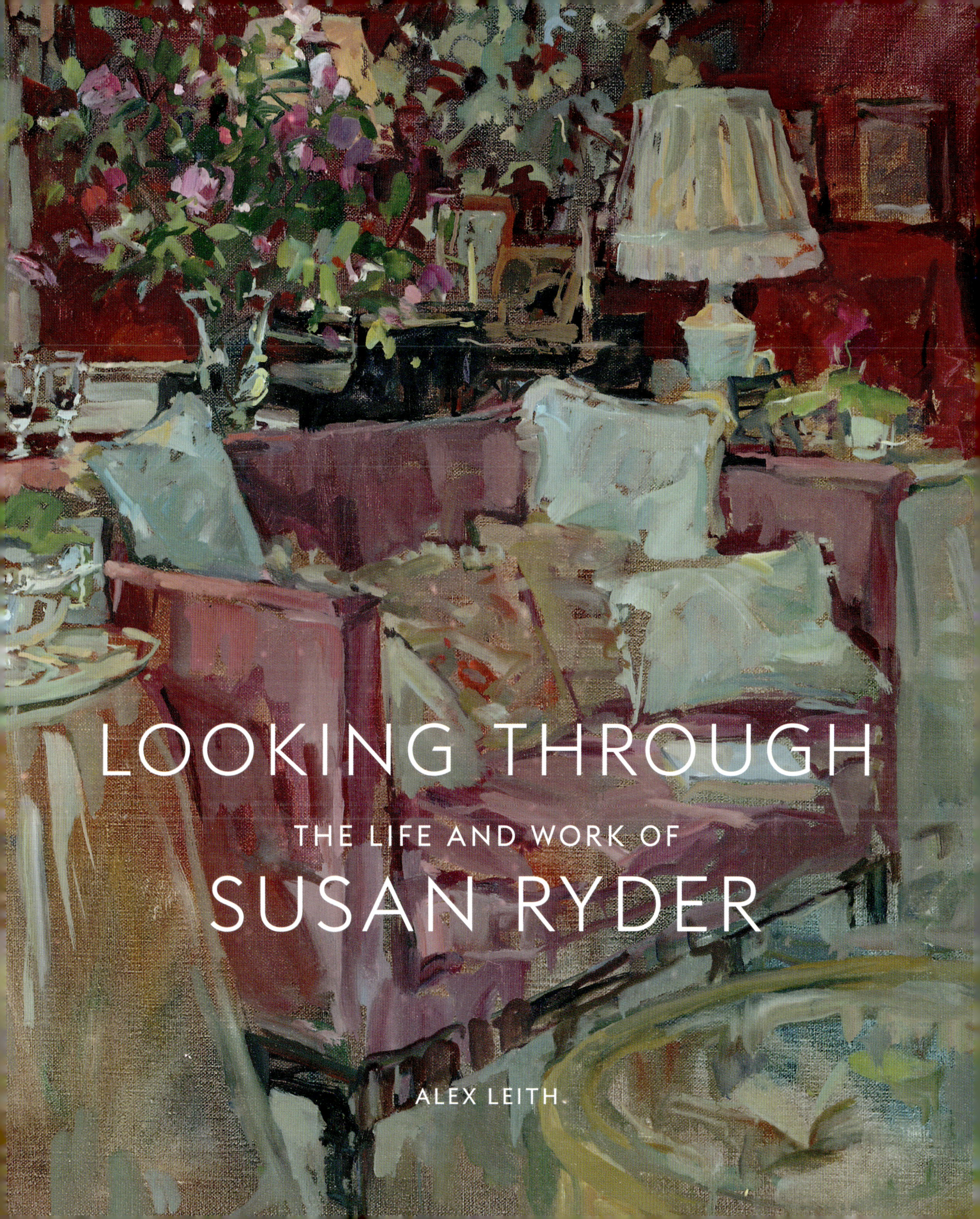

LOOKING THROUGH

THE LIFE AND WORK OF SUSAN RYDER

ALEX LEITH

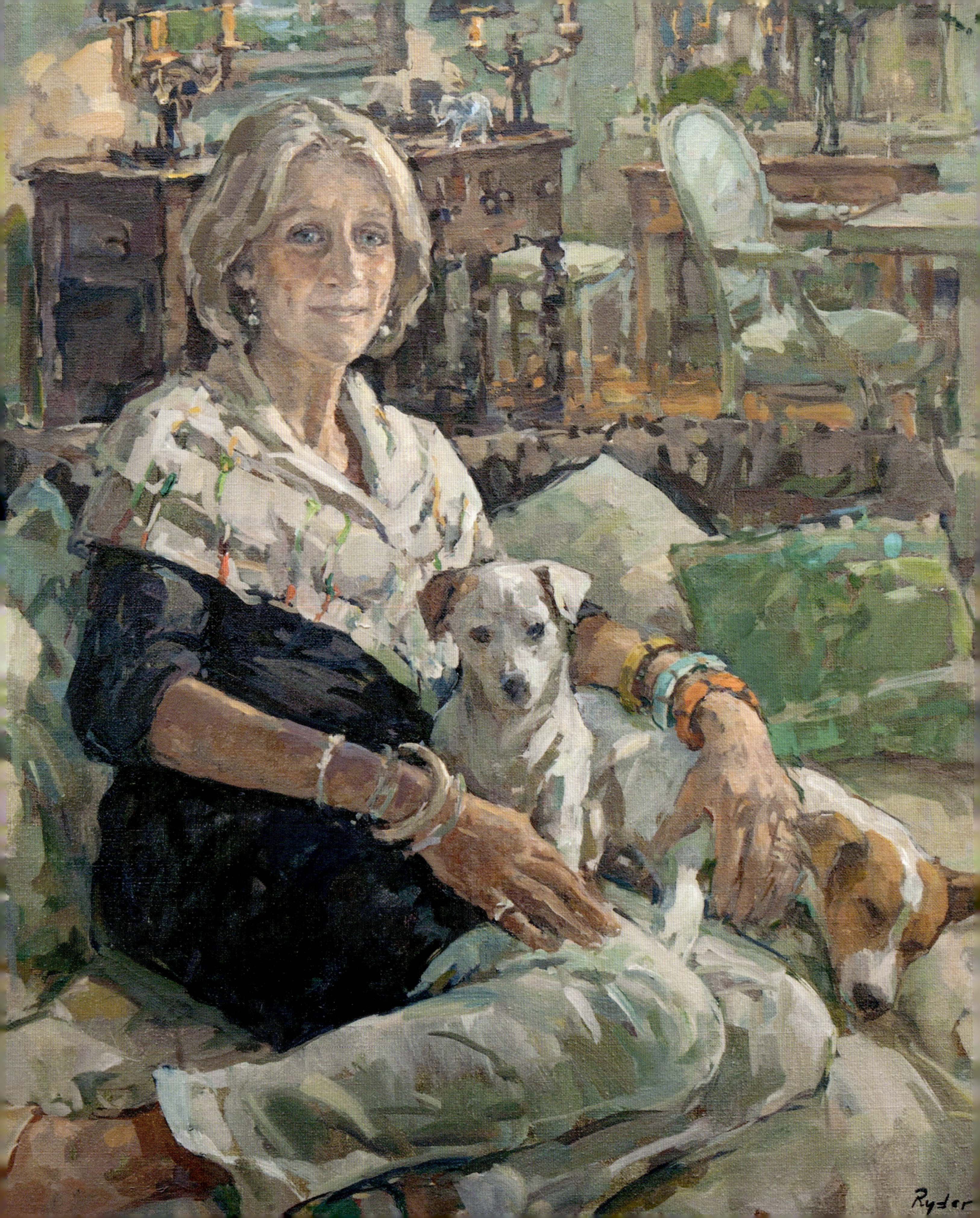
Ryder

CONTENTS

FOREWORD

When I first began a career in galleries the world was a very different place. The internet was the stuff of science fiction and contemporary artists were either painters or sculptors – judged principally by their ability to create something of beauty. The public were largely aware of the contemporary artists of the day through the mainstream exhibiting forums, chiefly the Royal Academy Summer Exhibition. From this annual pilgrimage to Piccadilly, a number of the more painterly Academicians grew quietly famous – solo shows generated queues and how-to painting books and videos became best sellers.

By the early 1990s a handful of artists were on every gallery owner's wish list – Ken Howard, Donald Hamilton Fraser, Bernard Dunstan, Fred Cuming and, of course, Susan Ryder. It is significant that all these artists' careers survived the deluge of *Sensation* and its aftermath. Today Susan's followers are as numerous and passionate about her work as ever. The internet-led resurgence of interest in *plein-air* painting has introduced her to a new international audience and a generation of young people starved of real-life experience.

Susan's consistent appeal across the decades is easy to explain. Through her paintings she maintains that perennial high wire act – the balance between traditional style and technique and the timeless quality in all those works of art that still speak to us now across centuries. Her interiors take us to a calm place, rooms in which we can imagine ourselves at peace, happy even. Low lighting, soft fabrics and well-loved furniture one can sink into after a long supper with friends. The fantasy of elegant living that they conjure may not resonate with everyone but the sense of home and belonging they engender is universal.

Throughout the decades her work has drawn on the depiction of light to create this sense of place. Drawing rooms and hallways are bathed in pools of lamplight by evening and terraces and flower borders dappled in sunlight by day. All rendered in her distinctive impressionist brushwork with an instinctive lightness of touch that breathes life into her subjects.

MATTHEW HALL

HALF TITLE **Self-Portait**, 30 × 24
TITLE PAGE **Red Walls, Red Sofa**, detail
PAGE 4 **Sorrel with her Terriers**, detail
FACING PAGE **Covered Terrace (Province)**, detail

ENDPAPERS
FRONT **The Empty Easel**, detail
BACK **Lamplight**, detail

All painting dimensions given in inches.

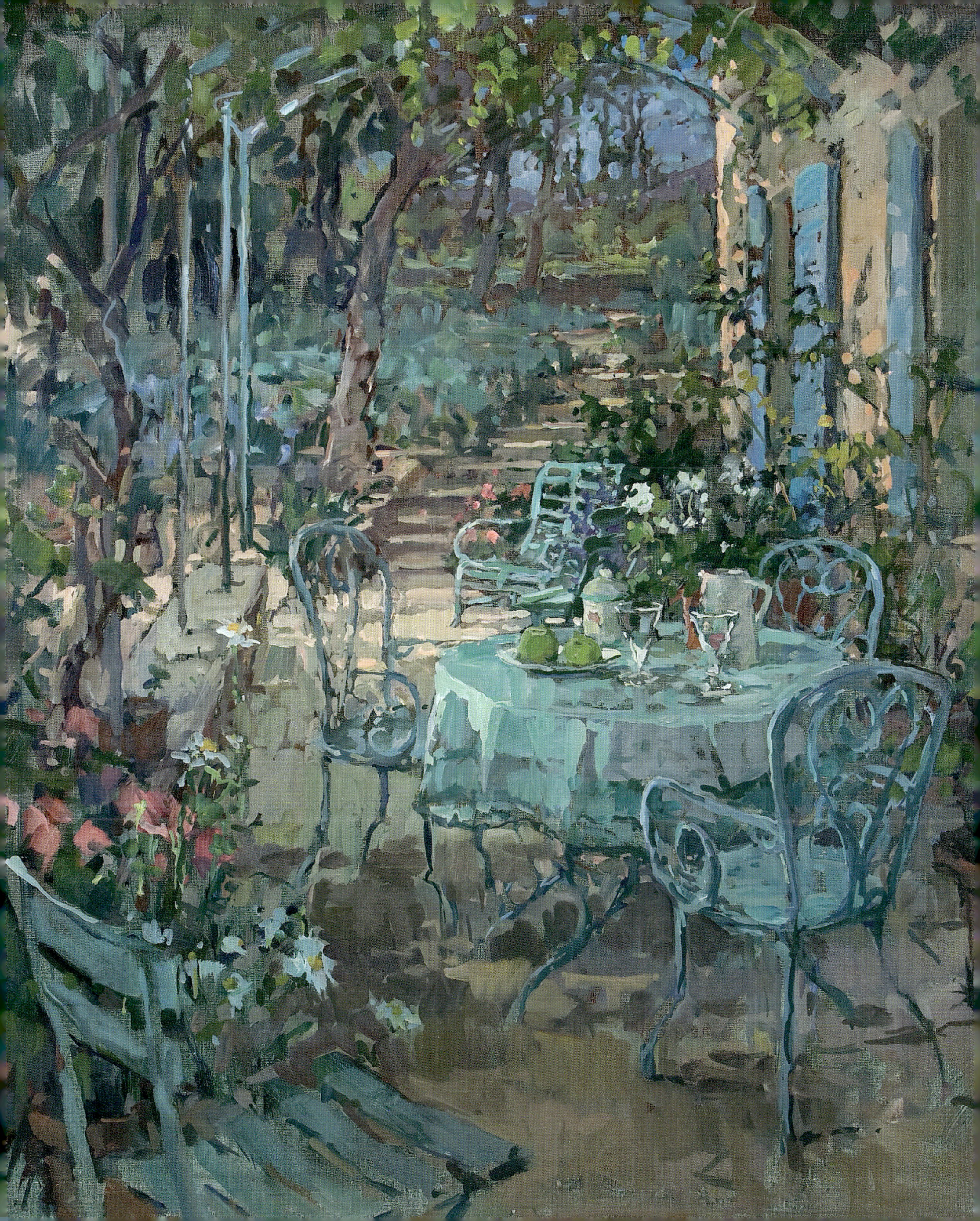

INTRODUCTION

A CHANCE ENCOUNTER

One question the painter Susan Ryder frequently gets asked is: 'How do you get your portrait commissions?' It's a difficult one to respond to, as there are many different possible answers. But no commission in her sixty-year career has had stranger origins than one that came about after a chance encounter in 2019.

Ryder and her husband, Martin Bates, were at Berwick Railway Station, in Northumberland, shortly to board an express train south to London. Martin, having had an operation on his back, was in a wheelchair: the main reason for the couple's journey south was to have a meeting with his surgeon to assess his progress. The porter had wheeled them to the waiting room, and promised to come back to help them on to the train when it arrived. They were not alone: also sitting there was an American couple, with whom they began chatting. Nothing consequential: no names were swapped, or anything like that. The couple revealed they had a holiday house near Melrose in the Scottish Borders, and were on their way back to the USA, via London. Ryder and Martin told them about *their* home, north of the border in Berwickshire, not far away.

The Americans kindly helped get Martin and their luggage onto the platform, and when the porter arrived to assist him onto the train, they all said their goodbyes and headed off to their reserved seats.

Unknown to Ryder at this point, the Americans, Mark and Cameil Moorman, were great lovers of art. Before they got their flight, they had an appointment at Panter & Hall Gallery on Pall Mall in London. They had reserved a painting they had found online and fallen in love with, and wanted to see it in the flesh before completing the purchase. The painting was called *Oak Room Chair with Violets*, and it was by… Susan Ryder. After the transaction was happily completed, they asked if they could find out more about the painter, and Matthew Hall pulled out a catalogue of Ryder's latest solo show to give them.

Leafing through the catalogue, largely featuring images of Ryder's exquisitely painted neo-impressionist interiors, they saw a photograph of Ryder, standing at her easel. 'Hey!' said Cameil, in amazement. 'Isn't that the lady we saw this morning at Berwick Railway Station?' 'Highly likely,' said Hall. 'She lives up there, and I know she's coming down to London this week!' He immediately rang Ryder, and, just a few hours after saying their goodbyes 350 miles north of London, their acquaintance was renewed.

The next time the Moormans came to England, they paid a visit to Ryder's house, and got to sit in the very oak chair that was portrayed in the painting they had bought. The two couples have become friends and, following the Covid pandemic, the Moormans have commissioned Ryder to paint a double portrait of themselves, as well as individual portraits of their three children, two of whom have since travelled over the Atlantic for that purpose.

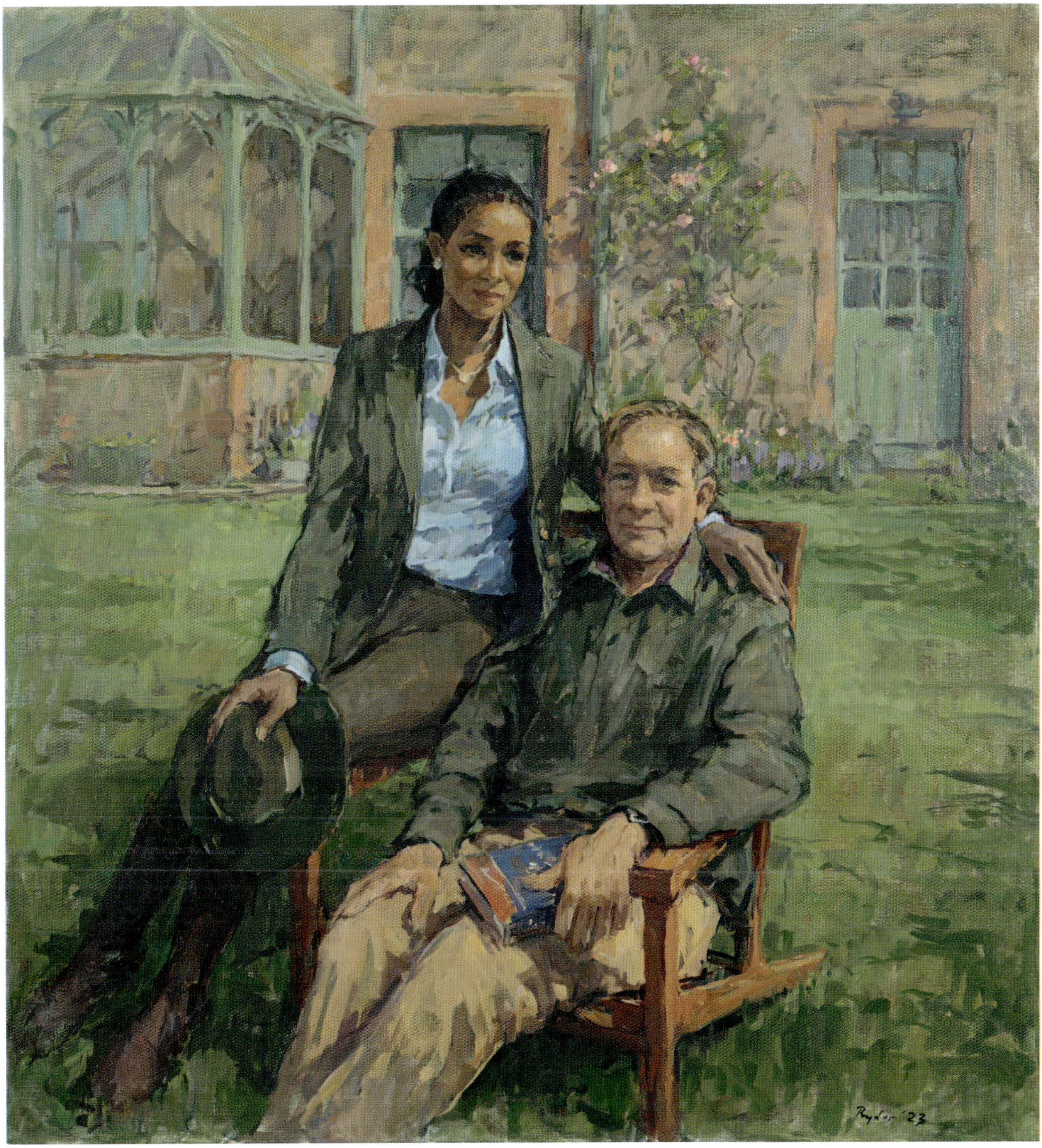

Mark and Cameil Moorman, 38 × 36

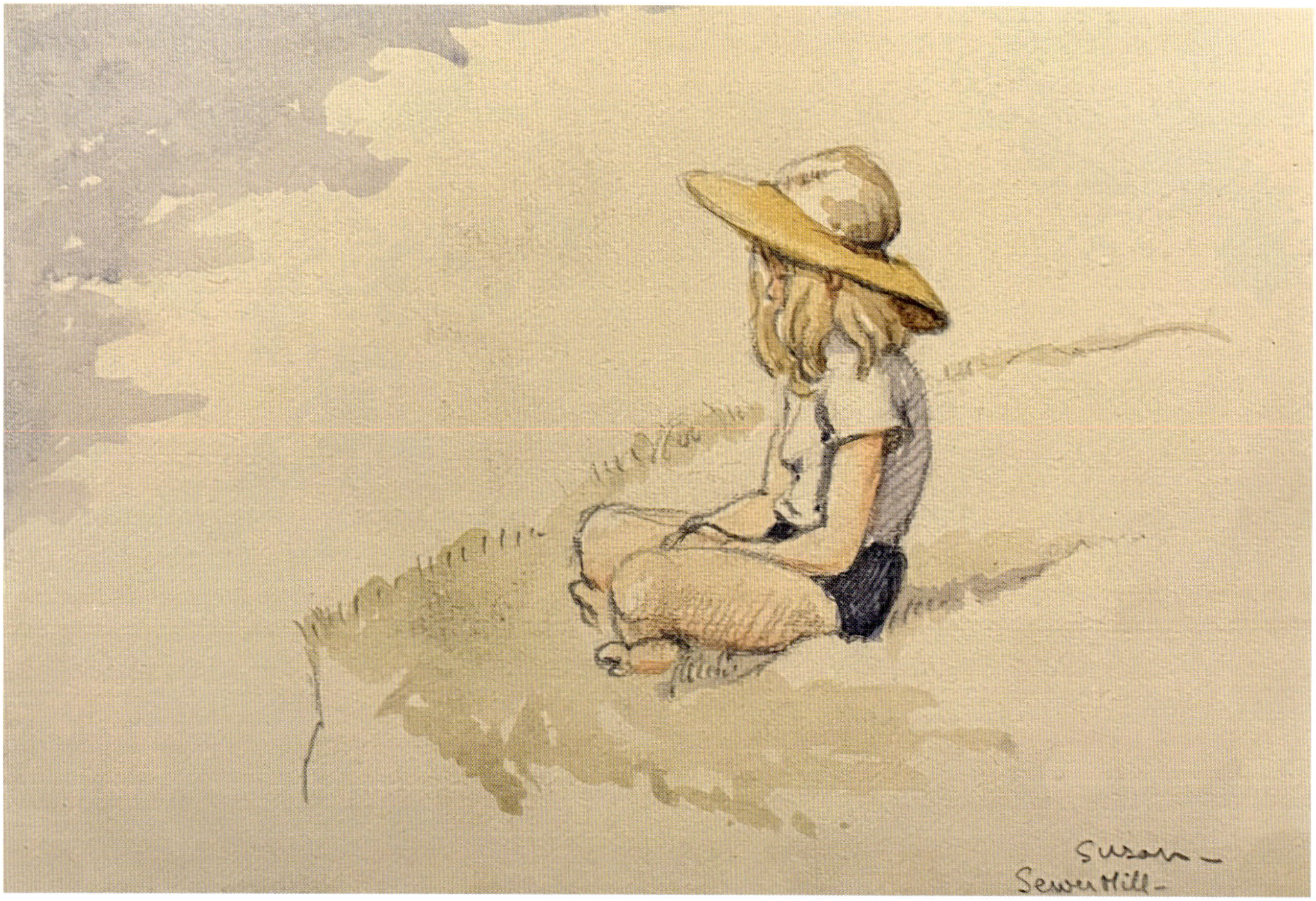

Susan by Felicity Green Wilkinson

CHILDHOOD

In June 1950, Robert and Hilaré Ryder attended an exhibition displaying artwork by children from all the primary schools in the Windsor area. They were delighted to discover that a landscape by their daughter Suky – aged six – had won first prize, and was prominently displayed on an easel in the middle of the hall. Their pride was amplified when the next edition of the local newspaper carried a report of the show, illustrated by a photograph of the painting, of three trees. 'It is too early to tell,' wrote the reporter, 'whether Suky Ryder will eventually ply her trade as a professional painter.'

That reporter clearly had an inkling that she would, and indeed she did, though not primarily as a landscape painter. 'Suky', now known as Susan Ryder, has enjoyed a prodigious six-decade career as one of the country's best-loved painters of both interiors and portraits.

Perhaps it was inevitable that Ryder would become an artist, for creativity was in her blood. Her father Robert is best remembered as an explorer and war hero (he was awarded the Victoria Cross in the Second World War) and later as a Conservative MP. But he was a talented amateur painter, too, and throughout his life produced landscapes in watercolour, pen and ink and oils. His sister, Enid Campbell, was also an accomplished watercolourist. Creativity came through the other side of the family, too. Her mother's sister, Felicity Green Wilkinson was a painter and graduate of the Slade School of Art.

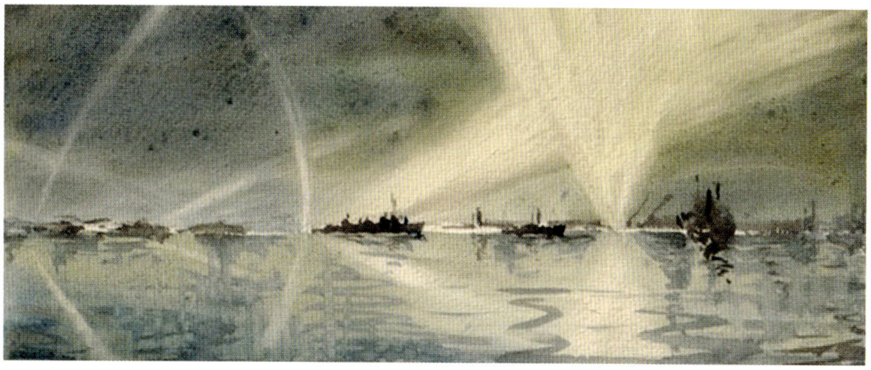

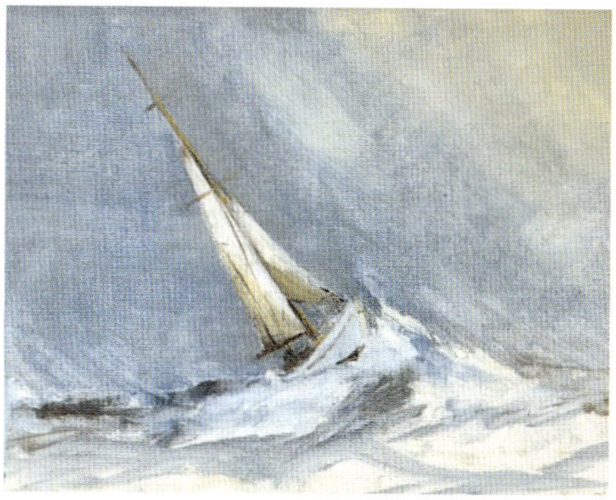

ABOVE LEFT

St Nazaire Raid, 1942
watercolour by Enid Campbell

ABOVE RIGHT

Oil sketch by Robert Ryder

Ryder was born in Windsor, in March 1944. Her parents and older brother Lisle had been offered temporary accommodation at St George's House, in the Horseshoe Cloister of the castle, by the Dean of Windsor, a friend of Hilaré's father, himself a clergyman. Between the ages of five and eight, she attended a nursery school in nearby Datchet, but received most of her significant early education from her parents: her father shared his love of history and geography, her mother imparted a love of literature and music.

Her father was a passionate sailor, who had entered the Royal Navy in 1926, aged eighteen. By 1950 he had left the service to become the Conservative MP for Merton and Morden, but he was never far from the deck of a boat, and it wasn't long before he bought a Buckie-built herring drifter which he converted into a family home-from-home. Every Easter, for a month, and every summer, for two, the family would take to the seas. It was on one such adventure in 1952 that an incident demonstrated the then eight-year-old Susan Ryder's preternatural ability to relate shapes in design. Her father had dropped anchor off the Brittany Coast, and the young Ryder, as ever, was drawing the scene she saw before her, in her well-thumbed sketchbook. 'The lighthouse has moved,' she announced, realising that the drawing she was completing no longer represented the landscape in front of her. 'Don't be silly,' replied her parents, before understanding that it wasn't

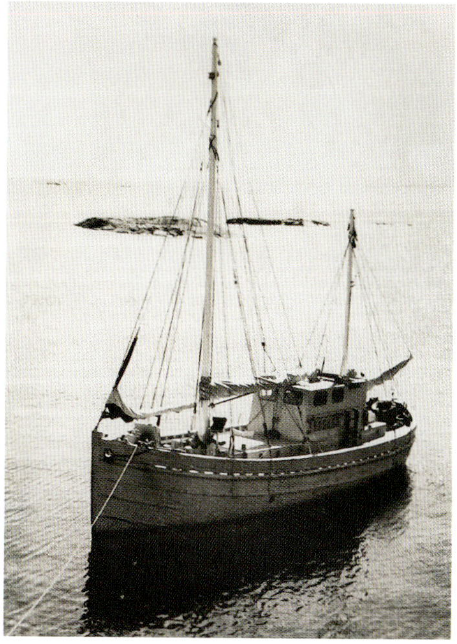

Yacht *Foresight*

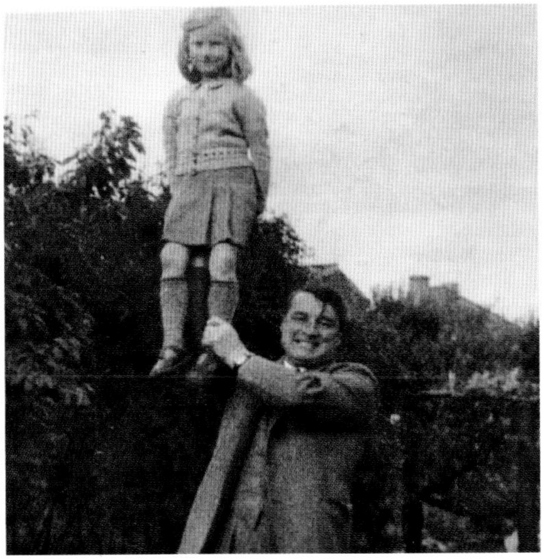

Susan Ryder held aloft by her father

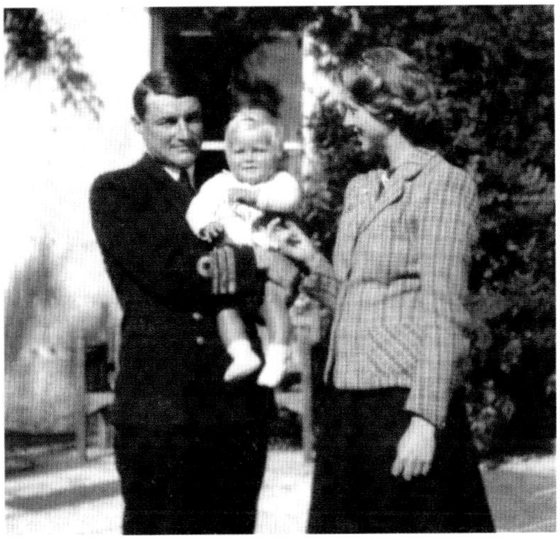

Lisle Ryder with his parents

the lighthouse that had moved, but the boat. The herring drifter was drifting: the anchor was dragging, and their daughter's visual acuity had saved them from potential calamity.

That autumn Ryder became a weekly boarder at Ibstock Place School, on the edge of Richmond Park, in Roehampton. It was a Froebel school, encouraging the children's creative side, and her artistic talent was further nurtured. By this time, the family had moved to a flat in Knightsbridge, which had belonged to Ryder's grandfather. Her passion for art was greatly encouraged by her father, who would take her on trips to the Natural History Museum to sketch the animals. He also encouraged her to practise painting, using his oils and canvases. Hilaré Ryder grew worried that her husband was over-enthusiastic about her daughter's painting career, and could put her off. That was far from being the case. She thrived on the encouragement, and to this day is grateful to her father.

The art classes at her next educational stepping stone, Beaufront Girls School, near Camberley, however, left a lot to be desired. Ryder tells how her teacher used to touch up their work to 'improve' it. She did, however, enjoy her role as the school play scenery designer, especially for a drama that she wrote with her father in the holidays. Ryder left the school at sixteen, with an A-Level art qualification, taken early and largely self-taught, under her belt.

After a six-month stay in Blois, in the Loire Valley (undertaken to brush up her French, but also incorporating informative art classes), Ryder enrolled at the Byam Shaw School of Art in Notting Hill Gate, a short bus ride from her Kensington home. She envisaged a career as a set designer, but her painting was encouraged by several inspiring teachers at the school, all successful practising artists, notably the principal Maurice de Sausmarez, Bernard Dunston RA, and in addition Peter Garrard, who taught her the importance of tone.

Dunston, a brilliant painter of post-impressionist figure-studies depicted in interior settings, was particularly important to her development. He was a kind, gentle man

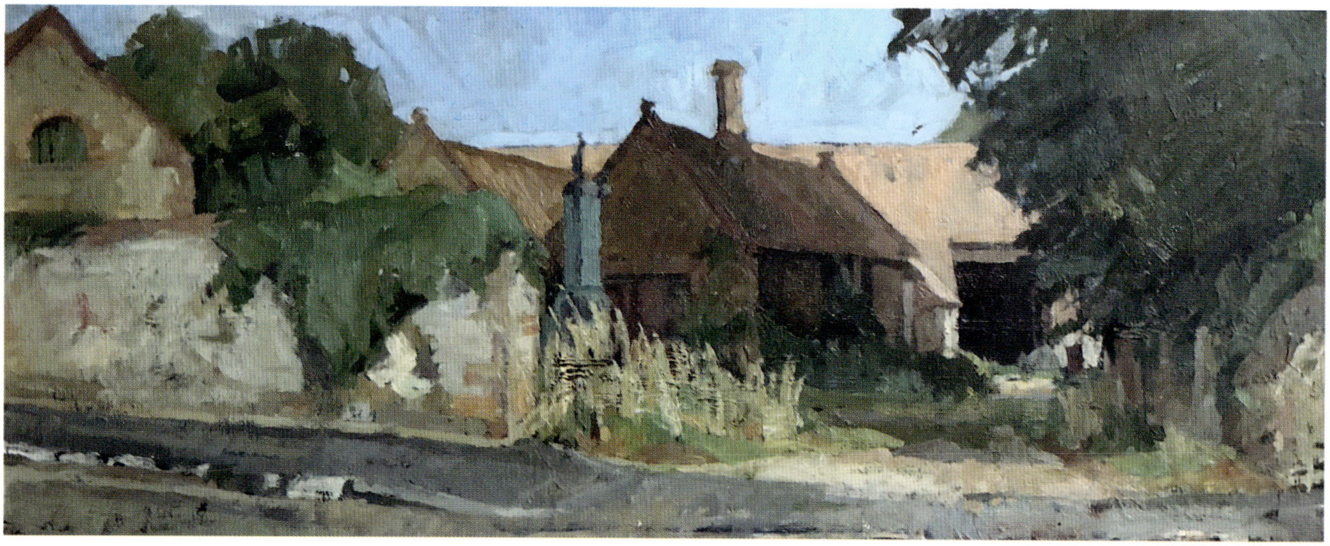

who favoured encouragement over instruction, which suited her. She describes him to this day as her 'main influence'. It is thanks to him that she became 'hooked' on interiors, and particularly the interplay between cool daylight and warm lamplight.

Norfolk Barns, 11 × 27

The first year was entirely dedicated to drawing. The students were encouraged to closely examine their subject matter: generally an inanimate object, such as a statue. Above all, they were taught to 'look'. It was only in the second year that they were allowed to paint, although Ryder had continued doing so in her spare time. This was the period when abstract art was in fashion, with Op Art and Pop Art taking off, but her teachers didn't even nod to these trends. Byam Shaw was all about figurative art. Ryder was happy about that, it suited her. She was doing what she loved.

She made good friends at the school, including Annabel Gosling, Diana Calvert and Jane Corsellis, all of whom have gone on to enjoy successful careers as artists, and who have become lifelong friends. (As we shall find out later, Ryder still enjoys annual painting holidays with them to France and further afield.)

Life drawing – and from the second year, life painting – was one of the staples of the students' education, and Ryder made an important breakthrough during one of these classes. An eight-year-old ballet dancer was modelling, and when the child's mother came to pick her up, she was so impressed with Ryder's impression of her daughter, she asked to buy the painting. She offered £5, and a commission to paint her other two children. Ryder's parents told their friends about her success, and during the next holiday she was asked by them to paint *their* children. She upped her price to £10 per painting. Her career as a portrait artist had begun, and the commissions have continued coming in, to this day.

Another breakthrough, at the end of her third and final year, came when one of her pieces was accepted into the *Royal Academy Summer Exhibition*. Ryder was chosen along with her three good friends. It was a thrill to see her work hanging in the Small South Room. The painting featured a seated figure bathed in warm firelight, countered by a fresher, cooler exterior light shining through the window.

Ryder left the Byam Shaw with a National Diploma of Design, and a strong vocation as an oil painter. Her dissertation compared the interior light of Vermeer and Vuillard, both significant influences on her work. She focused on the ways in which they captured 'the fall of light'.

She was also awarded a David Murray Scholarship, a £200 bursary to travel to a chosen destination to develop her landscape painting skills, with promised extra tuition from an RA artist. Most of the other award winners chose to go to Venice or Provence. Ryder decided to save money and spend her time 'camping' in an unfurnished early Victorian rectory in Wolferton, Norfolk, which her parents had just bought. Sadly, no RAs could be persuaded to make the rather unglamorous trip to East Anglia. The house overlooked the Wash, and Ryder was very taken by the wide Norfolk landscape. When she related her enthusiasm for the 'big skies' to an elderly relative, on a visit for tea, it was misheard as 'pigsties'.

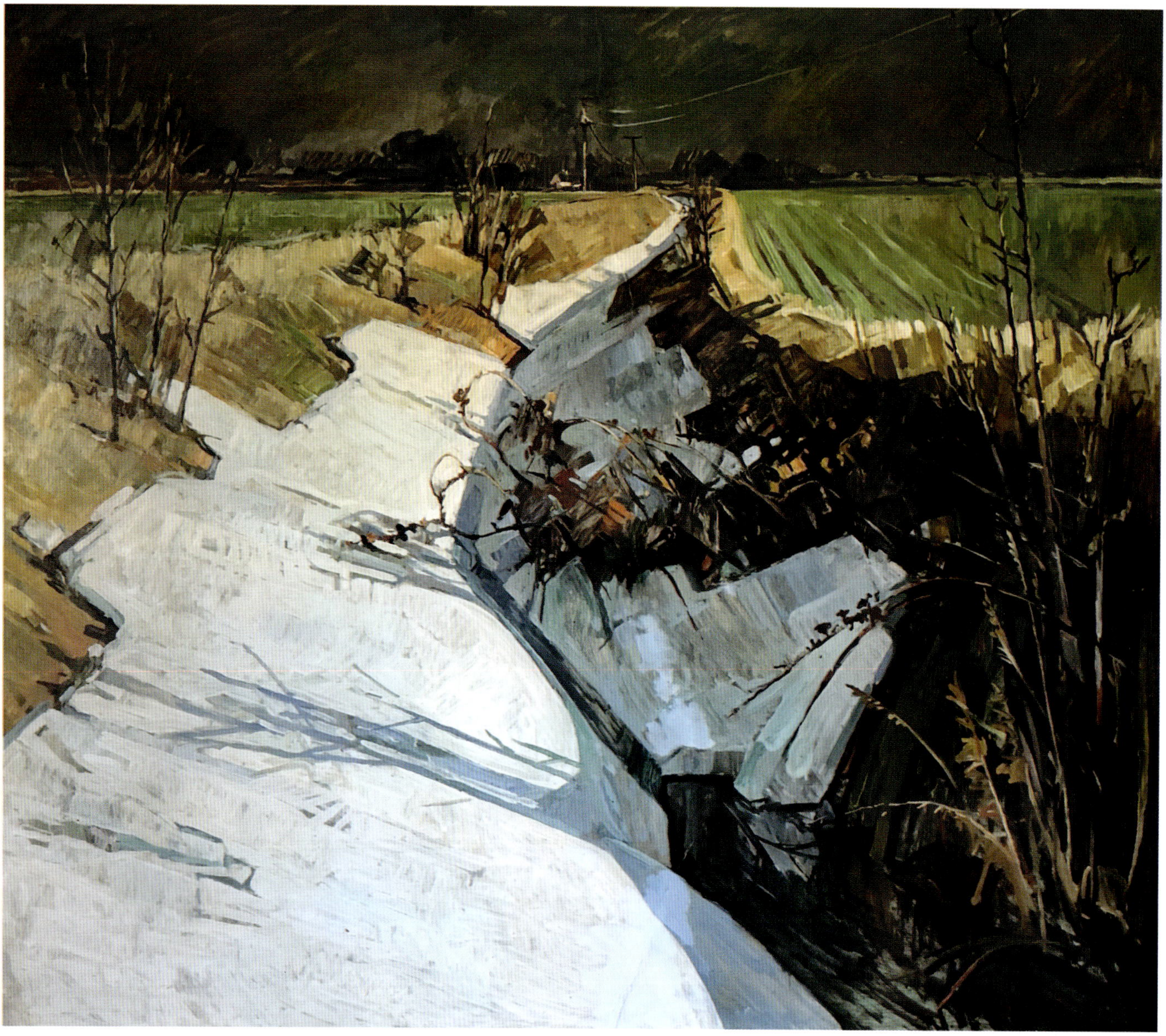

Last of the Snow, 48 × 56

I had this painting on the roof of my mini, collecting it from an exhibition when it blew off and snapped in half. I painted on hardboard in those days – I bundled the pieces into the car and my brother glued them together. It now hangs in pride of place in his hallway.

THE YOUNG ARTIST

An interesting early commission in the spring of 1964 gave Ryder the opportunity to show her talent to a wider audience. Her godmother, Lady Margaret Leese, and her husband were expert horticulturists, specialising in the cultivation of succulents and cacti. They held annual displays of these desert plants at the Chelsea Flower Show and asked Ryder to paint six 3 × 6-foot backdrops, featuring landscapes of the plants' desert habitats, for that year's show. The cacti came away with the gold medal.

It was to Lady Leese's parents that Ryder's mother, Hilaré, owed a short theatrical career. In the 1930s they hosted annual plays at Tabley House, the family's grand Palladian villa in Cheshire, overseen by the playwright and scriptwriter Ian Hay. Amateur performers – The Tabley Players – were invited to stay for a week to rehearse their parts and to perform in front of an audience of the great and good of the local area. Hilaré was chosen to perform in several of these plays. In 1938 she played the junior lead in a Hay-penned play called *The Education of Eve*, for which she won accolades in the local press, the *Liverpool Daily Post* suggesting her to be 'a continual delight', and 'a star among the lesser lights'. The play was scheduled, in 1940, for a West End run, with Peggy Ashcroft playing Hilaré's part. When Ashcroft became pregnant, Hilaré was asked to step in. Alas the performances were never held, as most West End theatres were closed down during the Blitz.

Without doubt, family connections helped the young Susan Ryder to win commissions. In 1964 she took a trip to

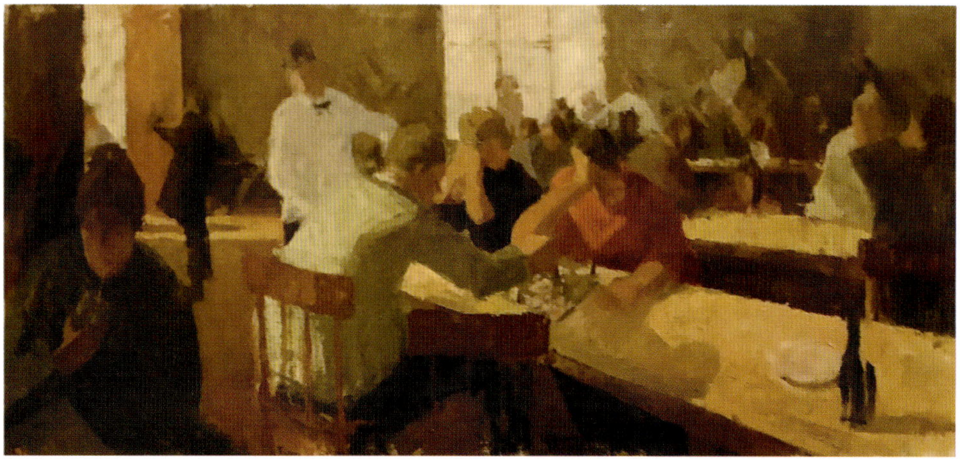

The Chess Players, 14 × 30

Yorkshire, in a blue Mini her parents had given her, to paint the portrait of a friend from Beaufront, Sarah Rossiter. While she was up north, one of her parents' friends, Richard Wood MP (the son of Lord Halifax, later Lord Holderness), discovered the purpose of her trip, and asked her to paint a portrait of him. He was the Conservative Minister of Pensions, and a director of the *Yorkshire Post*. It was an important break, Ryder's first 'society' portrait. And it was a challenging sit: the young painter had to persuade the cabinet minister that he shouldn't study on his Linguaphone while she was working on his likeness, because it would shut him off from the contact that is so vital between sitter and painter. Wood used the image on his Christmas cards that year, which further spread the word about the artist's ability.

Many years later she returned to Yorkshire to paint Richard Wood's son, Ed, who was something of a giant, at 6 ft 5 in. There was a lift in the Woods's drawing room, and they wanted a life-size portrait of their son to fill the 8 × 3 ft wall space when the unit was upstairs. Ryder, just 5 ft 2 in, had to kneel on the floor to paint his feet, and use a step ladder to paint his face.

Shortly after graduating from the Byam Shaw, Ryder was delighted to have a portrait accepted for the Royal Society of Portrait Painters' annual exhibition in their permanent gallery at 6½ Suffolk Street, in London's West End. When the porter saw the name 'Susan Ryder' on the label of Ryder's canvas, he said – to her amazement – 'It's an honour to be handling your work, miss'. He had confused Ryder with her namesake Sue Ryder, of the Sue Ryder charity. This marked the beginning of a lifelong association with the Royal Society of Portrait Painters.

In April 1965, Ryder was delighted to learn that no fewer than three of her paintings had been accepted for the *Royal Academy Summer Exhibition*.

By this time, she was being wooed by a handsome young shipping executive, Martin Bates, who she had met six weeks earlier, while skiing in the Alps. Some of her party, including her brother Lisle, who had met Martin by chance the previous day, were skiing in blizzard conditions: only the Brits were out. Martin, accompanied by a friend, spotted Lisle on the slopes and the two parties had lunch together in a mountain hut. It was love at first sight.

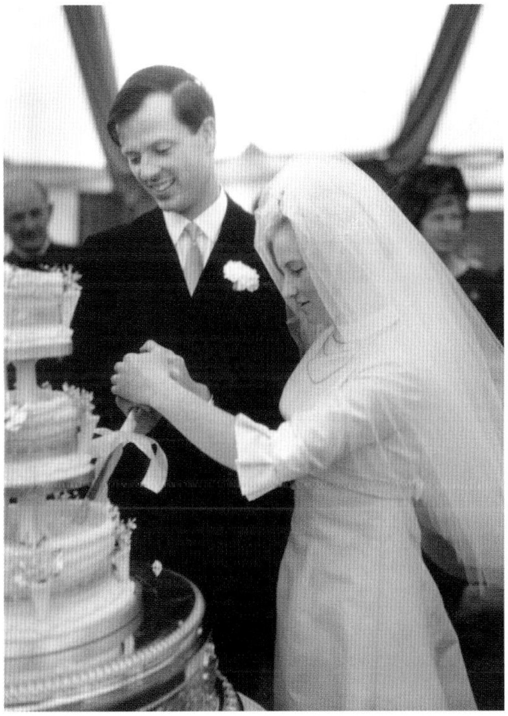

Cutting the wedding cake

The romance continued in London, after the holiday. That April evening, Ryder, before breaking the news of her RA success, announced: 'We've got something to celebrate tonight.' Bates was taken aback, as he had planned to propose marriage that very night. Had she second-guessed him?

And so, on 2 October 1965, Susan Ryder became Susan Bates. However, as she had already established an artistic reputation with her maiden name, she decided to continue using 'Susan Ryder' as her working moniker. She took to signing her paintings with just her surname, 'Ryder', so she wasn't pigeonholed as a female painter.

Martin's position at BOAC Cunard enabled the young couple to enjoy a wonderful honeymoon in Peru (where they visited the Inca ruins of Machu Picchu), having spent a week in Jamaica. Ryder packed her painting paraphernalia in her suitcase, of course, and painted landscapes when she could find the time. Martin contributed to the process by cleaning off her palette (a practice which discontinued when they got back home!). He was, however, to prove an enormous help to her career in other respects, later claiming he had developed 'prehensile arms' from years of lugging her canvases around.

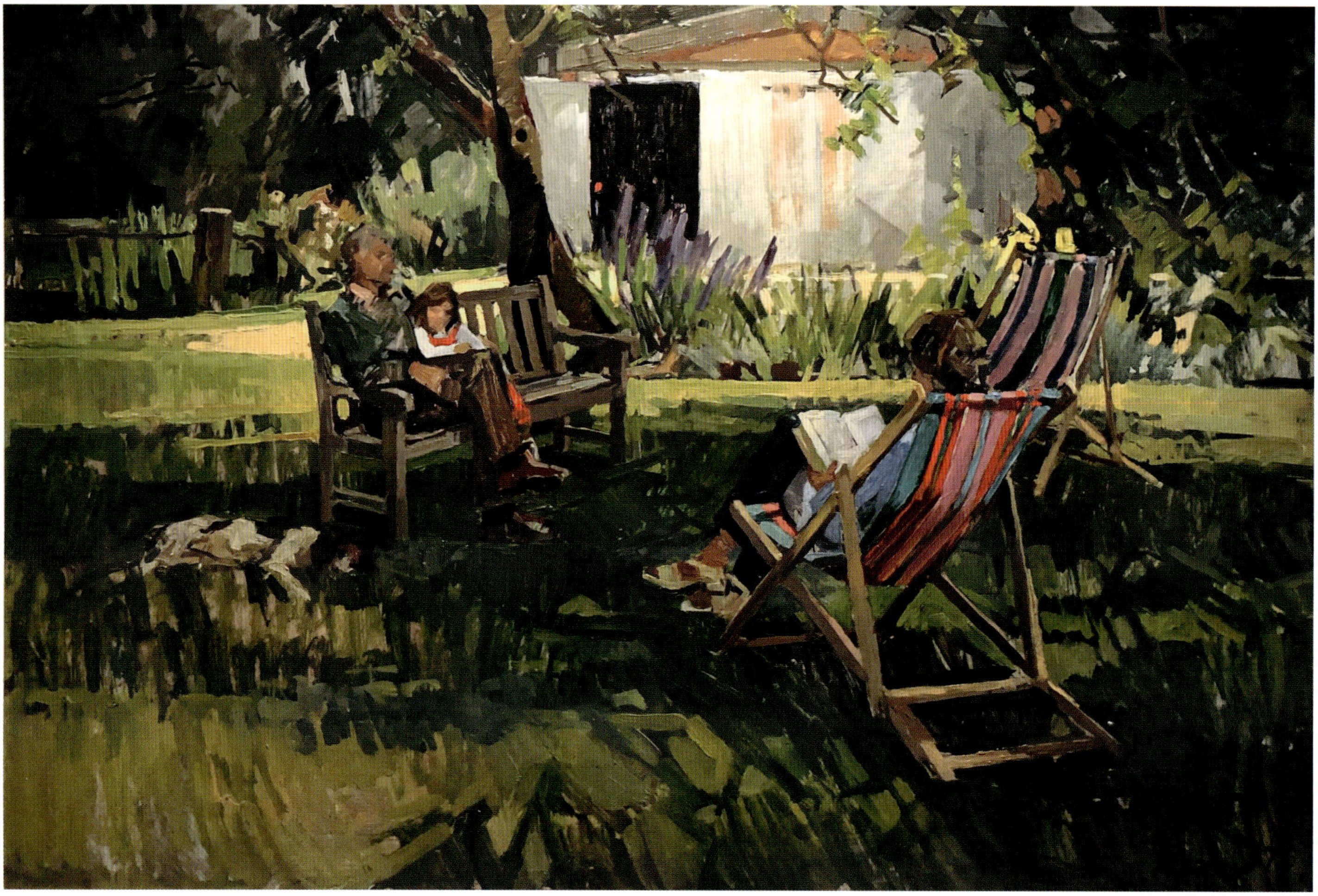

Child Care, 24 × 30

ART AND FAMILY

The history of art is full of examples of female artists whose careers have foundered when the exigencies of married life have suffocated their creative output. That Susan Ryder continued to develop her career despite five house moves in four years, and the birth of two children in quick succession (Oliver in 1969, and Susannah in 1970) is testament to her indomitable spirit and the invaluable support of her parents, especially her wonderful mother.

When first married, Ryder took a job teaching eight to twelve-year-old children at Claygate School in Esher, which she saw as an alternative career in case she was unable to make a living as a painter. She particularly enjoyed encouraging the girls who had little confidence in their ability, but in whom she saw potential. But this job came to an end when Martin's position at BOAC Cunard necessitated moves, first to Southampton, then to London, and finally to Liverpool. He eventually decided he wanted independence from a firm so connected with his family, so they moved to Suffolk where he ran a small shipping company in Felixstowe. At last they were settled.

Once the children started at nursery school, Ryder gave herself a year to explore the possibility of making enough money from painting, without turning to teaching as a back-up. It was her continuing commissions as a portrait painter that pulled her through, and persuaded her to carry on. As a busy mother of two, she wouldn't have been able to justify taking time off her household duties to paint landscapes, or build up a collection of works for an exhibition. But portrait commissions were different: she knew the exact date for the sitting, which meant she could arrange for support to be called in while she was away (she generally chose to paint her subjects in their own houses). Ryder would be the first to say that this critical stage of her career was blessed by the combined support of her parents who were always willing to come and look after the children, and her tremendous home help.

The choice to paint her subjects in their home surroundings was one that Ryder adopted early in her career, and has since stuck with, despite the necessary travelling it entails. There are several reasons for this. She finds that sitters are more relaxed in their own home, and she can surreptitiously study them at mealtimes, and while they are interacting naturally with their family (and animals). Furthermore, she is stimulated by the challenge of finding herself in front of a different setting, with a different play of light for every painting, adding an element of discovery, which she thrives on.

She painted at home, too, whenever she could find time, developing her skill at depicting interiors. One such occasion

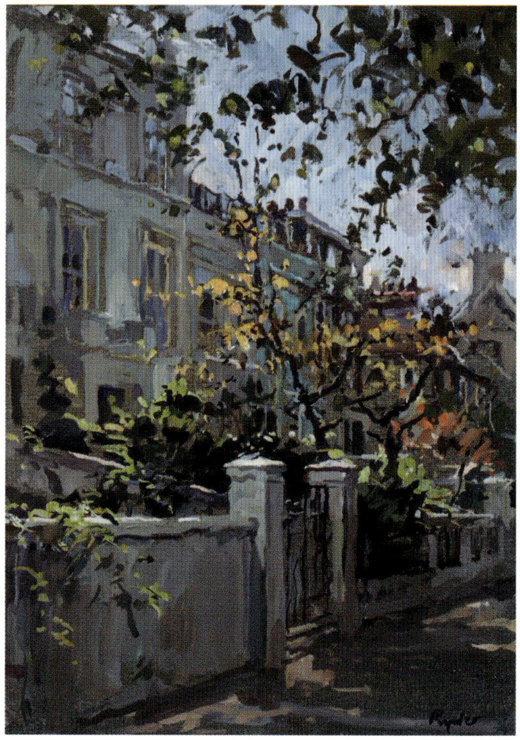

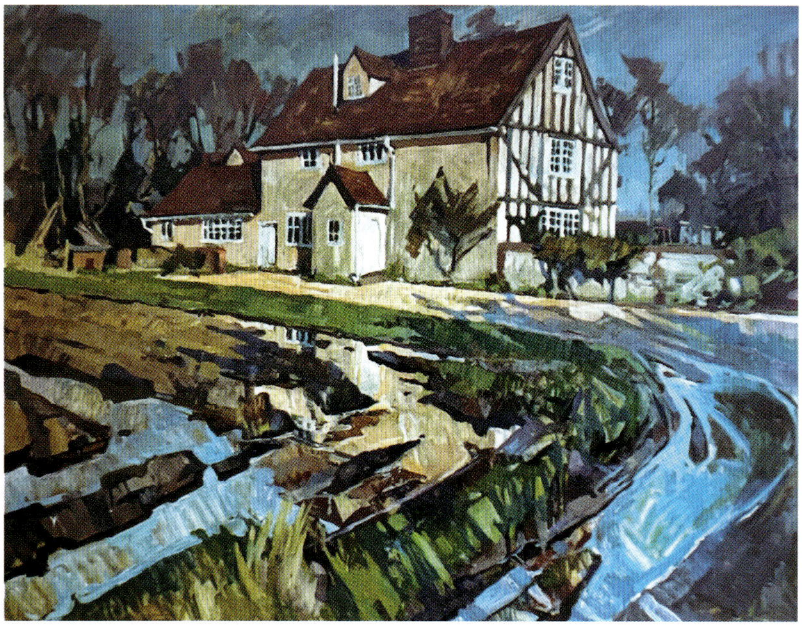

ABOVE

Ladbroke Grove, 16 × 12

LEFT

Hill Farm, 25 × 30

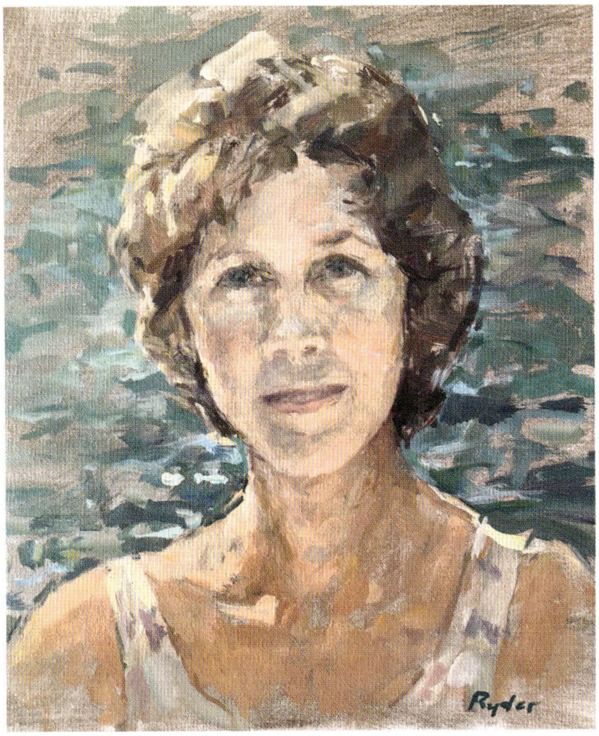

Hilaré Ryder, 14 × 12

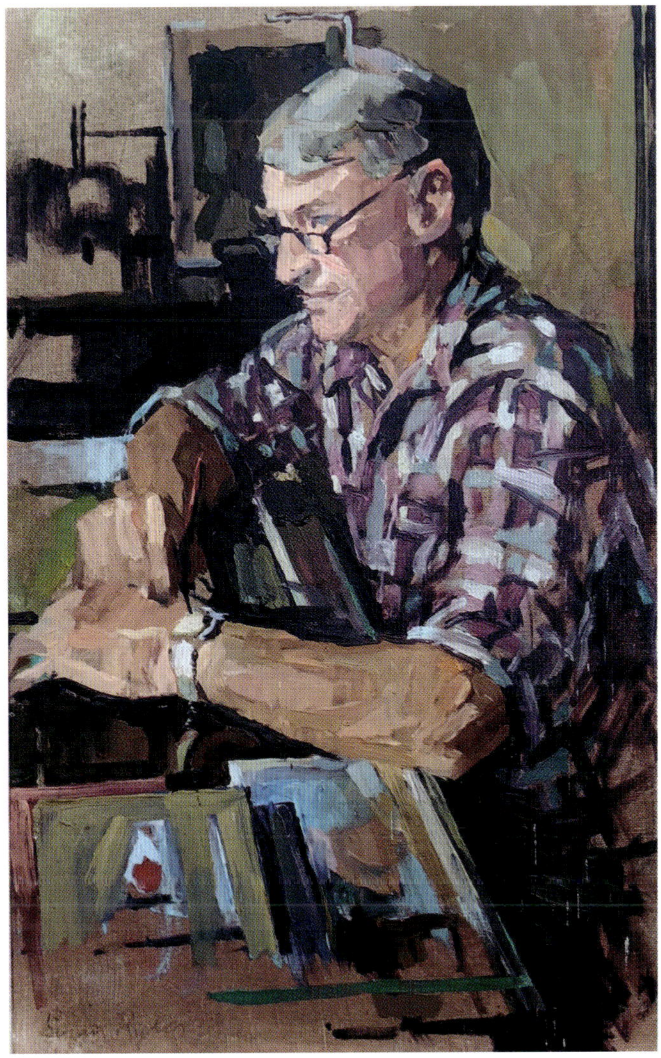

Robert Ryder, 12 × 18

arose in 1974, when Oliver, aged five, caught chickenpox. She placed him in bed, gave him some Fuzzy Felt and other toys to occupy him, and – combining simultaneous roles as nurse and artist – managed to knock out a very decent portrait of him, and the bedroom surroundings, which she still cherishes. An interesting footnote to this painting: it is dated '1974', one of the last pictures she put a date to. Soon afterwards she was told by one of the gallery owners that the addition of a date was frowned upon in the trade, as the practice shortened the shelf life of a painting.

One commission often led to another. Ryder was asked to paint someone her father knew, a Second World War fighter pilot who had fought in the Battle of Britain and been a Prisoner of War in Stalag Luft III (of *Great Escape* fame) named Alec Ingle. He had stayed on in the RAF until 1966, rising to the rank of Wing Commander. After retirement he had moved to a large, divided house in Sussex, in the same building as another higher-ranking RAF officer, an Air Vice Marshal, from whom Ryder had borrowed a chair appropriate to the sitting. The Wing Commander 'squeezed into' his old uniform. When the portrait was completed, the Air Vice Marshal came to look at it, liked it, and asked her to paint a portrait of him, too. Ryder thus stayed on in Sussex for a few more days, amused that the higher-ranking officer wished to be portrayed in an old jumper, rather than in his military dress suit, much to the astonishment of Wing Commander Ingle.

Not every commission was a complete success, such as when friends asked Ryder to paint their seven-year-old son. In those days, for head-and-shoulder portraits, she liked to use a north light (daylight coming through a north-facing window, which remains constant and creates softer shadows). She had found an upstairs room that fitted the bill, and set her easel up there. On the evening of the last sitting, she left the picture in the room (along with all her materials) so the father could have a look at it after he got back from work. He rang her to say that he liked it very much, as did the rest of the family.

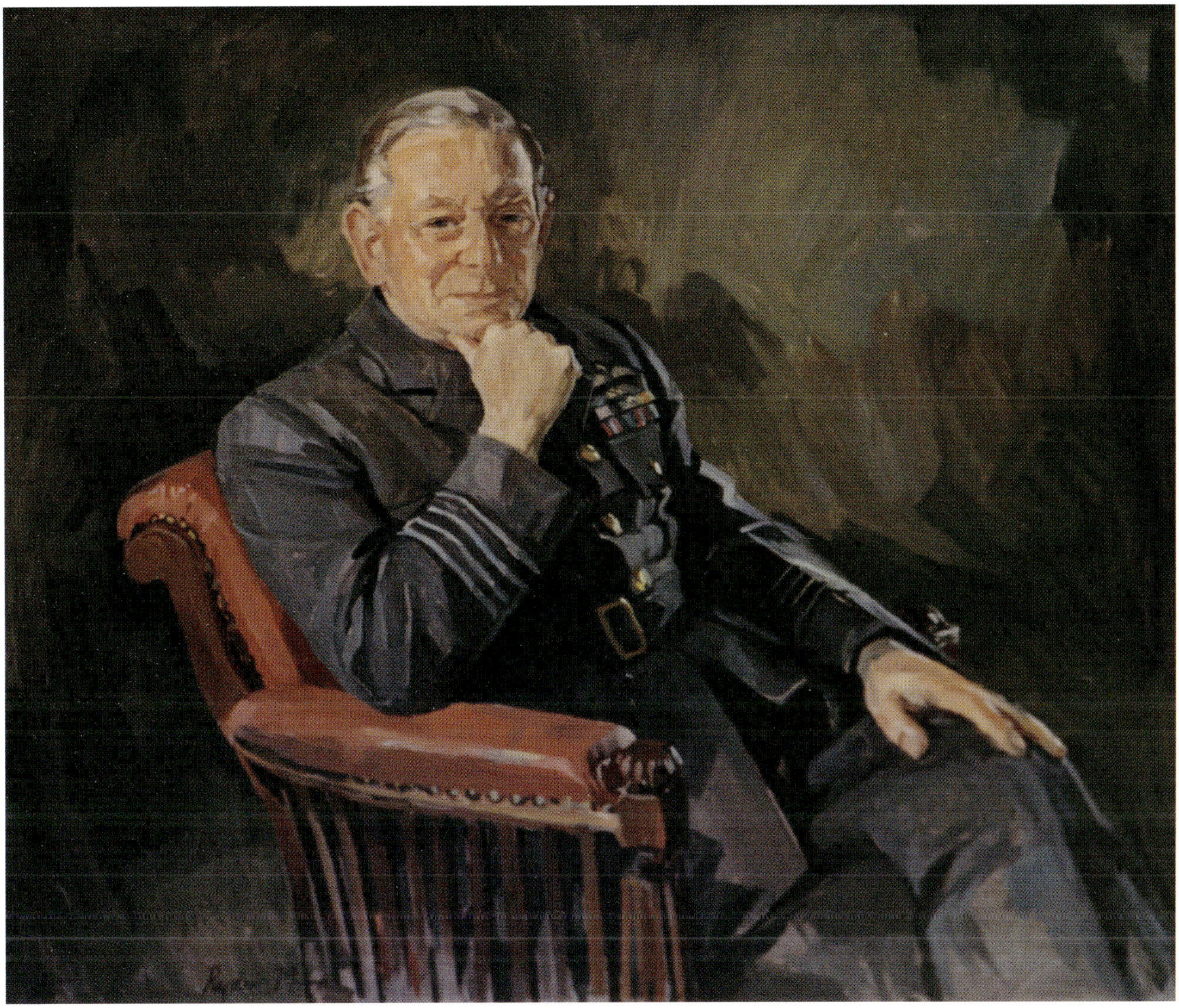

Group Capt Alec Ingle, 30 × 40

But before she returned the next day the family's three-year-old daughter had sneaked into the room and painted all over the canvas, 'finishing it off'. Ryder had to start all over again, and, what's more, the poor young lad had to sit again. She realised the second painting wasn't as successful as the first had been – it's difficult to muster your creative faculties when you're repeating yourself – but the family, if they shared that opinion, weren't in a position to say so.

Oliver and Susannah were enrolled in a school in Sudbury, and Ryder, before picking them up one afternoon in 1975, went into a framer in town, with a painting of dog roses she'd done in the summer. The man who ran the business popped an old-fashioned gilt frame on the painting, and Ryder was

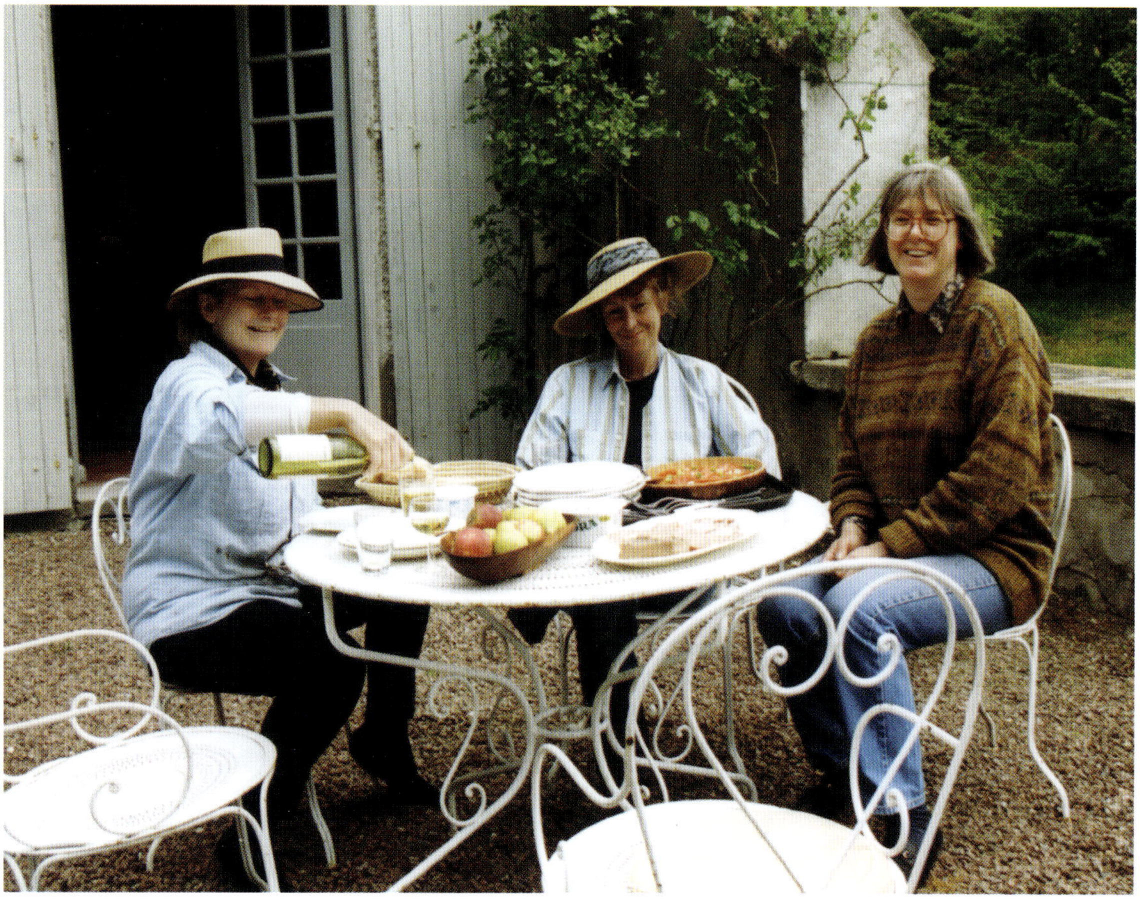

Corsellis, Gosling and Calvert

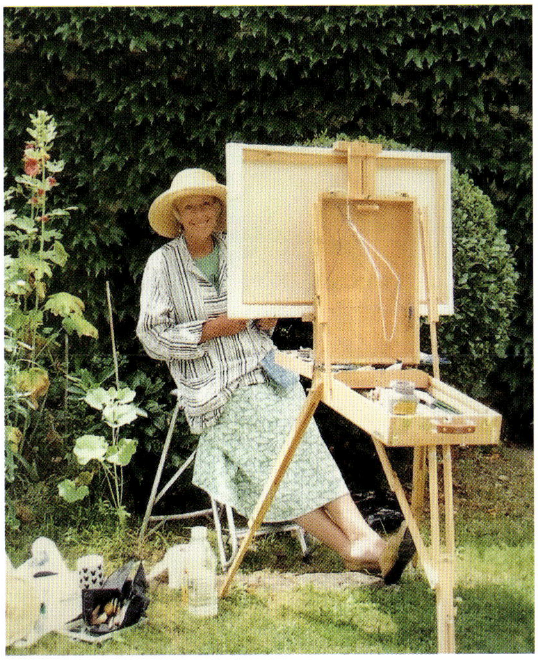

Annabel Gosling painting

astounded what a difference it made to the picture. She vowed to pay better attention to the framing of her pictures. She used the same framer until he retired, and then his successor, Andy Kinloch, whose frames continued greatly to enhance her work.

Ryder's job was not without its dangers, especially as a young woman. She has always loved travelling, and was delighted when asked to paint a Professor at the University of Rouen, a specialist in crop spraying. She stayed at a hotel where the sittings were to take place, but the landlord spent half the night knocking on her locked door, trying to persuade her that her painting would be much better if she slept with him.

France was also the setting for a rather more relaxing trip around that time, with her good friends from the Byam Shaw, Annabel Gosling, Diana Calvert and Jane Corsellis. The four artists rented a farmhouse in the Dordogne for a fortnight, with their husbands joining them for the second week. The women would spend the days painting while the men went off wine tasting. This became a regular event. One year Martin and Richard Martineau (Diana's husband) went home a couple of days early, piling a lot of paintings in the car. They were stopped at customs, suspected of smuggling works by French Impressionists, but were let through when the *douanes* realised that the paint on the canvases was still wet.

In November 1979, Ryder was given her first solo show, at the Haste Gallery in Great Colman Street in the centre of Ipswich. This space had been run by artist and businessman, Jack Haste, since 1953, alongside a shop selling art materials, and was one of the mainstays of the Suffolk art scene. Haste admired Ryder's portraits but encouraged her to put her hand to other subject matter, and Ryder enjoyed returning to landscape painting, notably of hedgerows and poppy fields; of snowscapes and sunlit estuaries. The show was a success, with most of the paintings finding new homes. However, her first small solo show in London, at the Gallery George in Marylebone, was a failure, selling only three works; a terrible disappointment.

An extremely important step in Ryder's career came in 1982, when she was elected as a member of the New English Art Club. This august society was founded in 1885, by a group of painters including John Singer Sargent, as an alternative to the academic (some might say 'stuffy') Royal Academy, which hadn't embraced the lessons learnt from French Impressionism. In latter years, the NEAC has set itself aside from the RA by its strict adherence to 'figurative, observational and painterly' art, unlike the RA, which had embraced abstract and conceptual art, as well. The club holds an annual exhibition for members' work and that of emerging artists whose ethos reflects its own, accepted after a selection process. Ryder's paintings had been chosen to be exhibited in the show – then as now held at the Mall Galleries – six or seven years running. Calvert and

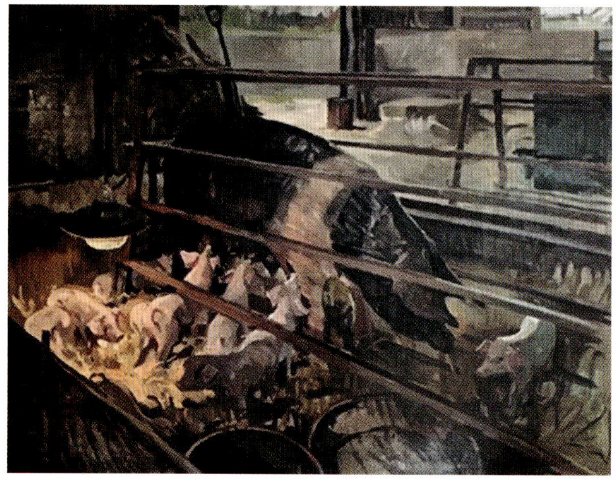

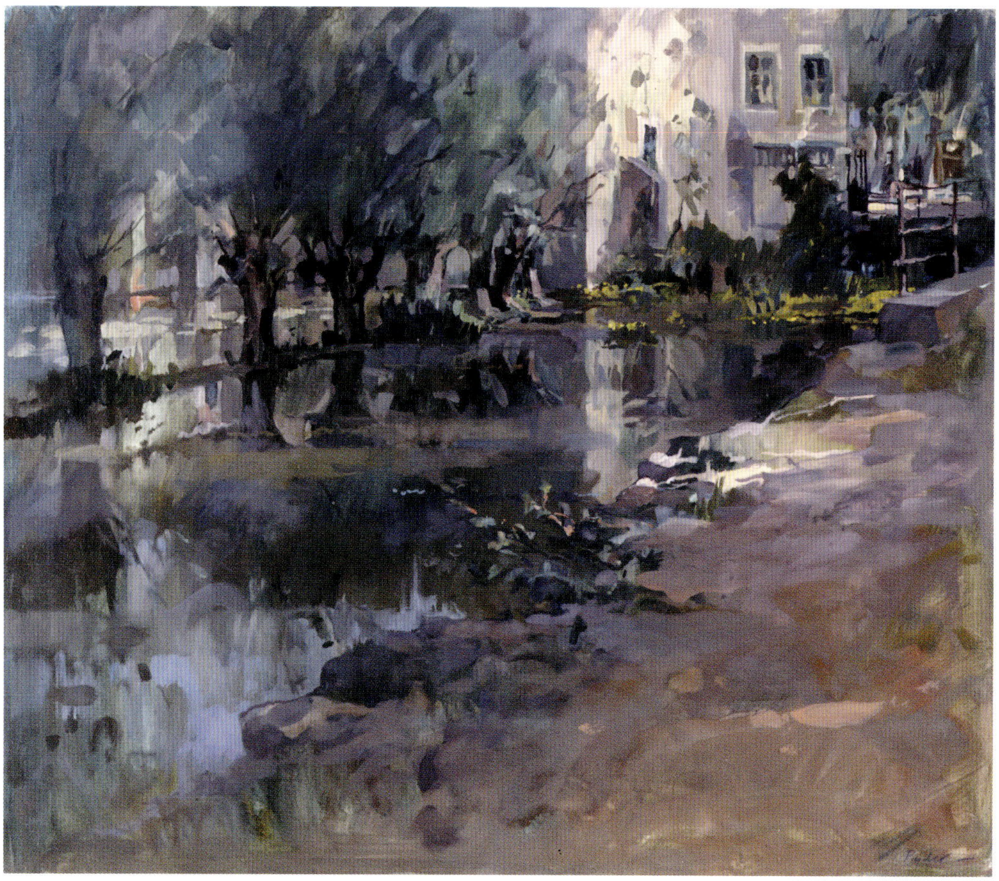

ABOVE

Pig Litters 30 × 36

LEFT

Canal at Eymet, Dordogne 30 × 36

Corsellis were already members, and persuaded her to apply to join. The two paintings she selected for the society's consideration were a canal scene she had painted in Eymet, in the Dordogne, and a large oil painting she had done of pigs and piglets in Suffolk (recalling her old aunt's mishearing of 'pigsties' for 'big skies'!). An interesting choice, then, showing off her versatility. She was duly elected.

An anecdote from the painting of the pigsty picture illustrates Ryder's curiosity and inventiveness. She noticed that, after each suckling session, one of the dozen piglets would approach its mother face to face, and touch snouts, as if to say: 'Thank you'. Wondering whether it was always the same piglet that did this, or whether they took it in turns, she daubed a white paint mark on the back of the piglet that had last performed the ritual. Sadly, while she remembers carrying out this experiment, she can't remember its result.

Around that time, at an NEAC private view, Ryder was introduced to a big player in the art business. Manya Igel, a famous dealer of contemporary art, also represented Ryder's teachers Bernard Dunstan RA and Diana Armfield RA, and was a devotee of the New English Art Club ethos. Art dealer John White told her: 'If she takes you up, you're made'. Igel *did* take her up, and over the years was a huge help to her career, selling her works all over the world. The dealer was a flamboyant character, who had escaped Nazi persecution on the last Kindertransport to leave her native Danzig (now Gdansk), in September 1939. She was confident enough in her eye to buy paintings outright from artists, instead of following the usual practice of dealing with them sale or return. This endeared her to artists and instilled trust in her buyers, that what she was selling was worth purchasing. She particularly loved Ryder's red interiors, for which she found a hungry market. She also found she could sell Ryder's larger pictures better than her smaller ones, which encouraged the artist to work on a bigger scale.

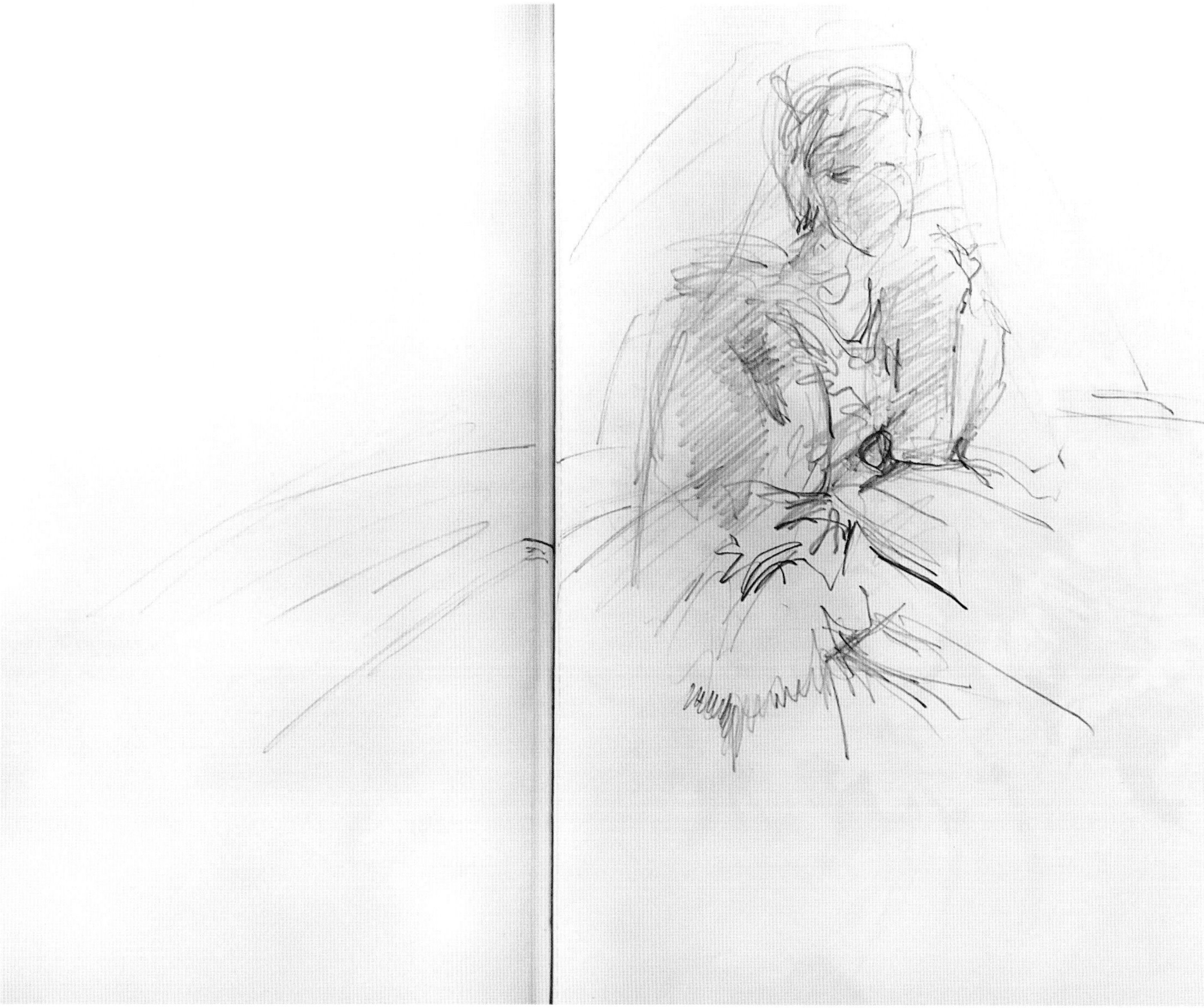

Preliminary sketch for HRH Princess Diana

PORTRAIT OF A PRINCESS

In November 1981 Ryder was commissioned to paint the Queen Mother's homeopathic doctor, in Wisbech, Norfolk. As often happened, one commission led to another – in this case the most important in Ryder's career so far.

While carrying out the commission, she stayed with the Queen's Sandringham Land Agent and his wife, friends of her parents. The couple were also hosting another guest, Sir Oliver Millar, Surveyor of the Queen's Pictures (a job Millar had taken over, incidentally, from Soviet spy Anthony Blunt). Millar, having learnt Ryder's occupation, and understanding that her latest portrait was on site, asked if she would take him to look at it. While he was inspecting it, she admitted she was worried she'd got the subject's hands wrong. 'Don't touch them,' Millar replied. 'They're perfect.'

A week later, back home in Suffolk, Ryder returned from a Christmas shopping expedition in Ipswich, to learn that Millar had called her, and wanted her to call back, urgently. Prince Charles, it turned out, had asked him to suggest an artist to paint the Princess (who he had, of course, married in July of that year) in her wedding dress. The gown, designed by David and Elizabeth Emanuel, was soon to go on a tour of the country, so the portrait needed to be completed in double-quick time. He had suggested Ryder for the job. Would she like to do it? Of course, she said she would.

The royal couple's Highgrove House residence was still being refurbished, and they were at that time living in Buckingham Palace, where Ryder was summoned to appear three days later, to be shown where the sittings were to take place. This was to be in the Yellow Drawing Room, the traditional venue for royal portraits.

This was the second portrait of the Princess commissioned since Charles and Diana's engagement, the first being an acrylic painting by Bryan Organ, also executed in the Yellow Drawing Room, featuring a demure-looking Diana in a black trouser suit before the wedding. The painting, nicknamed 'Shy Di' by the tabloid press, was commissioned by the National Portrait Gallery, but was at the time being restored after being attacked with a knife by an anti-monarchist.

Ryder's portrait was a private rather than an official commission. At 5×4 ft, it was bigger than any work she had previously painted. So big, in fact, she had to order the canvas from a new supplier, Bird & Davis, who delivered it to the Palace. (She was so pleased with their service she continues to use them to this day.) Ryder had a week to plan the composition of the portrait to show Sir Oliver for his approval. In the end it was the Prince of Wales who decided that he wanted the whole dress to be included.

The Princess was scheduled to undertake four one-hour sittings, over six days. For the first two, she was to wear the wedding dress, which would then be sent off on tour. In the second two, she was to wear casual clothing. Ryder was informed that she would be allowed to stay in the Yellow Drawing Room after the first two sittings to continue painting the dress, with a dummy substituting for the Princess. Nevertheless, she had her work cut out.

The painter was thirty-six years old, the Princess – by now pregnant with William – was twenty. Ryder, who, as ever, started by making a pencil sketch on paper to work out the form the painting would take, found Diana to be kind and considerate, though admitting to suffering from morning sickness. When the preliminary sketching process was over, and Ryder had started working with her oils on the canvas, the Princess thoughtfully remarked: 'You look much happier now you're painting.'

For the third and fourth session, Diana appeared wearing casual jerseys (red, then blue), when Ryder had wanted her to wear a white shirt, for the sake of continuity. No matter, she found that the box that had contained the dress also held some leftover taffeta, which she draped around her subject's shoulders.

Most of the canvas is taken up by Ryder's rendition of the voluptuous folds of the ivory silk and antique lace dress, the Princess's head framed by the tulle veil, cascading on to the floor. Diana's face announces an alluring mix of confidence and coyness. It is, above all, a sympathetic portrait, romantic in style, balancing the humanity of its subject, with the exuberant magnificence of her wedding garment, perhaps the most talked-about item of clothing of the twentieth century. And, as you might imagine from Ryder, the rendition of light on the folds of the dress is most skilfully rendered. This is set off by the plainness of the cloudy-green background.

The painting of the portrait, being a private commission, didn't attract the attention of the press, and the public was not to see it – or even know about it – until April 1982. Ryder asked the Palace permission to exhibit the piece in that summer's *Royal Society of Portrait Painters Exhibition*, at the Mall Galleries. They agreed, and the RSPP, after some deliberation, accepted her entry (she was not yet a member), welcoming the publicity the painting would attract, and recognising its quality. Accordingly, they hung it on the most prominent wall of the gallery, behind glass, as a security measure.

Ryder was rather embarrassed that she had been chosen to paint the picture due to a fortuitous meeting with the Surveyor of the Queen's Pictures. But she also surmised that Prince Charles had been looking for a *young* artist to paint the portrait, so as to support a burgeoning career.

The press view was jammed with photographers and journalists: this was a real s*tory*. The Palace had made sure that Ryder was prepared for their questions, putting her in touch with Bryan Organ to advise her on what she should and

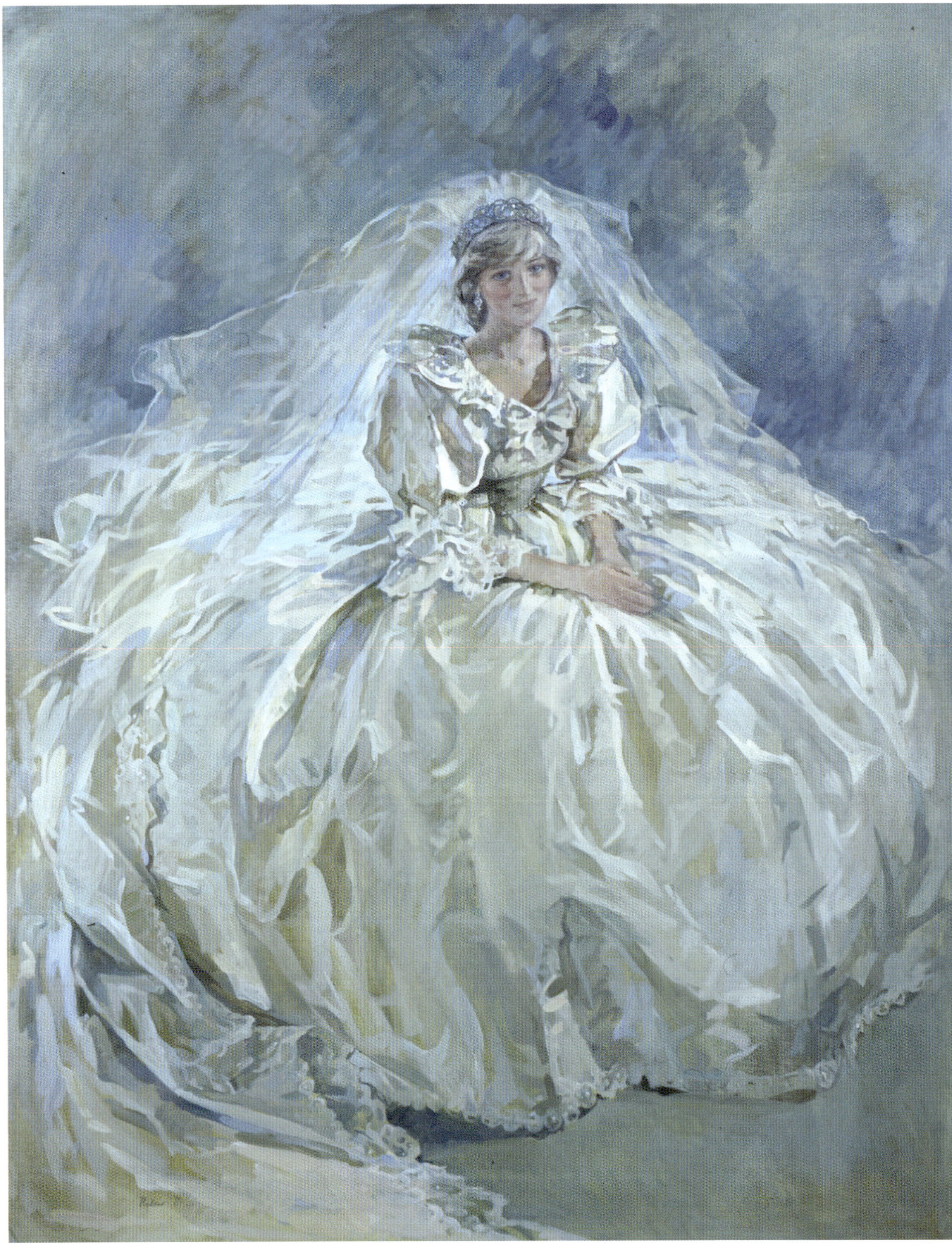

shouldn't say, when she was interviewed. When the female reporter from the *Daily Mail* asked her for an exclusive interview, she politely refused. 'You silly girl,' responded the journalist, and Ryder suspected that this would not be the end of the matter.

The next day, the *Mail* ran an article under the headline 'Chocolate-box vision of the fairytale Princess', suggesting the image might be best suited for the cover of a novel by Diana's step-grandmother Barbara Cartland. Acerbic art critic, Brian Sewell, writing in *Tatler*, was even more scathing about the painting (no surprise there), writing: 'I've never really seen anything so awful. It looks like the Princess has been dropped in a puddle of ice-cream.'

Other newspapers were better. The *Express*'s Mike Parry interviewed established royal portrait painter, Michael Noakes, who said: 'Miss [sic] Ryder's painting is very romantic. It looks enough like the Princess. It's nicely handled in a loose style. The billowing effect is impressive. I like the colours.'

Ryder was delighted with the *good* press, and, understanding all the limelight would be positive for her career, didn't let herself become upset by the criticism. She was particularly amused by a cartoon in the *Daily Mail*, depicting a forlorn conceptual artist being comforted by his girlfriend. Behind him is a pile of mud, crowned by an upturned bucket on a stick, and labelled with a wooden sign reading 'Di'. In front of him, on the floor, is a newspaper, bearing the headline NEW PORTRAIT OF DIANA. The caption, voicing the words of the girl, reads 'Oh, come on, love – you were pipped at the post, that's all…'

Looking back at all the press cuttings today, she finds Brian Sewell's comments bother her now, much more than they did back then, as she subsequently realised what an impressive critic he was.

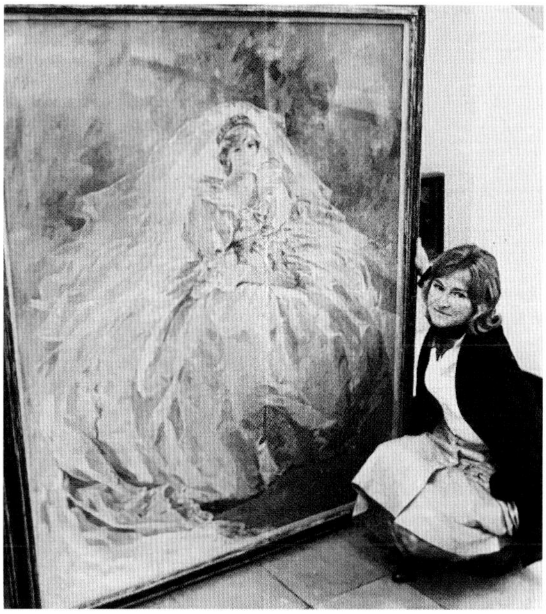

'artist Sue Ryder with her portrait of the Princess of Wales in her wedding dress, commissioned by the Prince of Wales.'

The Lady, 29 April 1982

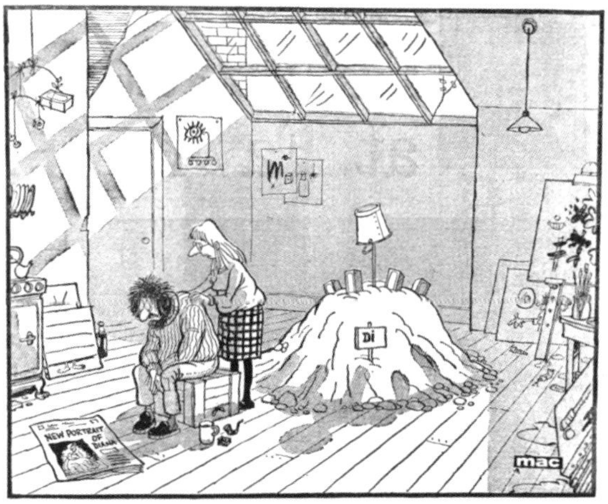

'Oh, come on, love—you were pipped at the post, that's all . . .'

Daily Mail, 21 April 1982

HRH Diana Princess of Wales, 60 × 50

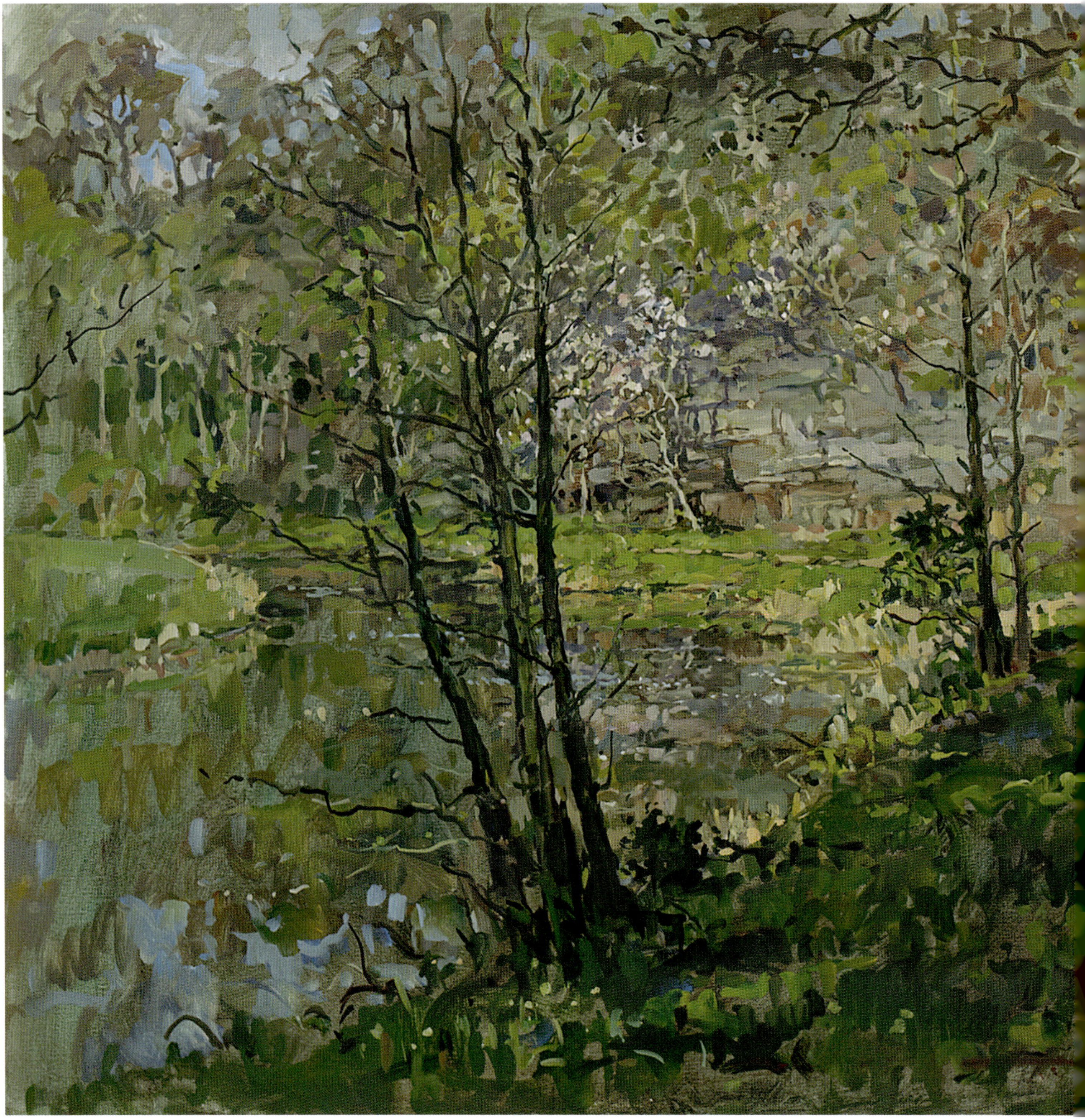

River Till, Springtime, 36 × 52

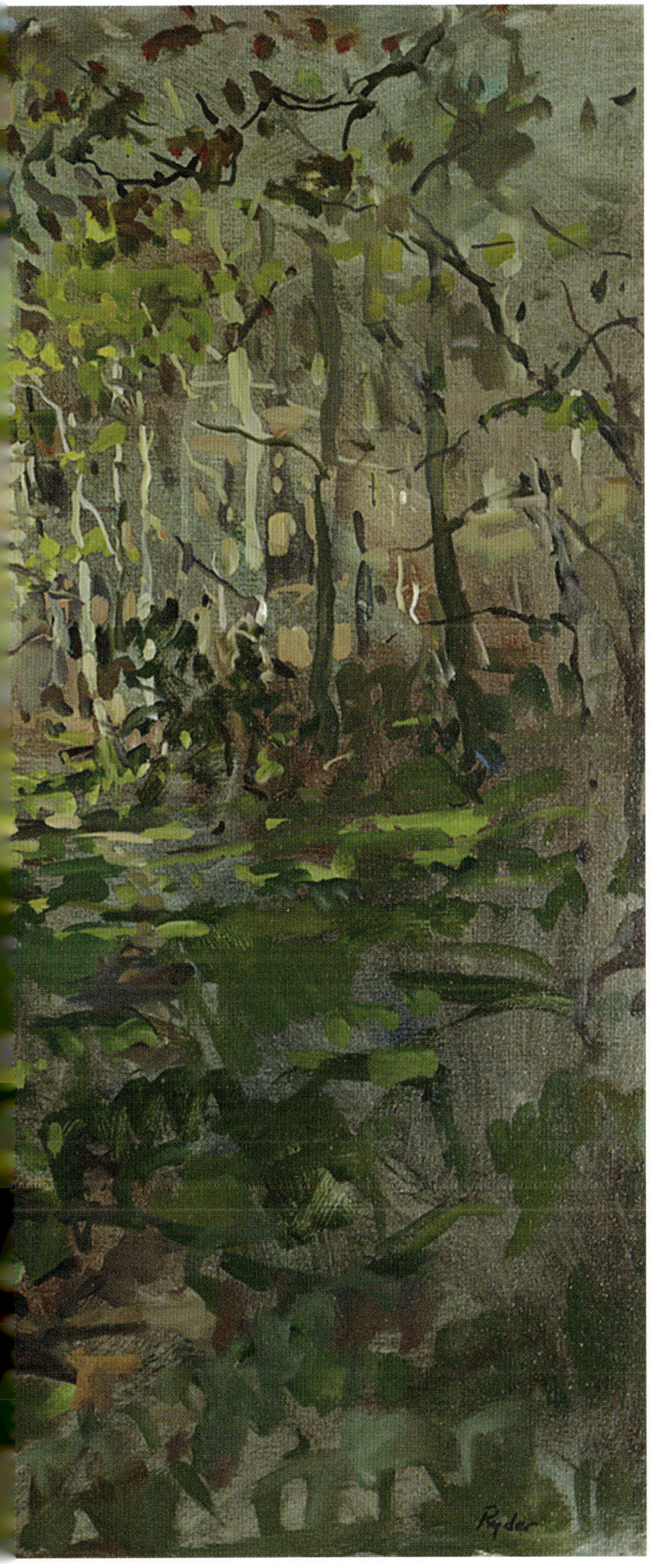

AN ESTABLISHED ARTIST

In 1982, Martin Bates and Susan Ryder made the big decision to take on a family home in the Scottish Borders, close to Martin's brother, Jeremy. Belchester House had been lived in by Martin's family since the fourteenth century. Leaving Suffolk, and with Martin still working in the City, they bought a three-bedroom town house in Earl's Court, living in London and spending holidays at Belchester, 'camping' in the house while their property was still being 'reroofed, rewired, re-everythinged'. This process took several years, prolonged by the fact that the children, when consulted, prioritised the construction of a tennis court over the decoration of the drawing room. When they did get down to restoring the drawing room, they employed local interior designer, Hugh Poole Warren, who has since become a close family friend. Ryder painted his wife Sarah, followed by a portrait of Hugh, the latter reproduced on page 97.

Before leaving her Suffolk home, Ryder built a bonfire from forty-odd paintings she hadn't sold or didn't like, which had been clogging up the attic, and burnt the lot of them, a symbolic gesture signalling a new start in her career.

There was one last hurrah, however, in Suffolk: a second solo exhibition at the Haste Gallery in Ipswich in October 1982, in which Ryder showed forty-six paintings, mostly East Anglian landscapes with descriptive titles such as *January Sunrise Catterwade Creek*, *Flight Pond at Congham* and *Mudflats at Manningtree*. There were also several flower paintings, and a couple of portraits, including one of her daughter, Susannah, and the one of Wing Commander Ingle. The show was a great commercial and critical success, with the *East Anglian Daily*

Times commenting on the 'Artist's sparkling mastery of paint [which] lifts her above the norm of Suffolk scene painting', and comparing her to John Singer Sargent, Franz Hals and Edouard Manet.

The exhibition took place just after the family had moved to London, a dramatic shift in circumstances that placed Ryder geographically at the heart of the art scene. Bolstered by the reputation she had gained from the Princess Diana portrait, and her membership of the New English Art Club, her career blossomed. The move also suited Martin, who had given up his work in the freight business, and become a shipping lawyer in the City. What's more, the artist's extended stays in Scotland gave her access to the beautiful homes belonging to friends they made in the area, such as Thirlestane Castle, near Lauder, Manderston House, near Duns, and Chillingham Castle, over

Christina Leder with her team, 30 × 38

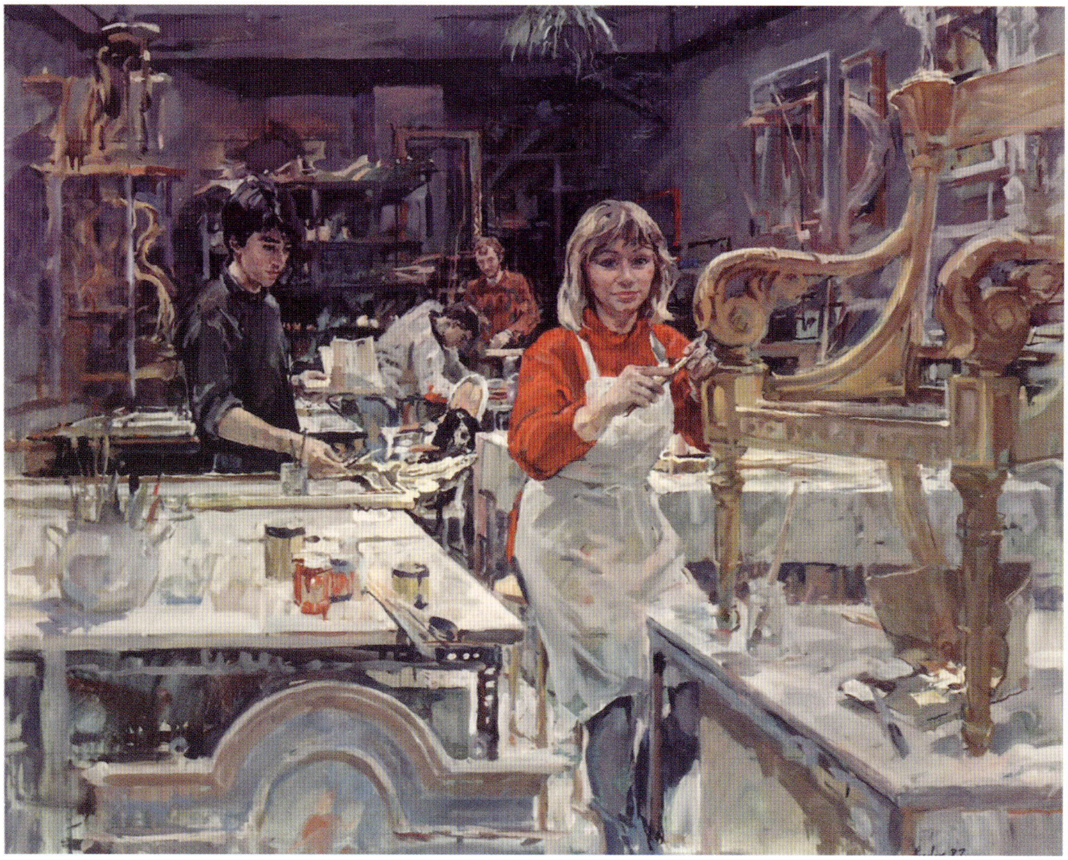

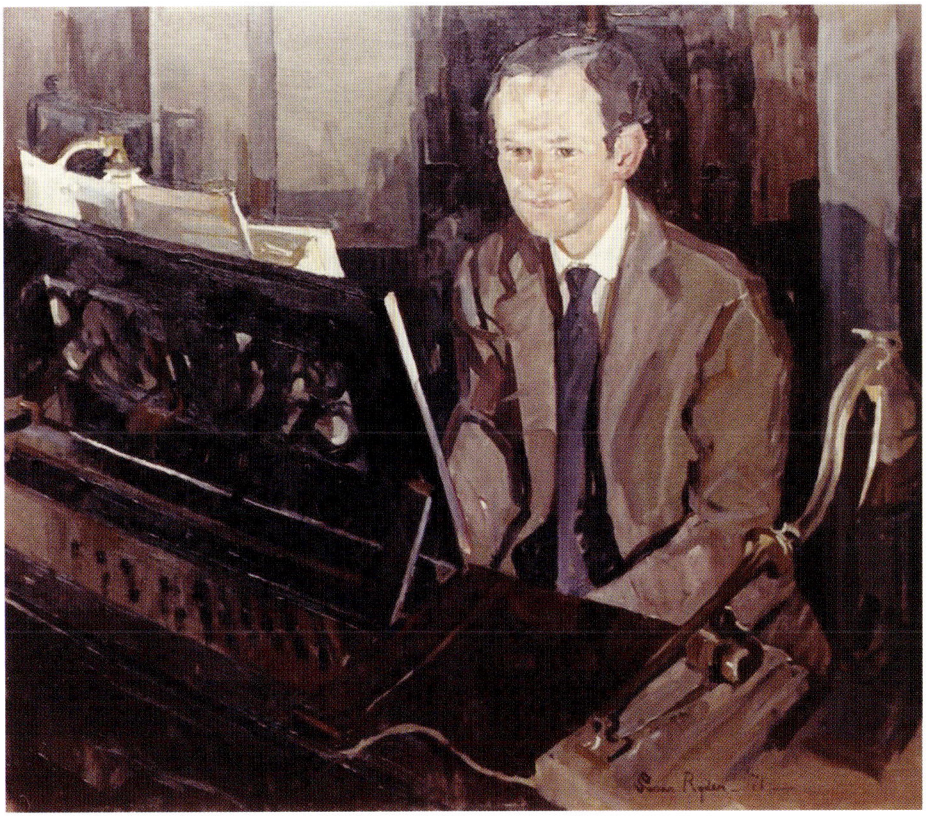

Jeremy, 26 × 30

the border in Northumberland. In such inspiring settings she was able to develop her passion for painting interiors.

The move to London also necessitated her leaving her Suffolk framer, Andy Kinloch, and finding a new one. She soon discovered the workshop of Christina Leder, in nearby Parsons Green. Leder, an expert gilder as well as a framer, had built an extensive client list of prominent painters, including Ken Howard and Mary Fedden. Her skill lay not only in her gilding, but in the huge range of styles and personal attention to colour and shape of frame. Ryder soon painted a portrait of Leder, at work gilding a chair in her studio, with three team members tooling away behind her, and a spaniel resting in one of her gilded chairs. Leder still uses the portrait on the portal of her website, and Ryder still uses her services, delighted for her paintings to be enhanced by a master craftswoman's carefully wrought frames.

Once Belchester was fully restored, the family lived half in London, half in Berwickshire, while Oliver and Susannah grew up. They and Martin, of course, sat for many portraits, while Ryder continued to take on commissions. She was aided enormously by first the Greys and then Sue and Chris Hewitt helping with the housework and gardening, freeing her up to continue painting. Ryder's portrait of Sue Hewitt now hangs in the Royal Society of Portrait Painters collection at Girton College, Cambridge.

In 1984 Pears Soap's marketing department contacted Ryder, asking her to paint that year's Miss Pears winner, four-year-old Jenny Curran. Pears' director, Thomas J. Barratt, had implemented a revolutionary and highly successful branding campaign for the soap company in the 1880s, using images of cute children posed in elegant interiors to promote his product (including an adulterated version of Sir John Everett Millais's famous *Bubbles* painting). In 1958 Pears launched a new campaign, annually crowning a young girl 'Miss Pears' and choosing a prominent portrait painter to fashion their likeness. This was one of the rare occasions Ryder painted a portrait in her own home, devising a set-up whereby the girl was cutting up newspapers with a pair of red scissors, notionally making cuttings of all the publicity about her winning the award (rather a 'meta' concept, it must be said!). The little girl, Ryder remembers, wasn't the most compliant of sitters, and when asked not to disturb the carefully arranged newspapers on the floor, proceeded to kick them around. 'Don't tell her what to do, because she'll just do the opposite', said her mother. The unveiling of the portrait, of course, garnered much media attention, as it was designed to do, and further enhanced Ryder's reputation.

Doors started opening for Ryder, as she became more established. She caught the attention of Bill Patterson, an experienced art dealer who ran the prestigious gallery W.H. Patterson on Albemarle Street in Mayfair. The affable dealer, who had been in the trade since being demobbed from the RAF after the war, selected six of Ryder's works for a show featuring seven NEAC artists, including Diana Armfield RA, Tom Coates and Ken Howard RA. Delighted that all her

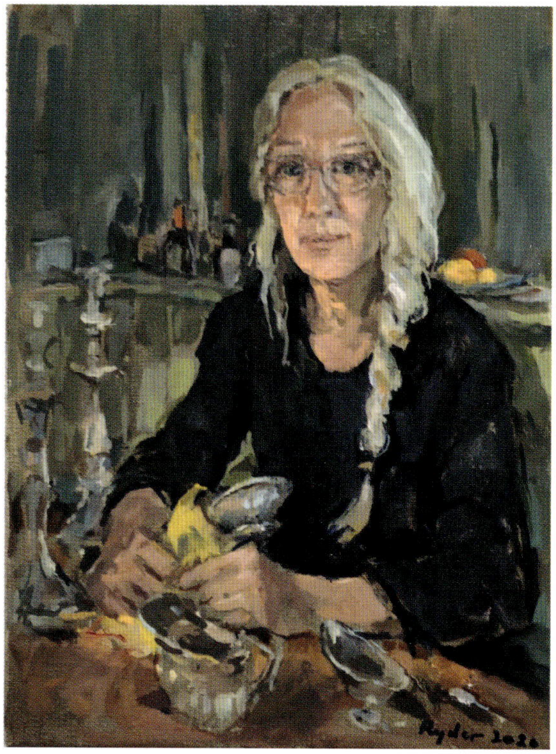

Sue cleaning silver, 20 × 16

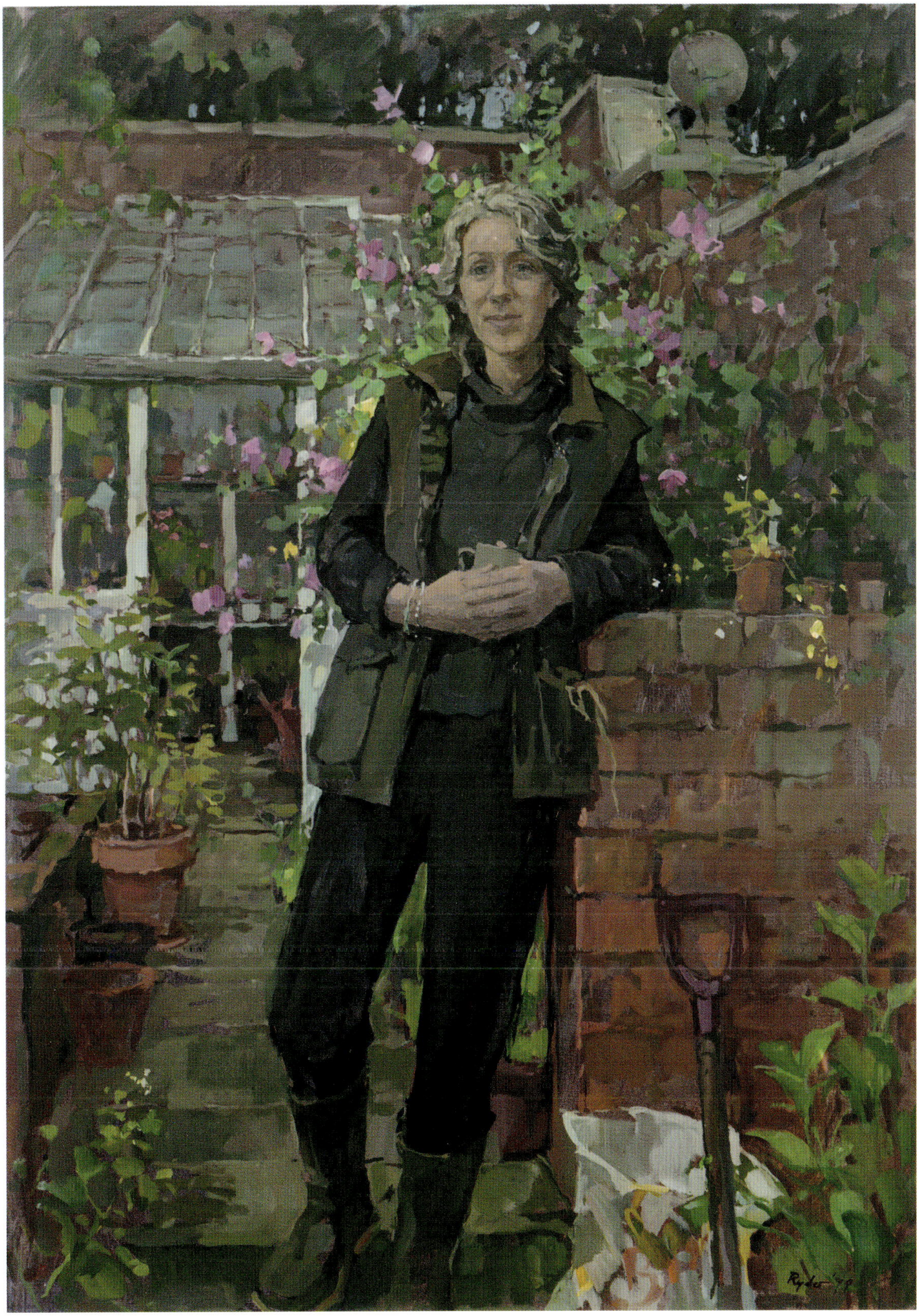

Sue Hewitt, Gardener, 36 × 28

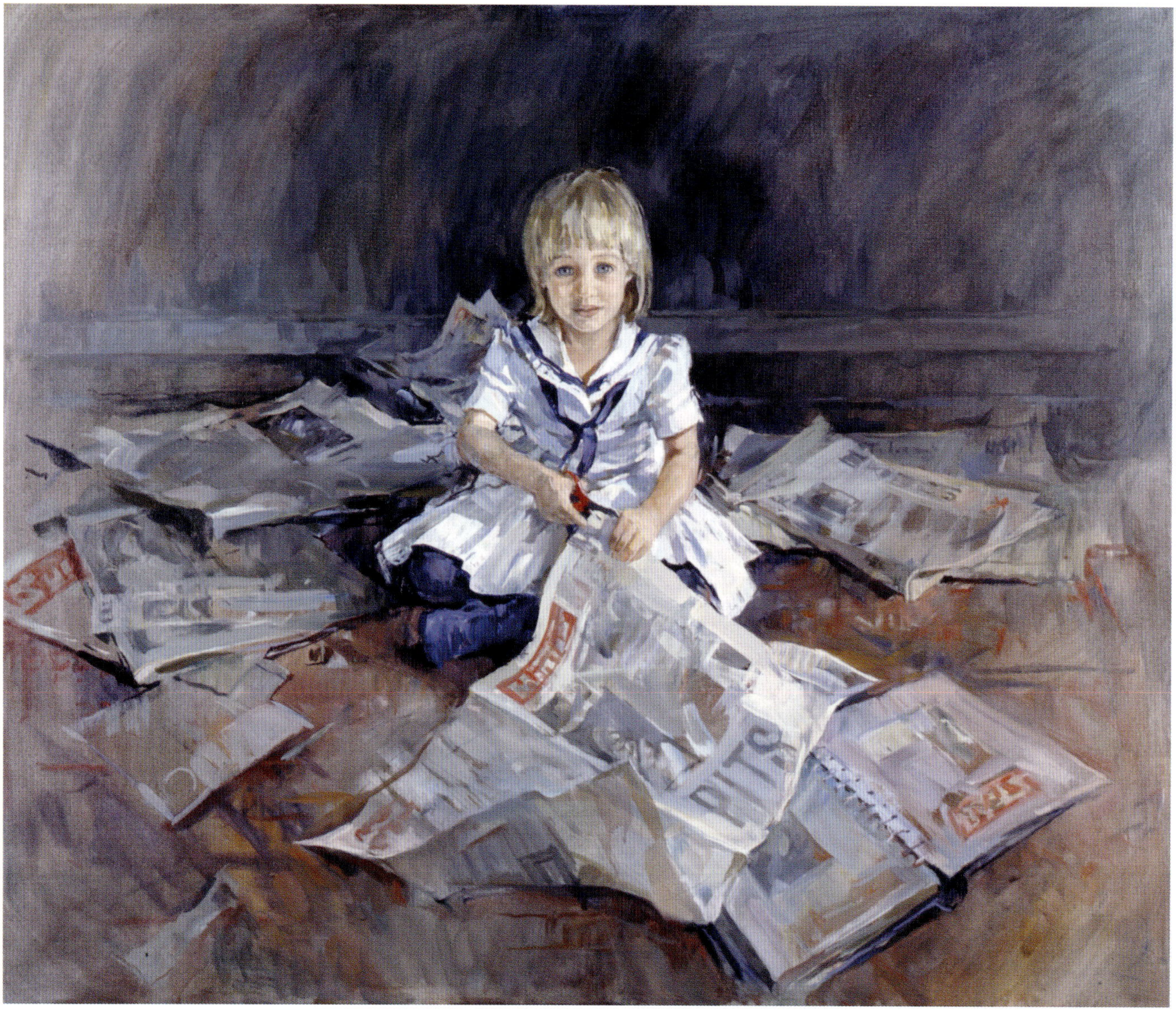

Miss Pears, 1984, 40 × 50

paintings had sold, she plucked up the courage to ask Patterson (and fellow director John White) for a solo show, and they accepted, telling her they were about to ask her, anyway. She went on to have a succession of sell-out solo shows at 'Pattersons', in 1989, 1994 and 1999.

In 1989 Ryder was given the opportunity to practise her landscape painting, on a trip to India. Susannah, now eighteen, had found a teaching job in the southern region of Tamil Nadu, and Ryder and her husband linked a visit to her with a trip to Kashmir, where the son-in-law of friends ran shooting trips. They organised a party of ten ('six guns, four wives'), to stay on a houseboat, and Ryder spent the daytime painting the spectacular lakes and mountains in winter sunlight, while her husband joined the other men shooting.

By this time an annual painting trip to France with friends had been long established in Ryder's calendar. This practice began in 1980 and has continued for the subsequent four decades. Jane Corsellis showed the way, joined by Annabel Gosling and Ryder, with Diana Calvert persuaded to later join them. In later years Ryder's artist friend Julia Trotter came

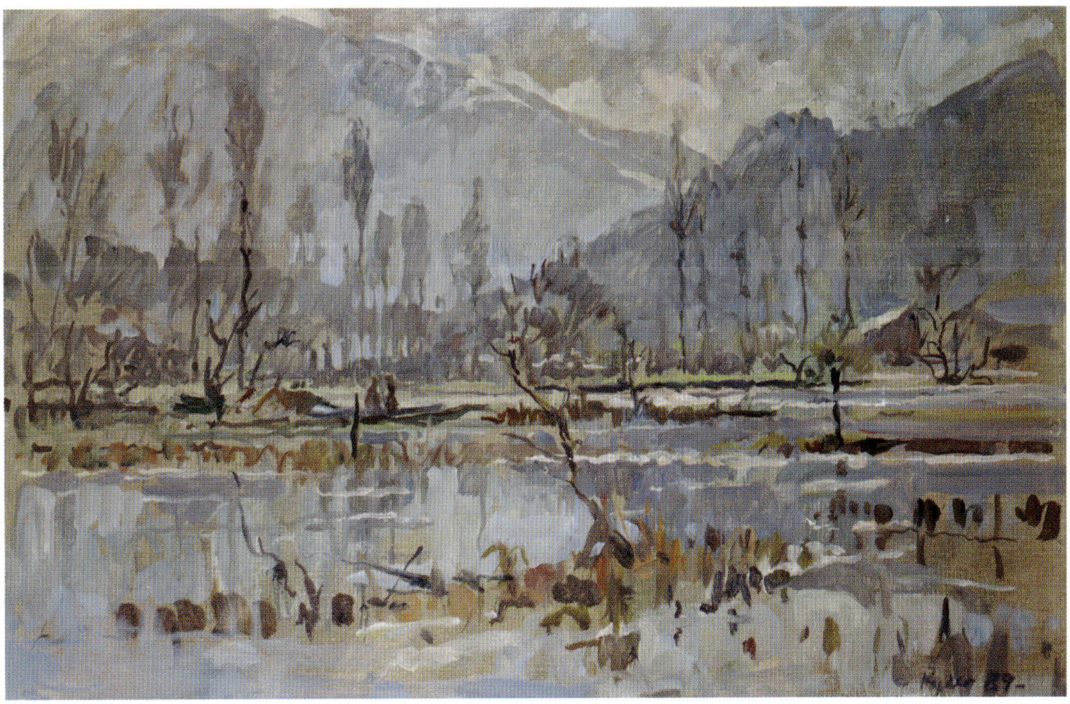

Kashmir, 12 × 18

with her and Gosling on many trips. Generally, the painters' husbands would join them in the second week, spending their days on wine tasting trips, or playing golf, and trying not to get in the way, though adding hugely to the fun (a golf bag being covered in oil paint being the least of their worries).

The maximum number of painter friends for a trip is three: more than that and they find they get in one another's way, as they set up terrace scenes and interiors, with landscapes also being a popular subject. Often it was just Gosling and Ryder, with their car loaded with canvases and props, destination Provence, the Loire, the Dordogne, or Normandy. In 2018 American artist Hope Reis was to join Ryder and Trotter, having first met over the internet. Variety of venue has always been a consideration: only twice have they returned to the same inspiring place.

On one occasion, the sixty-year-old property owner asked the painters if he could bring his mother to meet them. They were surprised when he later showed up with a glamorous forty-year-old woman. . . until they realised he had said 'La Maire' (the Mayoress), and not 'Ma mère'.

Ryder has also enjoyed regular foreign painting trips courtesy of friends who own properties abroad. They have been incredibly kind and welcoming over many years, and have enabled Ryder to broaden the range of her interiors and landscapes.

As the eighties turned into the nineties, there was further success at private galleries. Ryder's work was shown at the Peter Keyser Gallery in Dorset, the Richard Hagen Gallery on Broadway and the Brian Sinfield Gallery, in Burford. In September 1991, Sinfield included Ryder in a show of contemporary British artists, *Against the Light*, which also included her former teachers Brian Dunstan and Diana Armfield, as well as Ken Howard and Fred Cuming. Sinfield used a Ryder painting, *The Red Chairs* (of an al fresco dining table in a French courtyard), to illustrate the private view's invitation card. Soon afterwards, he gave her a solo show in his prestigious Cotswolds gallery.

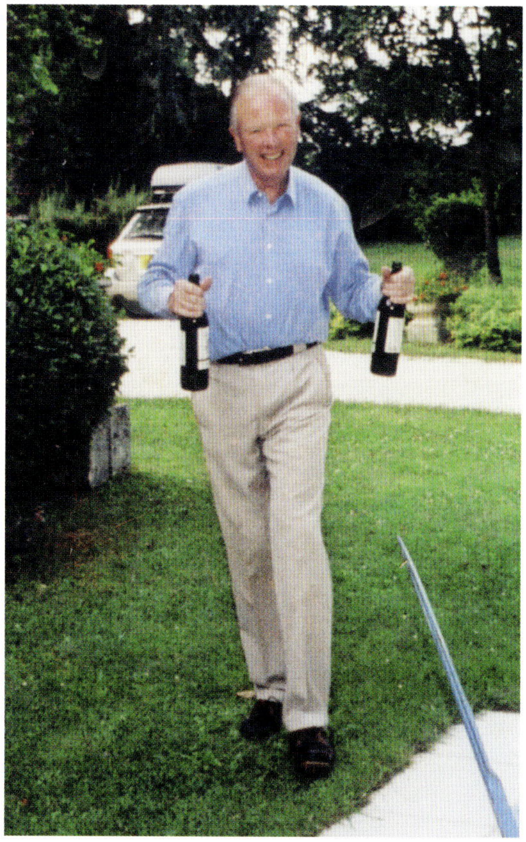

Martin Bates

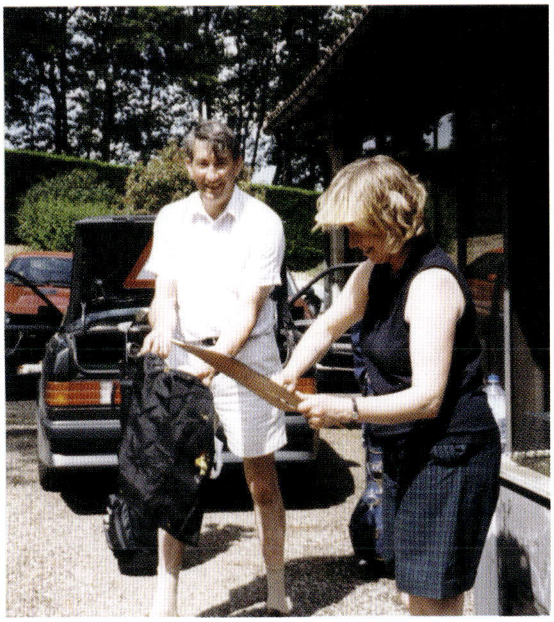

Alexander and Julie Trotter

That same year, Alexon Fashion House chose five women artists to paint five female celebrities. Ryder was chosen to paint the actor, Nicola Paget. The venue was her dressing room at the Aldwych Theatre. Sittings were spread over four Wednesday mornings, before the matinees. By an extraordinary coincidence the same taxi that dropped off Ryder and her blank canvas was passing to pick her up after the final sitting.

Ryder is an honorary member of the Society of Women Artists and in 1992, after twenty years of exhibiting, Ryder was elected as a member of the Royal Society of Portrait Painters. This was after her good friend George Bruce, a renowned portrait painter, talented mimic and lover of adventurous sports, had become president of the society. Bruce, also a Byam Shaw graduate, had long been an important ally; gallery manager John Deston and the society's commissions consultant Annabel Elton were also very supportive. It was Elton's job to put the right artists in touch with the right sitters, which led to a good deal of interesting work for Ryder.

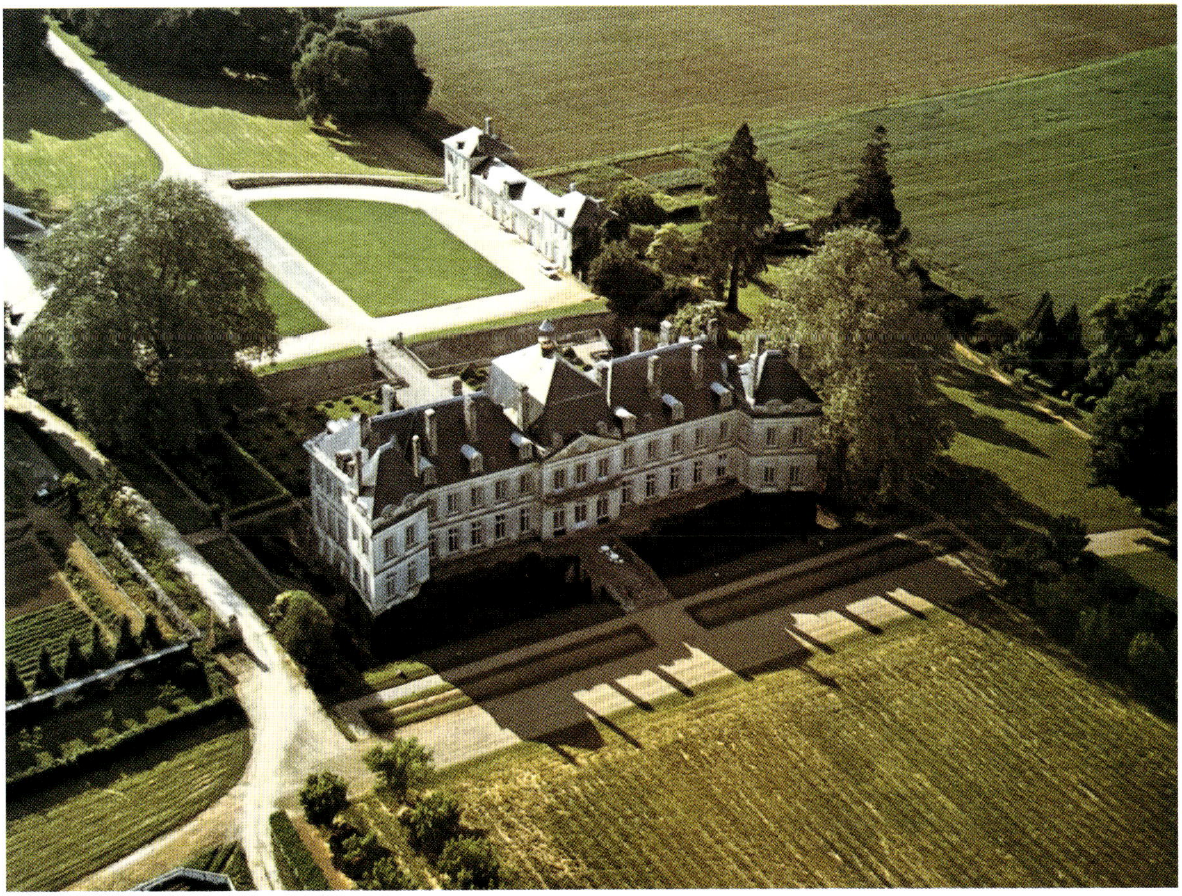

Château de Plassac

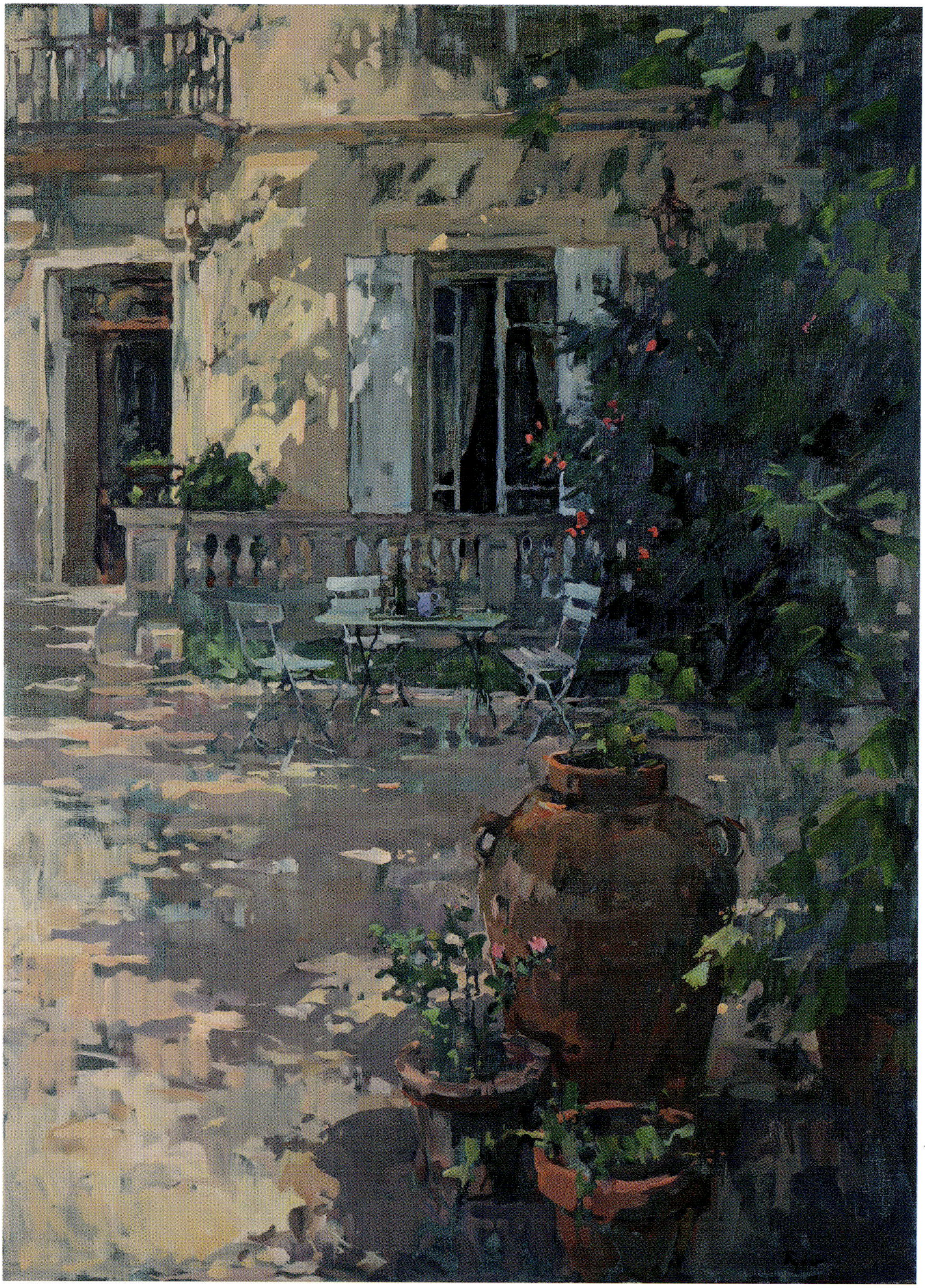

FACING PAGE

Terrace Urns, Province, 25 × 34

RIGHT

Kitchen Table – Mas de la Rose, 34 × 38

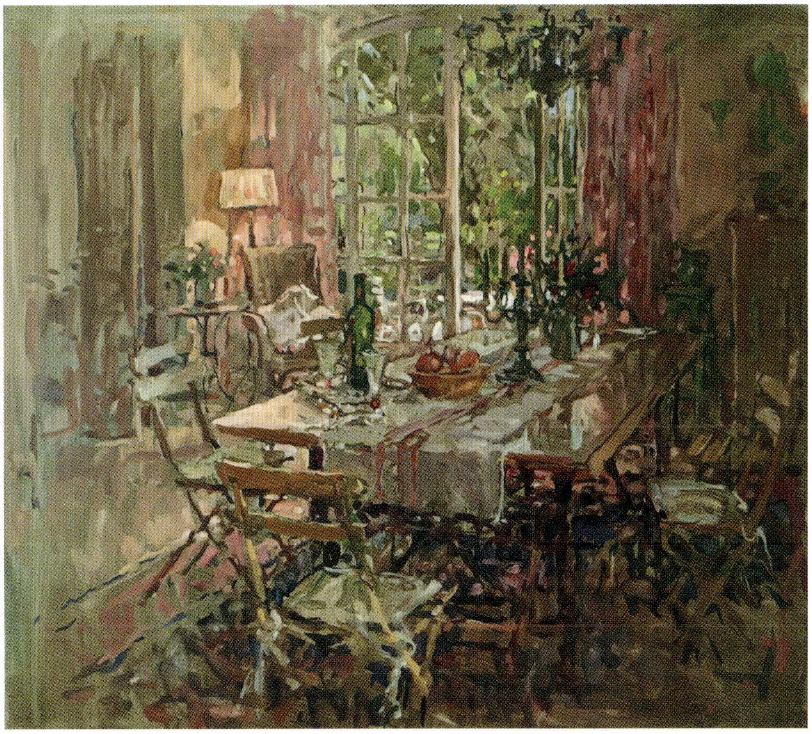

Courtyard Drinks, Feraillou 14 × 20

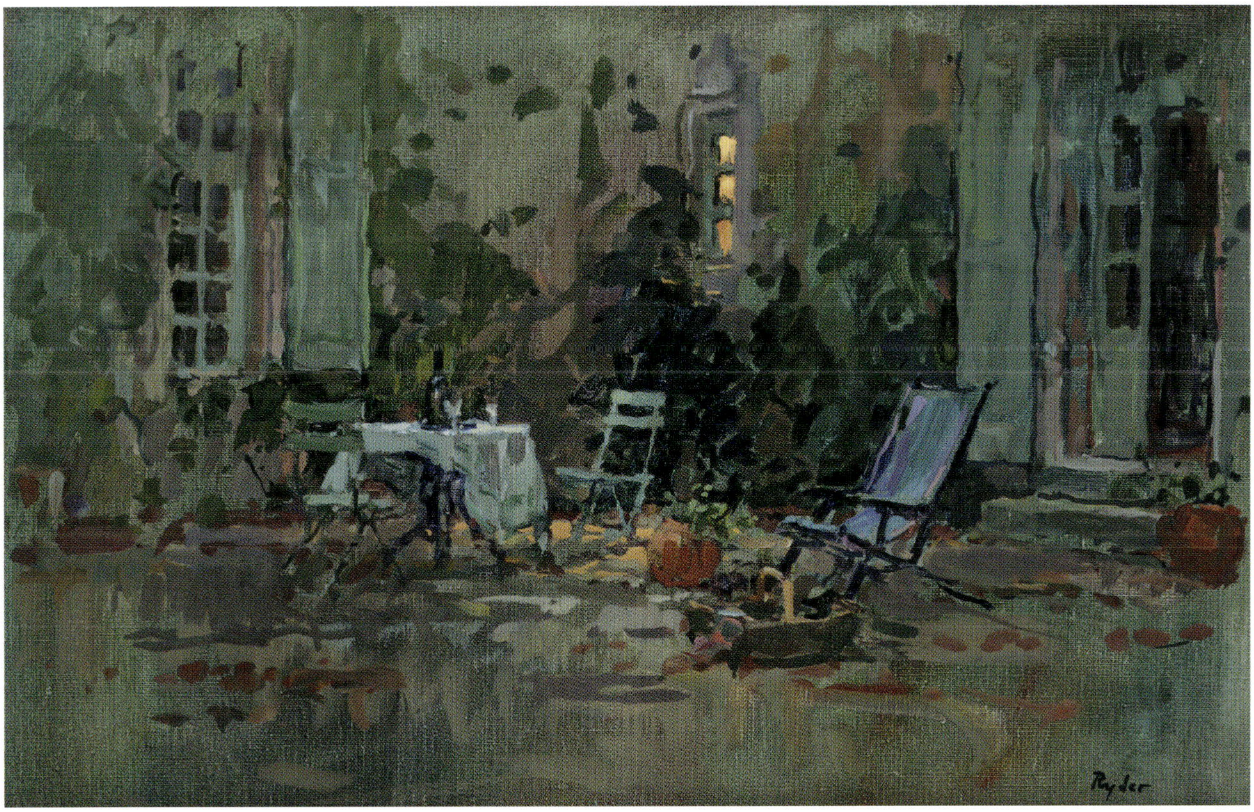

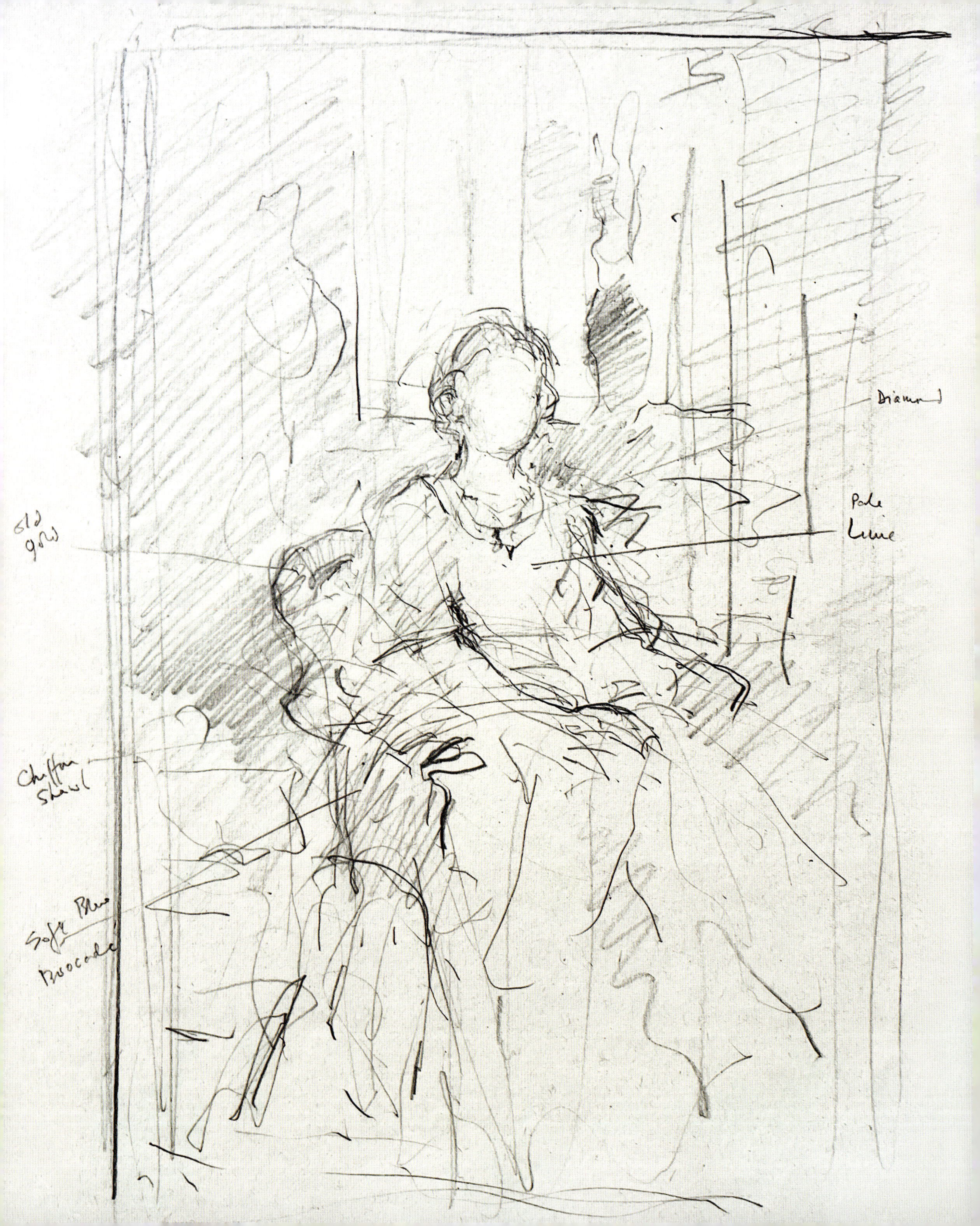
Diamond
Pale
Lime
Old
gold
Chiffon
Shawl
Soft Blue
Brocade

PAINTING QUEEN ELIZABETH

In March 1996, Ryder was called into the Pall Mall headquarters of the Royal Automobile Club, to be interviewed by a panel of three executive members. She was rather excited: because it was the one hundredth anniversary of the RAC's foundation, they wanted to mark the occasion with a royal portrait, to hang in the clubhouse. She assumed that the subject would be Prince Michael of Kent, then President of the RAC. At the end of the interview, she was told that that wasn't the case. The portrait was to be of Queen Elizabeth.

Painting the monarch is, of course, an enormous honour for a portrait artist. Over the next few days, as the RAC executives pondered over which artist in their shortlist of three would be chosen to be honoured with the commission, Ryder was naturally nervous. Every phone call might be them, with the news. She decided to keep the possible commission a secret, so as not to disappoint her friends and family if the decision went against her.

A few days later some great friends arrived for lunch, and were still in the hallway when a telephone call did prove to be from the RAC. The news was good, and Ryder couldn't contain her joy as it was confirmed. The friends overheard her side of the conversation, and gathered exactly what had happened. When she hung up, they joked: 'Shall we curtsey?' It was a happy lunch party.

There were extensive deliberations with the Queen's Dresser, Angela Kelly. The RAC had proposed that Her Majesty should wear a cocktail dress. Ryder thought this inappropriate, as the Queen's legs would be at eye level when the painting was eventually hung. When the artist suggested an informal evening dress, Kelly, on the telephone, outlined no fewer than nine garments that might suit, describing each one in some detail.

Preliminary sketch for
HM Queen Elizabeth II

On arriving at the Palace to choose between these, Ryder was told by a rather crestfallen Kelly that the Queen had since become involved in the decision-making process, and had whittled the nine down to two. One was made of 'plummy-coloured' dark wool, the other was a 'rather wonderful' green chiffon affair. Ryder suspected that Her Majesty was gently forcing her hand: she happily chose the chiffon dress.

Ryder was given six one-hour sittings in the Yellow Drawing Room, where she had painted Diana back in 1981. On that occasion she hadn't painted the interior of the room, preferring a simple background to accentuate the splendour of Diana's wedding dress. Sixteen years down the line, and by now an accomplished interiors painter, she decided to make the background an integral part of the painting, as she had come to do in all her portraits. She was allowed to wander round the Palace with a porter, to choose which chair to use. She rigged up her usual Hollywood lamp, to cast light on her royal subject.

Ryder found the Queen to be a charming sitter. Not the stillest, but full of conversation and gentle humour. The artist always encourages conversation during the painting process, as it brings out the personality of the sitter, and helps her to animate the portrait. But she had heard that one wasn't supposed to initiate a conversation with the monarch. Happily, on asking the Equerry, he said Her Majesty would like to be treated like other sitters.

Ryder normally starts a portrait by doing several pencil sketches on paper, in order to work out the composition, but in this case, with little time in front of such an important subject, she made one quick sketch before going straight into the painting process. The Queen's warm, chatty manner soon put her at ease: in fact, she kept having to remind herself that she was painting the country's reigning monarch. The conversation ranged far and wide, as she applied paint to canvas. Michael Fagan, the man who had broken into Buckingham Palace in 1982, had just been imprisoned (for another unrelated offence) so that episode was discussed, among many others. The first sitting lasted longer than the hour she had been allocated; the Queen didn't call a halt to proceedings. Ryder wanted to maximise the time at her

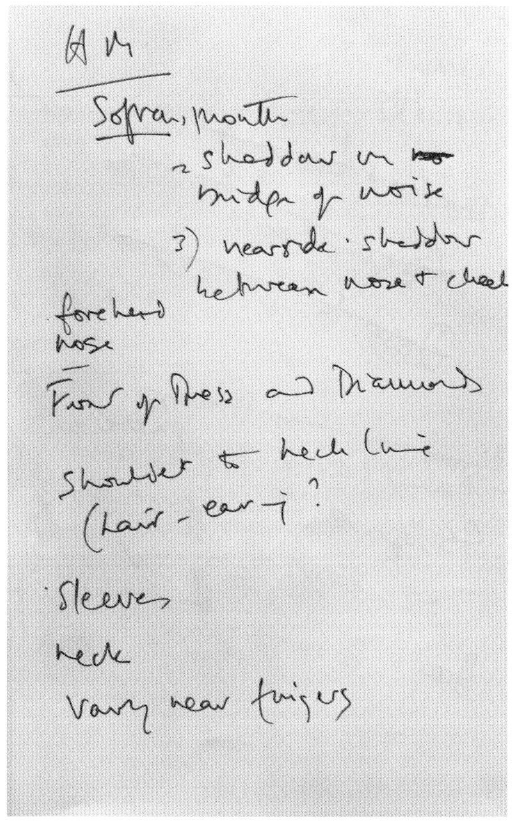
HM

2 shaddow on bridge of nose

3) nearside shaddow between nose & cheek

forehead

nose

Front of Dress and Diamonds

Shoulder to neck line

Sleeves

neck

Vary near fingers

Ryder's notes for HM Queen Elizabeth II

disposal, so she didn't say anything, making good use of the supplementary fifteen minutes.

Towards the end of the first sitting, Ryder asked Her Majesty if she wanted to have a look at how the painting was developing. The Queen came round to look at the canvas, before amusingly remarking that she had actually been following progress all along in a mirror behind Ryder. It's just as well the painter didn't realise this: she has never liked being watched while in the process of painting, it makes her strokes self-conscious, and takes her out of the zone in which her mark making becomes intuitive.

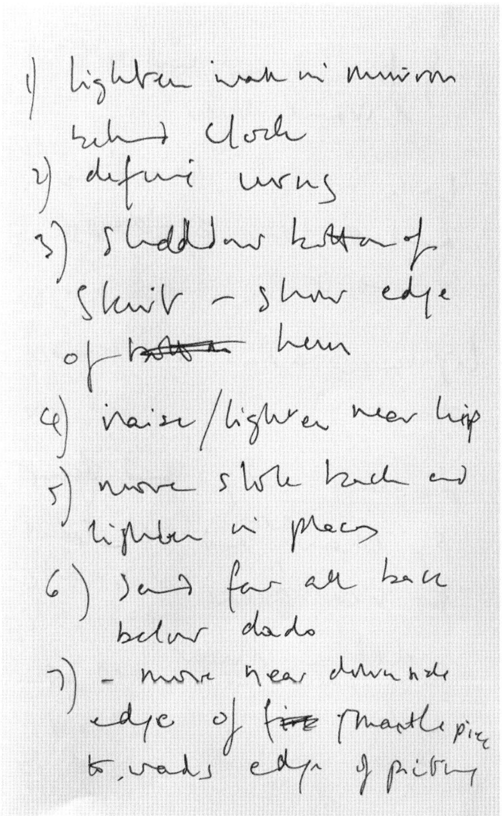

At the end of the first session, as Her Majesty took her leave, Ryder was slightly confused when the Queen remained standing in the doorway for several seconds, smiling, as if waiting for something, before eventually making her exit. An anxious moment: she later realised that etiquette demanded a curtsey on saying farewell. Nobody had told her (she made sure to remember after subsequent sittings). After the Queen's departure, Ryder was allowed to continue painting in the drawing room for as long as required.

The schedule of six, weekly sittings was broken by a three-week hiatus. The room was needed for a state visit by South African President Nelson Mandela, who was put up at the Palace. This presented a problem for Ryder. Between sittings she normally records the exact placement and angle of the sitter's chair and her easel with masking tape on the floor, so she can resume her work with everything as it has been during the last session. This became impossible. Instead, she used staples, invisible to the eye, hoping they wouldn't later be hoovered up. She was happy to find, on resuming the painting process, that they were still there.

After the last sitting with the Queen, Ryder took the painting back to her Berwickshire studio to apply some finishing touches, which felt like something of a secret mission. Carefully bubble-wrapped, the 60×40-inch canvas was duly loaded into the back of her car, and she drove it the 330 miles back home, up the A1. When told of this plan, the Queen expressed her worry that if Ryder had to make a sudden stop, she might be decapitated by the painting. She made sure to drive more carefully than she had ever driven before, more concerned about the safety of the painting than the safety of her head.

The portrait was unveiled at the annual *Royal Society of Portrait Painters Exhibition* at the Mall Galleries, round the corner from the Palace, in July 1998. Prince Michael of Kent did the honours, and there was a mob of press photographers and journalists there for the occasion. A comparison with Antony Williams's warts-and-all portrait of the year before was inevitably made, and the artist was asked if her rendition of the Queen was designed to flatter. 'I wanted to capture her overall warmth,' she replied, amid camera clicks and flashes. 'There are no wrinkles, I don't paint in such detail, but I don't think I've flattered Her Majesty. I've painted her as I saw her, and I saw her as an attractive person.'

As might be expected, there was a mixed response to the portrait in the many press reviews over the following days. *Art Review*, a magazine which championed the Young British Artists movement and all things conceptual, called it 'ridiculously obsequious'. Tony Winterton, the winner of that year's Ondaatje Prize, suggested, when pressed, that he found it 'too chocolate box', which was reported in some papers. But most of the pro-monarchy newspapers admired the painting, pleased that it wiped away memories of the less-than-flattering official portrait of the Queen, painted in 1996 by Antony Williams. The *Daily Mail*'s headline read 'The Queen is shown in the best of lights'. The *Evening Standard* announced: 'How the RAC restored our gracious Queen'. A Reuters report that was placed in local papers all over the country, began: 'A year has passed, yet the Queen looks younger. The latest portrait of the Queen, now aged seventy-one, shows her rejuvenated and recaptures a warm majesty'.

After the exhibition, the painting was moved to its permanent home at the RAC's London clubhouse at 89 Pall Mall. When later interviewed by the *Evening News*, in her Berwickshire home, Ryder was asked to compare her portrait of the Queen, to that of Antony Williams. 'I think they're very different views of the same person, and I admire his work,' she stated. 'But his portrait wasn't how I saw the Queen. He has a young man's view of a seventy-year-old while I have a fifty-three-year-old's view.'

HM Queen Elizabeth II, 60 × 40

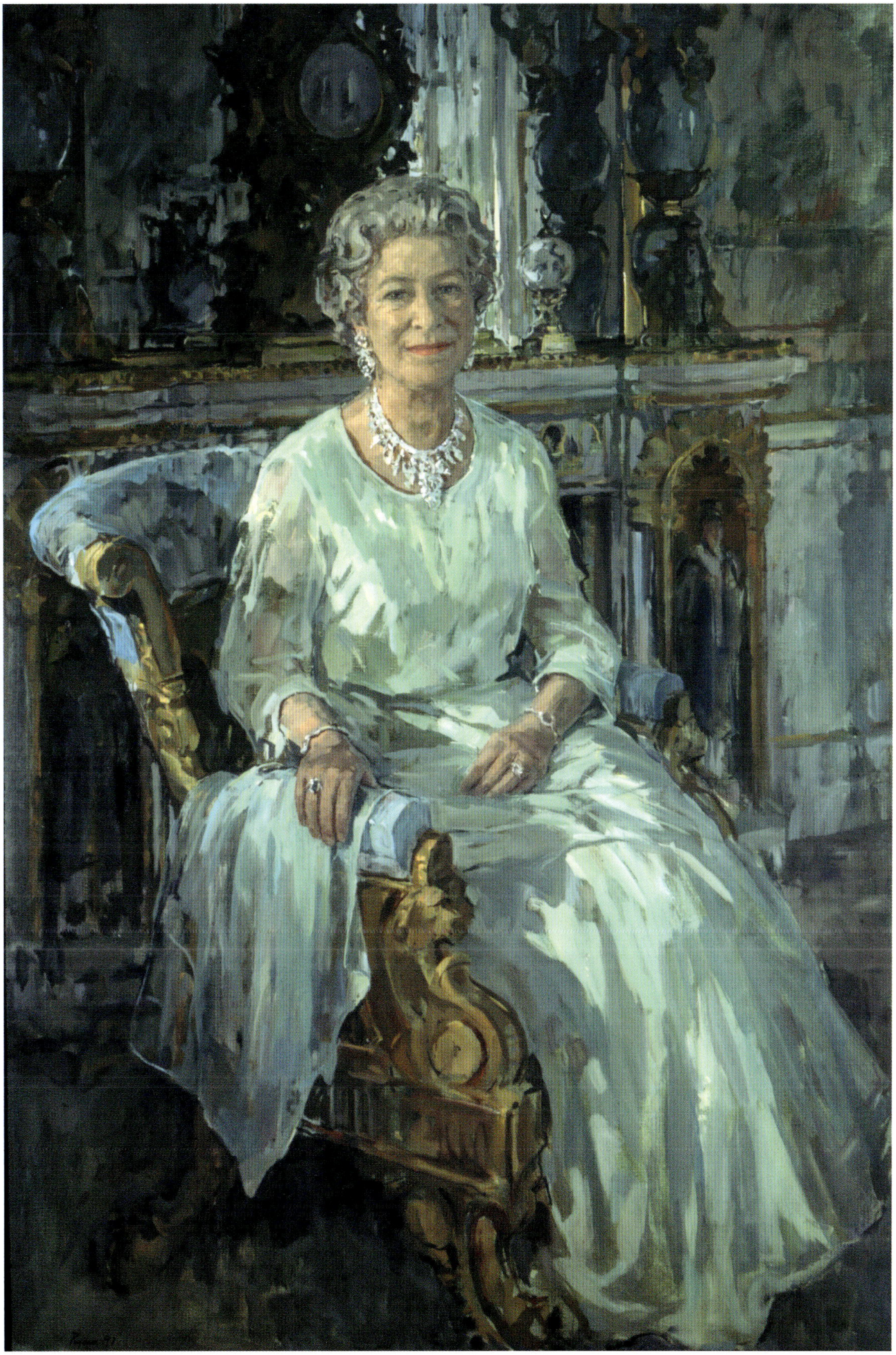

TRAVEL

In 2002 Ryder was honoured to be made Vice President of the Royal Society of Portrait Painters, working alongside that era's President Andrew Festing, and executive officer Meri Benham. She was called on to help organise committee meetings, private views and lunches. She had plenty of business in London during this busy period. After the death of Bill Patterson and John White, Ryder was taken on by James Kayll, first at the Oakham Gallery, in Bury Street, and then at Ackermanns in Knightsbridge. She found Kayll to be extremely supportive.

Around this time, Ryder discovered film footage that her father Robert Ryder had featured in as a young man, shot by the scientist Launcelot Fleming (later to become Bishop of Norwich, and her godfather), documenting an extraordinary voyage he had made between 1934 and 1936, while serving in the Royal Navy. Having successfully sailed the ketch *Tai-Mo-Shan* from Shanghai to Dartmouth the previous year, aged twenty-three, Lieutenant Ryder was chosen to be the skipper of the schooner *Penola*, on a surveying expedition to Antarctica, led by Australian explorer John Rymill. The expedition was fraught with problems – *Penola* wasn't well equipped to make such an arduous voyage – but was nevertheless a great success, charting new areas of the continent that had previously not been seen by man, and discovering that Graham Land was part of the continent of Antarctica and not an archipelago, as previously imagined. Robert Ryder was awarded the Polar Medal for the part he played in the expedition.

Susan and Martin's close friends Anthony and Nicky Clifton-Brown had made a trip to Antarctica on a converted

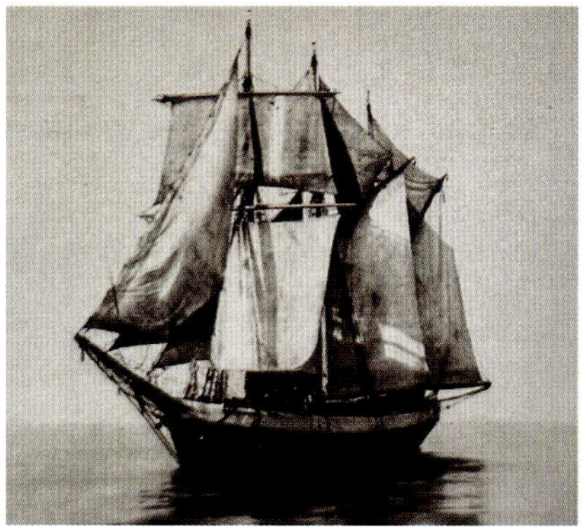

Penola under sail

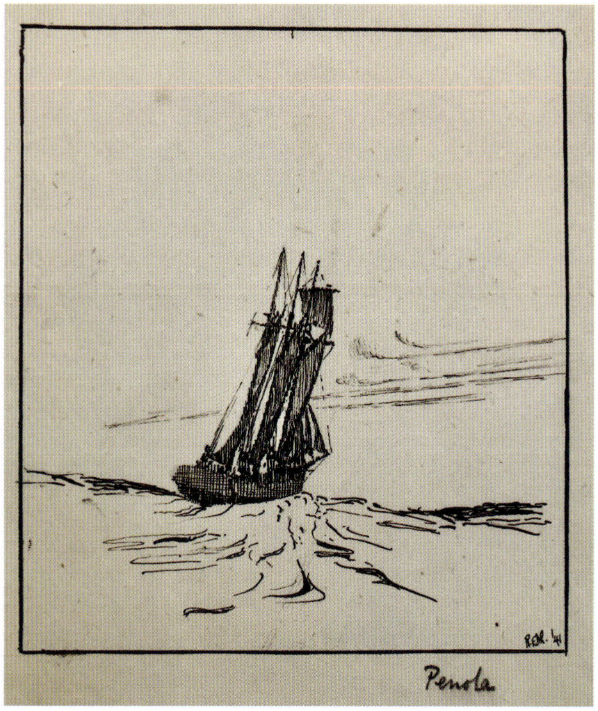

Robert Ryder's pen and ink sketch of the *Penola*

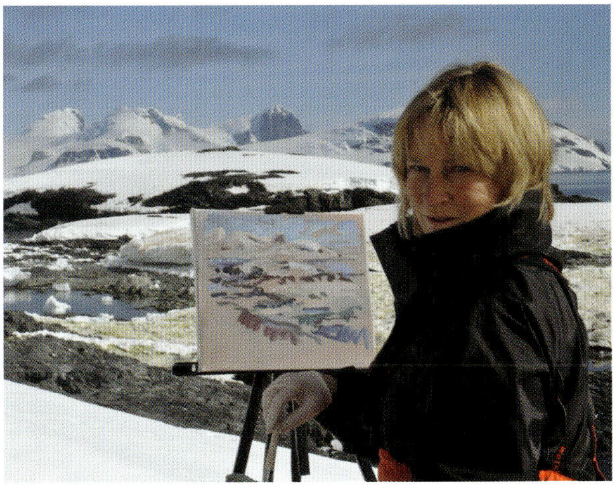

Ryder painting in Antarctica

Russian survey ship in 2002, and, having borrowed Fleming's video, had shown it to the skipper and crew, pointing out their connection with Lieutenant Ryder's daughter. This led the ship's captain and the Clifton-Browns to suggest that Susan Ryder and Martin should make the trip themselves. Martin had by now retired, and Ryder was eager to follow in her father's footsteps, so they decided to go, leaving England in February 2010.

Robert Ryder had painted scores of watercolour sketches on his voyage, as had his elder brother Lisle, also a member of the *Penola* crew. His daughter, who had inherited some of these paintings, and greatly cherished them, planned to follow suit, but deemed it too difficult to take all her oil painting paraphernalia with her on such an adventure. She was persuaded otherwise, however, when she made a preparatory visit to the British Arctic Survey venue, in Cambridge, before departure. There she was presented with a book of Edward Seago's oil paintings, which he had accomplished on a trip to Antarctica on HMY *Britannia* with Prince Philip in 1956 and 1957. Inspired, Ryder decided that she too must take her oils.

Making careful preparations for the journey, she assembled nine canvases in three different sizes, stretching three layers of canvas on each frame. She tinted each one with a light blue wash, and packed them in her suitcase. She also took her travel easel, oil paints and palette, as well as watercolours and paper so she could accomplish her landscapes in both mediums.

The couple stopped off on the way in Bueno Aires, to visit their friends Ana and Nick Livingston. Ryder had got to know Ana, a fine painter of still lifes and landscapes, while staying with good friends in Provence. It was summer in Argentina, so they left their summer clothes at the Livingstons before embarking south to Ushuaia, joining friends Damon and Sam De Laszlo on the Russian vessel *Sergey Vavilov*.

The ship, carrying ninety-five passengers, took them as far as the southern base of Robert Ryder's *Penola* expedition, and Ryder was thrilled to be able to paint exactly the same scenes as her father had painted, nearly seventy-five years before. She felt that these works were an act of remembrance for her father, who she had loved dearly, and who had been such an influence on her career as an artist. Robert Ryder was much missed, having died suddenly in 1987 of a heart attack, fittingly on the deck of his own yacht off the Channel Islands.

One afternoon, Ryder, left on her own on the shore, as the others went off exploring, set up her easel to paint the icy scene before her. She had been told in no uncertain terms never to go within 5 metres of any wildlife she encountered, so as not to distress the animals, or to carry disease from one Antarctic landing place to another. She was amused, then, when several penguins came up to her to investigate what she was up to, clambering over her rucksack and her boots, and well and truly breaking the sacred 5-metre rule. The penguins became the subject of that afternoon's painting.

Ryder returned from Antarctica having accomplished nine oil paintings and scores of watercolours. These, shown alongside works by her father and her uncle Lisle, formed half of an exhibition of her work, in June 2011, at the Ackermann Gallery.

The other half of the exhibition came from another trip Ryder made together with her husband, in May of the same year, to China. Again, her subject matter involved following in the footsteps of an intrepid relative, in this case her paternal grandfather Charles Ryder. Ryder had been an officer in the Royal Engineers and explorer who rose to become the Surveyor General of India just after the First World War.

This adventure came in several parts. First the couple went to Nanjing, a place of great interest to Bates, who was researching the life of fifteenth-century explorer Zheng He. A symposium on that topic had been arranged for Bates by Nanjing University. After that they joined Anthony and Nicky Clifton-Brown canoeing along the Dragon River, in Yangshuo County. Finally, retracing Charles Ryder's footsteps, they explored the territory around the Tibetan border.

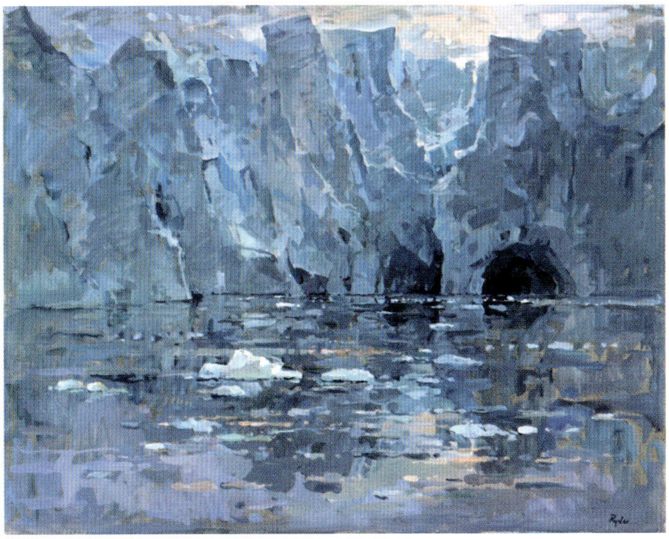

Ice cliffs and caves, Antarctic Peninsula, 28 × 36

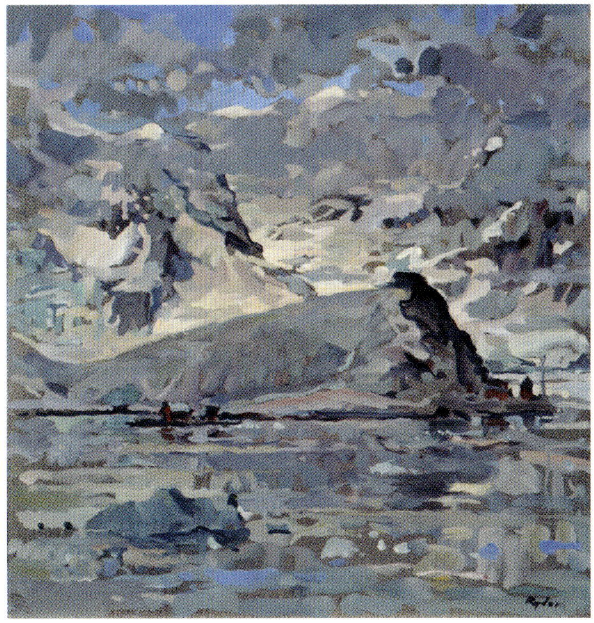

Near Port Lochroy, 24 × 24

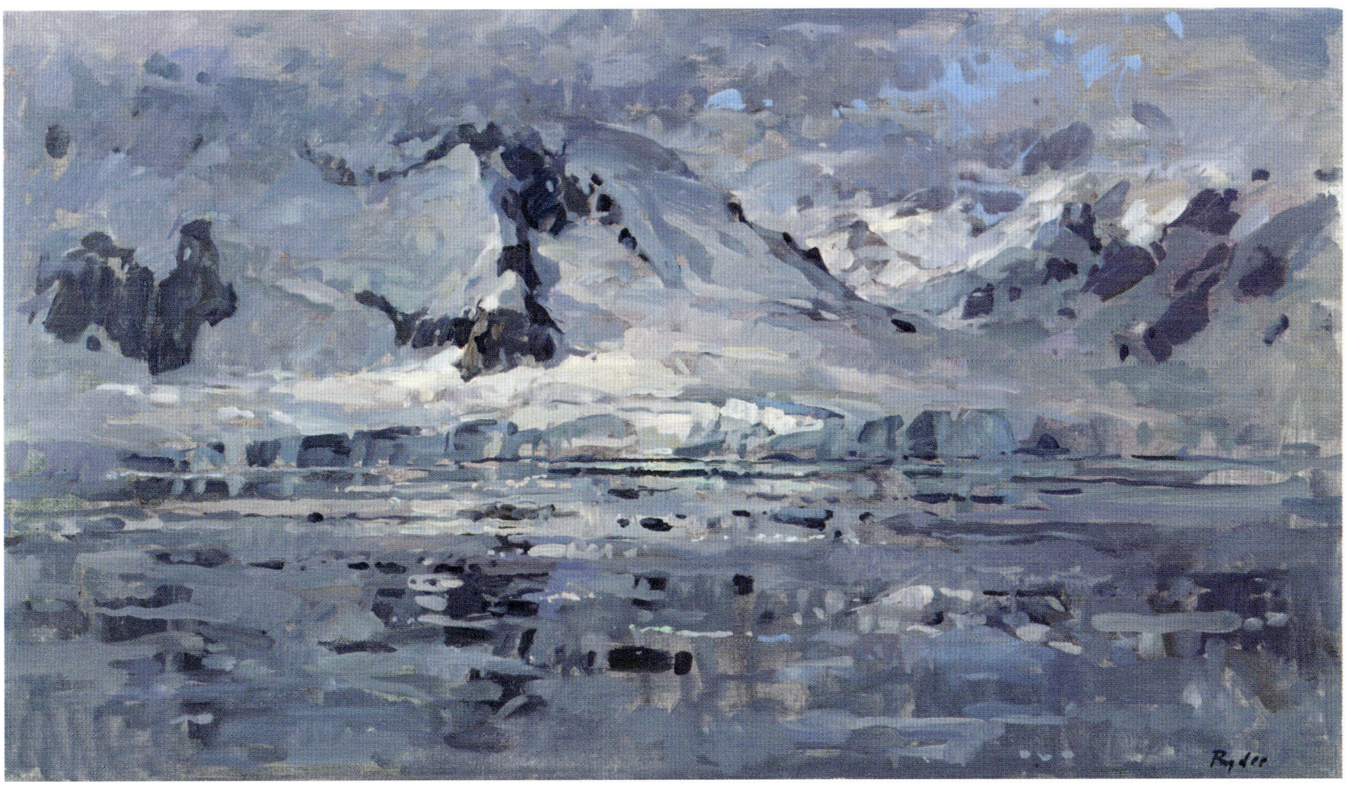

The Gerlach Strait, 18 × 30

2010 had been an exciting and fascinating year for Susan Ryder, taken right out of her professional comfort zone of quiet interiors and gentle portraits. Ryder came home with many watercolours: the resulting exhibition at the Ackermann Gallery was a great success, showcasing the artist's skill in capturing the nuances of the fall of light, whether describing the reflections of shimmering ice cliffs in frozen Antarctica, or the warmth of scores of red lanterns in a crowded Yunnan Province marketplace.

It was her last exhibition at Ackermanns, which closed the following year. In 2011, art dealer/gallery owners Matthew Hall and Tiffany Panter persuaded Ryder to return to the Oakham Gallery, where she enjoyed further successful solo shows. Soon they changed the name of the gallery to Panter & Hall, subsequently moving it to its present location in Pall Mall. Ryder enjoys solo exhibitions in the gallery every four years, largely featuring her exquisite interiors and terrace scenes, as well as occasional still lifes and landscapes. The carefully chosen titles of her shows reflect both her subject matter, and her talent for describing external and interior

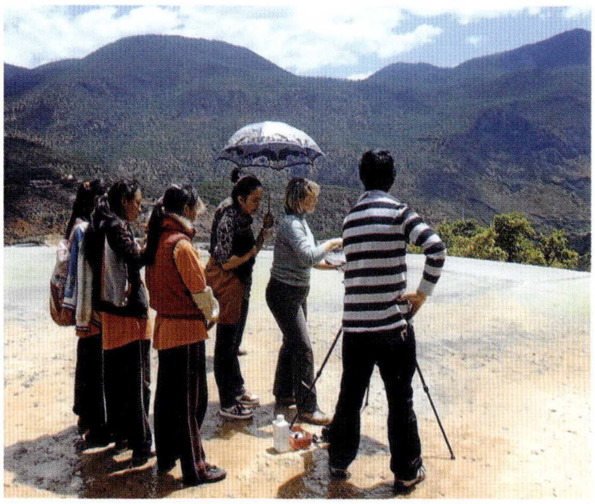

Ryder painting in China

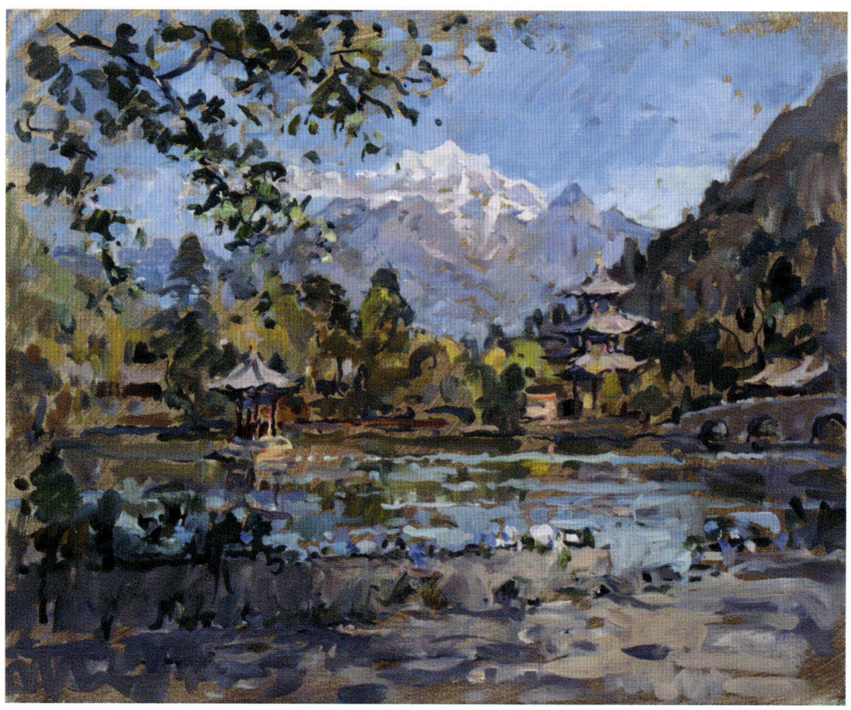

Black Dragon Mountain Pool, Lijiang, 16 × 20

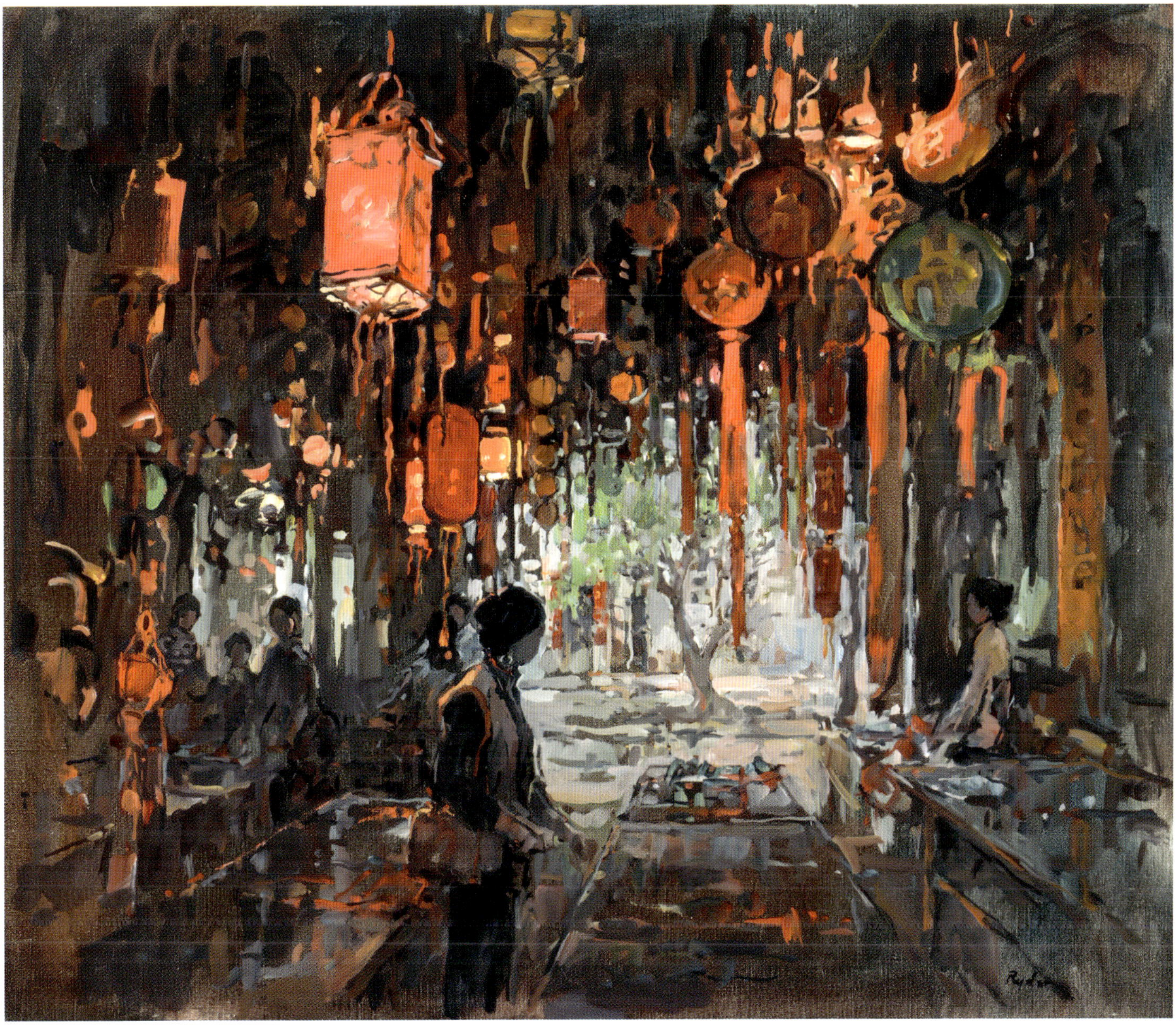

The Lantern Shop, Lijiang, 30 × 32

light, in her neo-impressionist style: *Reflected Light* in 2013 was followed by *Lamplight & Flowers* (2016) and *Looking Through* (2020). All have been near sell-out shows.

After the death of Manya Igel in 2017, the dealer who now sells most of Ryder's work between solo exhibitions is Sarah Samuels Fine Art in Cheshire.

General Sir John Swinton with his daughter Tilda, 32 × 36

Not all Ryder's portraits are commissions. In 2015 she attended the funeral of her friend and neighbour, Judy Swinton, mother of the actor Tilda Swinton. She had previously been commissioned to paint a double portrait of General Sir John and Lady Swinton. Knowing that Sir John would be lonely, Ryder suggested to Tilda that she should paint father and daughter together, over several sittings, when Tilda was next in Berwickshire. This was arranged, and Tilda had a hand in the composition of the painting, suggesting she should wear her red slipper shoes to link with her father's jacket. Ryder made several sketches, and – unusually – decided to take a number of photographs as well, in case they came in handy. And indeed they did: halfway through the second sitting Sir John fell over and bashed his head so badly he was rushed to hospital. Ryder was able to complete the portrait – which she later gifted to the Swintons – using the photographs she had taken. On the evening of the accident Tilda and Sir John, with a bandaged head, visited Ryder to inspect the painting, and share a celebratory glass of wine. From that day on Ryder has taken photos of her subjects, which she occasionally finds useful.

In June 2017, Ryder attended a talk by then Conservative minister Rory Stewart at the Borders Book Festival in Melrose. Stewart was giving a talk about (and a reading from) his forthcoming memoir *The Marches: Border Walks with My Father*. During the Q&A session, Stewart mentioned that his father, Brian, had had his portrait painted a few years before his death in 2015, and expressed his regret that this hadn't occurred many years before, when he was still in his prime. Ryder spoke

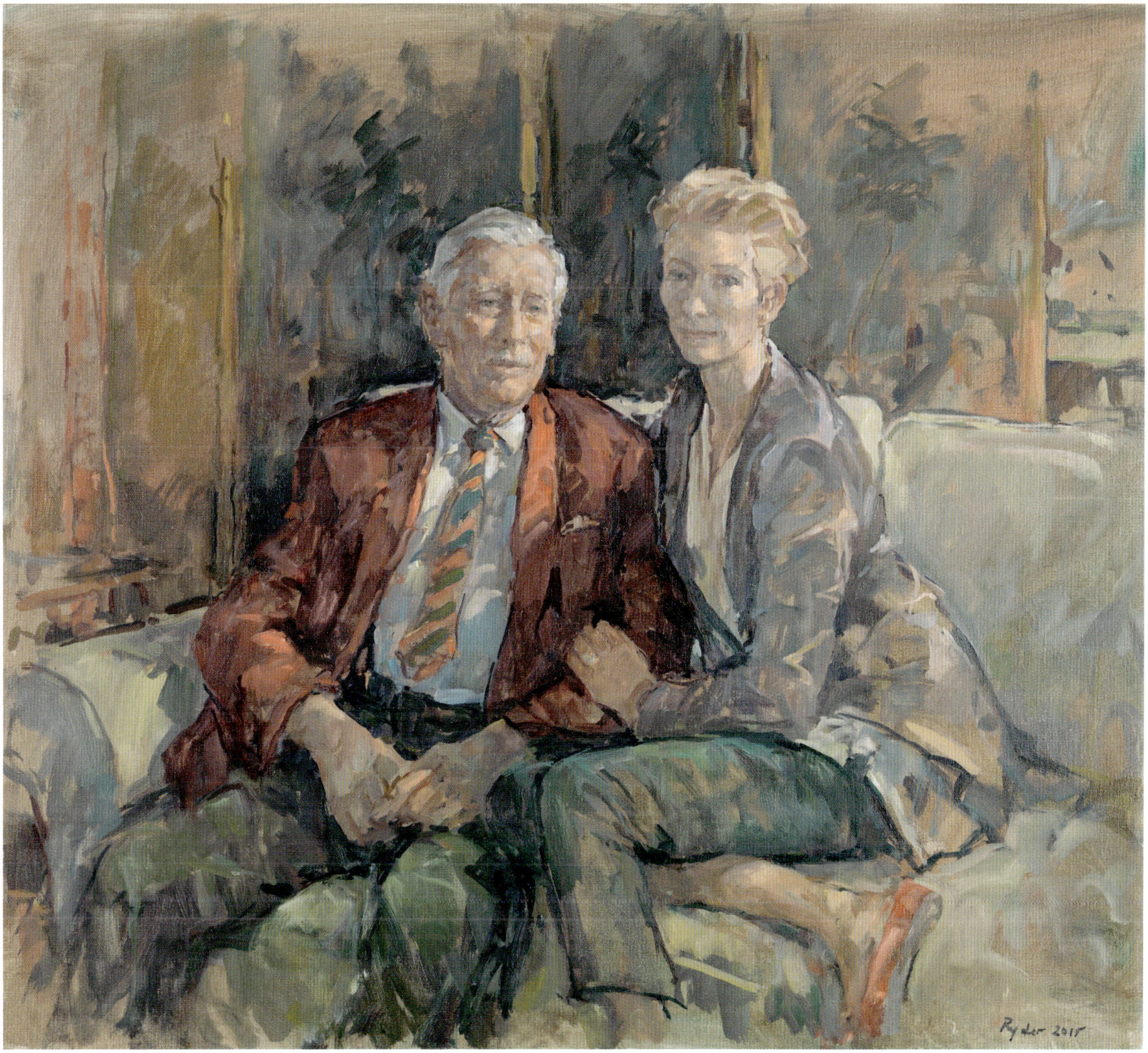
Ryder 2015

to Rory after the talk, offering to paint the politician, while *he* was still in his prime. Rory chose to be portrayed wearing a kilt in the Royal Stewart tartan, surrounded by props which were connected to his father's distinguished career in the army and the diplomatic service. The portrait was shown at the *2018 Royal Society of Portrait Painters Exhibition* at the Mall Galleries, after which Ryder gave it to the Stewarts.

The natural setting for Ryder's work to be displayed is on a wall, whether that be in a prestigious gallery or a drawing room. But she was recently alerted to a very different showcase for her mark making. The artist was highly amused to be forwarded a Facebook post showing one of her interior paintings, tattooed on to someone's leg in an Italian tattoo parlour!

Ryder is kept extremely busy with portrait commissions, but that doesn't stop her from finding time to paint her favourite subjects: members of her family. A watercolour of her father hangs prominently on the wall of her sitting room, the painting she most values in the world. Her mother was a frequent sitter, as has been Martin (reading a book, as ever) and, as we have seen, her two children Oliver and Susannah. In recent years there have been a son and daughter-in-law, followed by grandchildren, all of whom have sat for their grandmother so she can capture their likeness and personality: first Phoebe, then Archie, followed by Alec, and finally William. Recently Oliver has moved into the Belchester House with his family, and Ryder and Martin have moved into the converted stables next door. One of the latest portraits Ryder has completed is of her granddaughter Phoebe, in a white dress, now aged twenty-one. Phoebe is currently reading Graphic Design at Edinburgh University: with all the inherited artistic talent running through the family, she is ready to enjoy a creative future.

Rory Stewart, 30 × 25

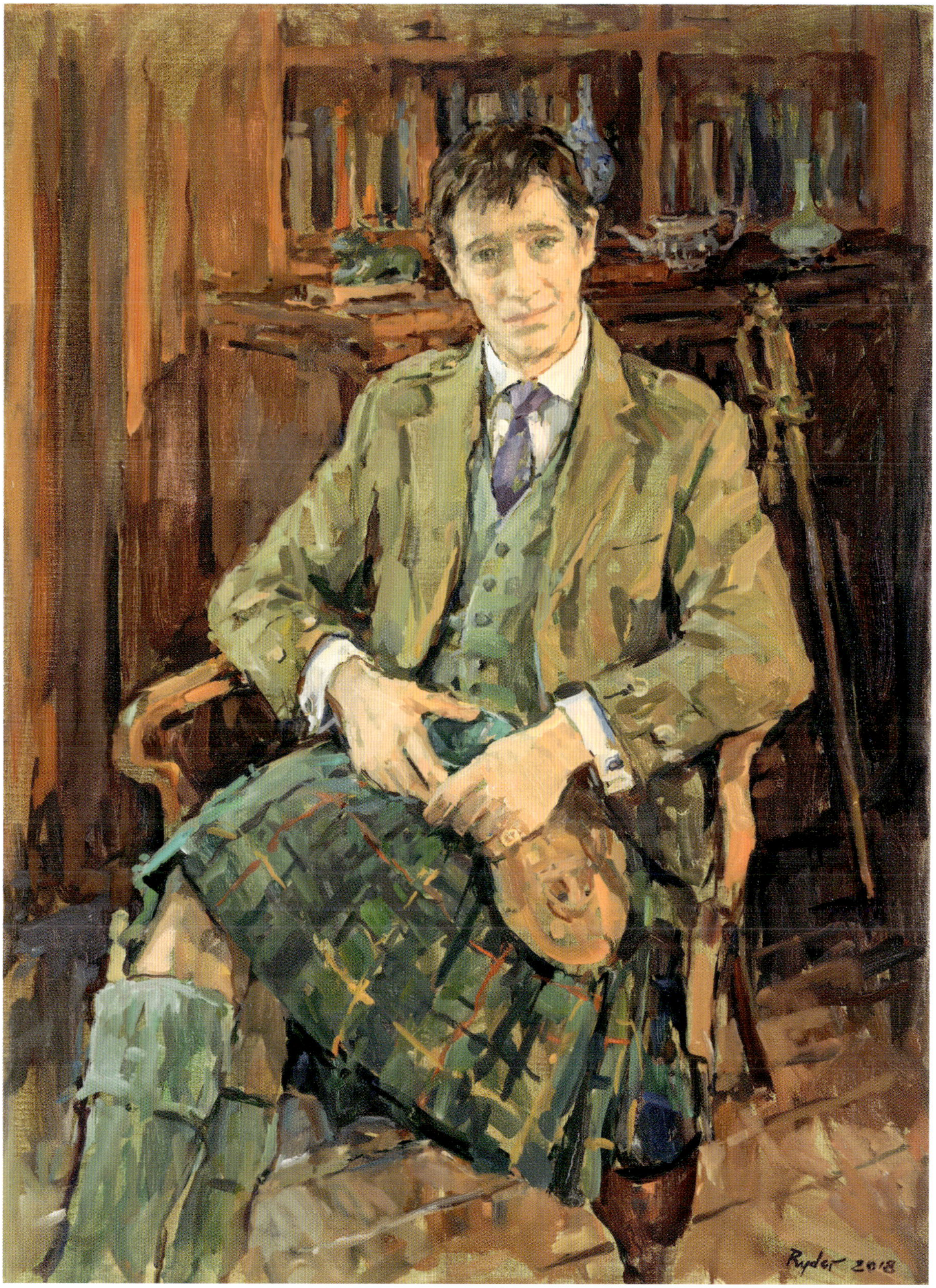
Ryder 2018

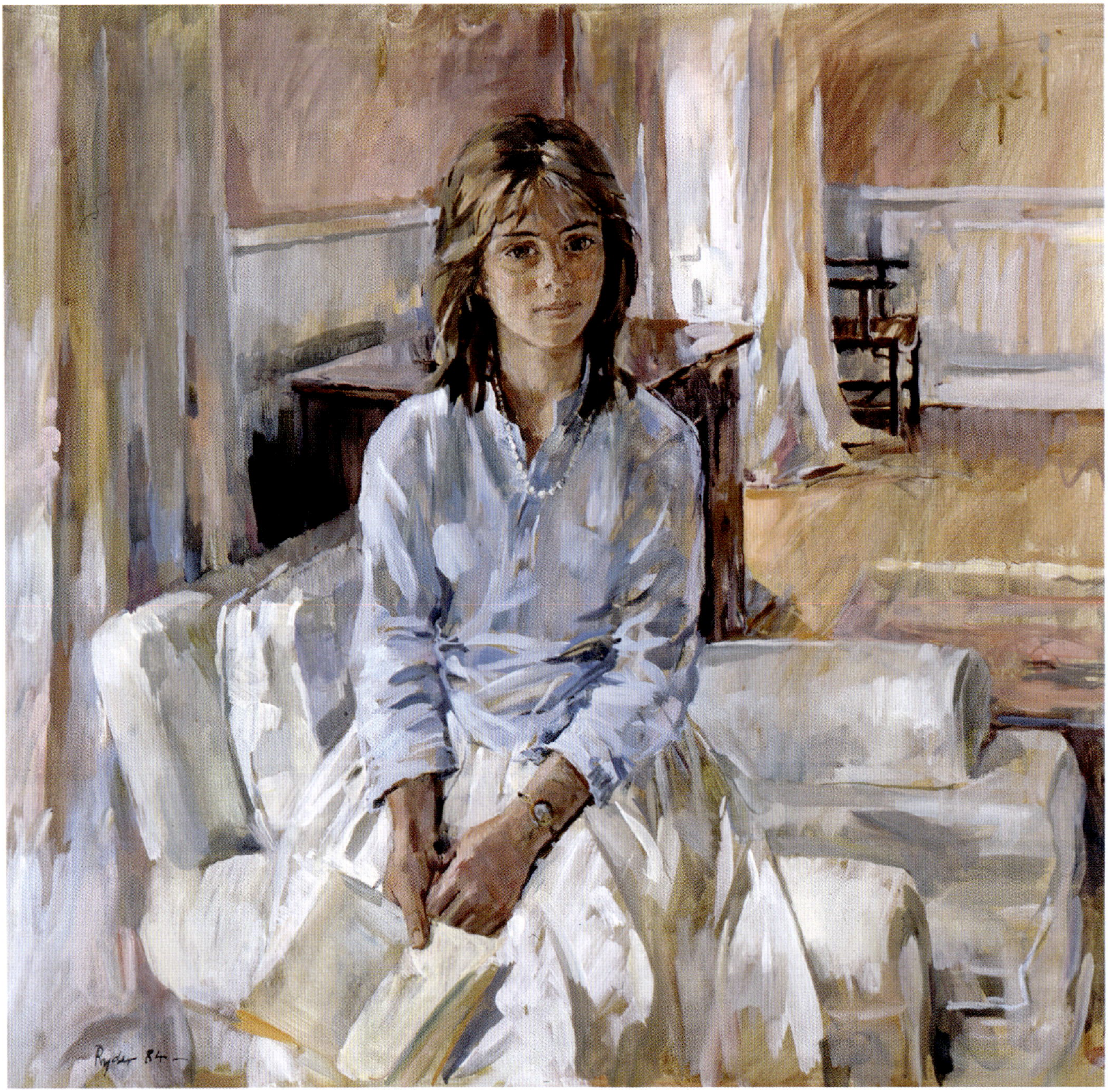

Susannah, 34 × 36

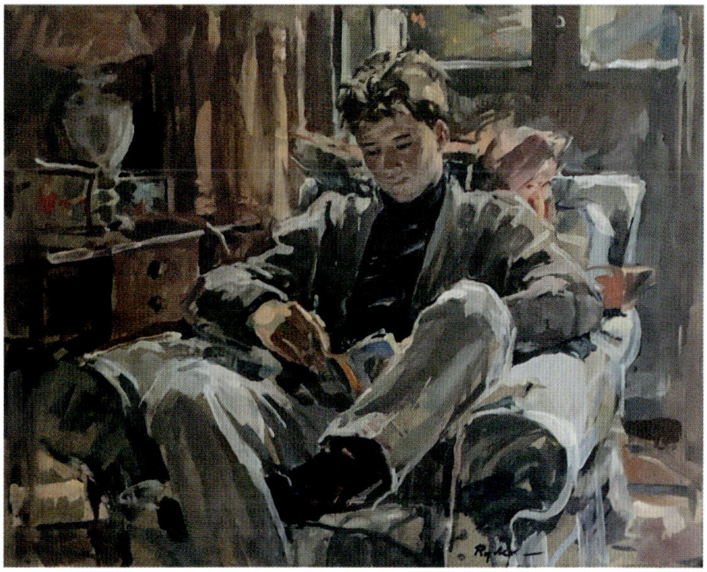

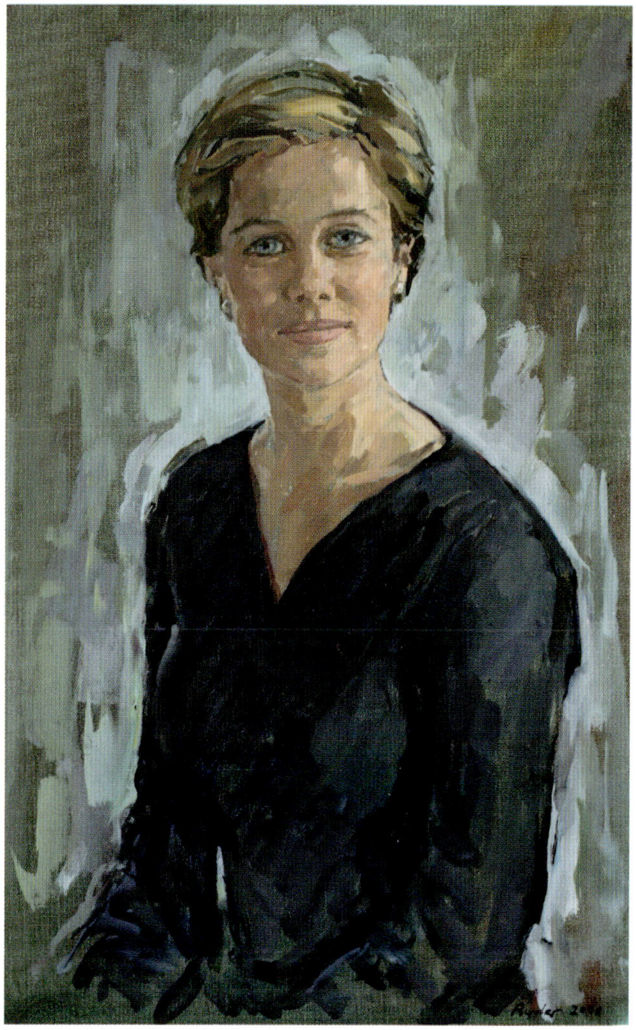

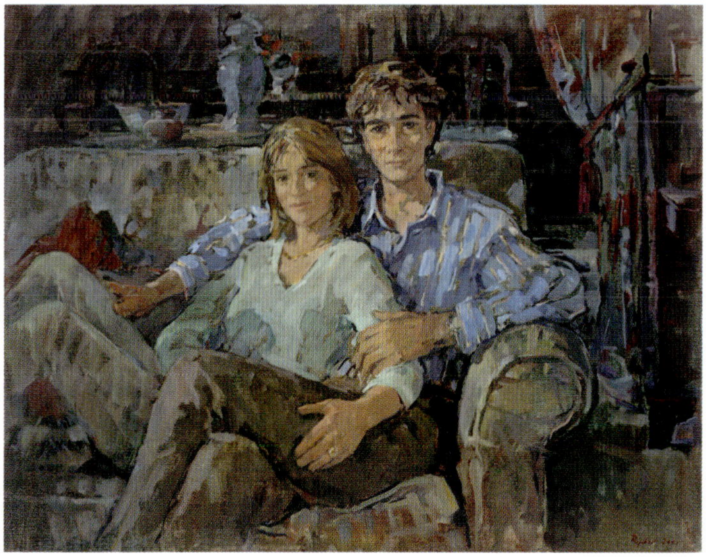

Annabel, 20 × 16

I painted this portrait of Annabel as a secret wedding present for Oliver. It was exhibited at the Royal Society of Portrait Painters in 2001 but sadly was stolen or collected in error from the Mall Galleries at the end of the show. If anyone finds it the family would be so grateful.

ABOVE LEFT

Oliver studying the Highway Code,
oil on board, 17 × 22

LEFT

Robin and Susannah, 28 × 36

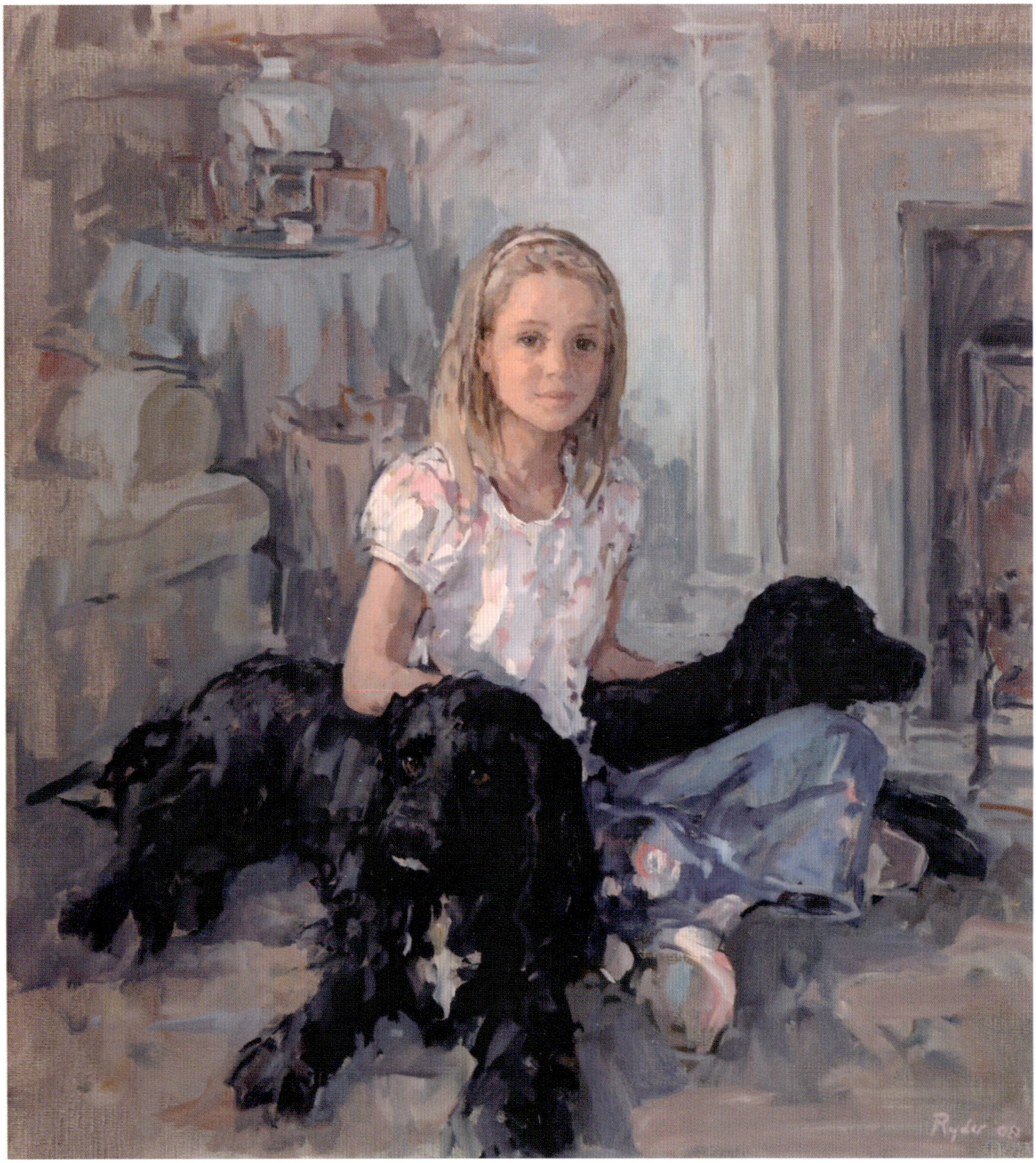

Phoebe with Molly and Mungo, 26 × 25

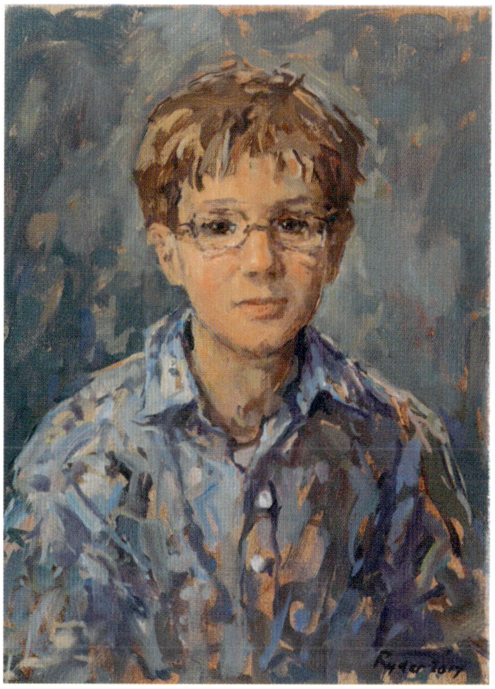

Archie, 20 × 16

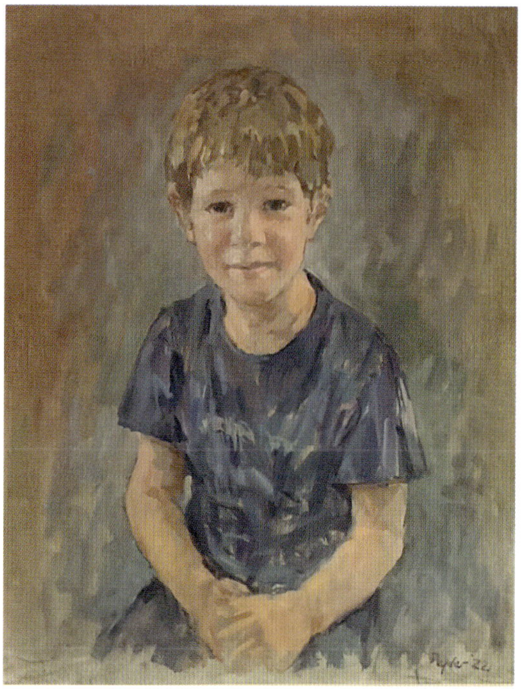

William, 20 × 16

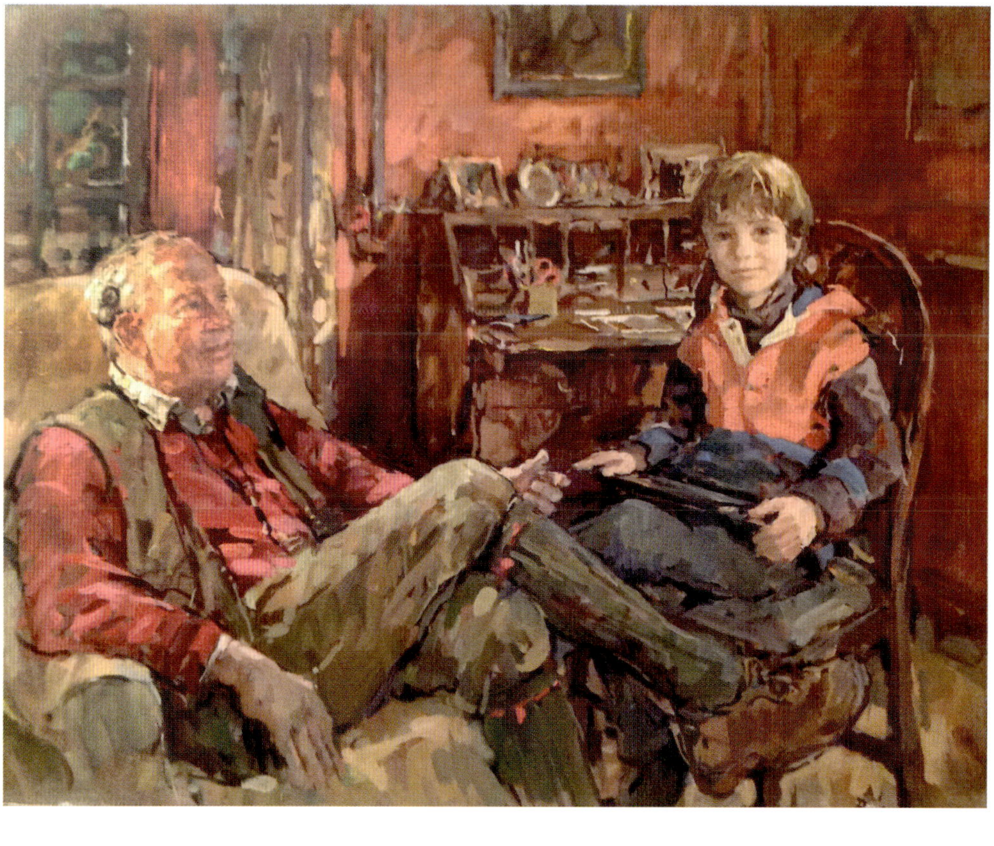

Alex with Papa, 20 × 24

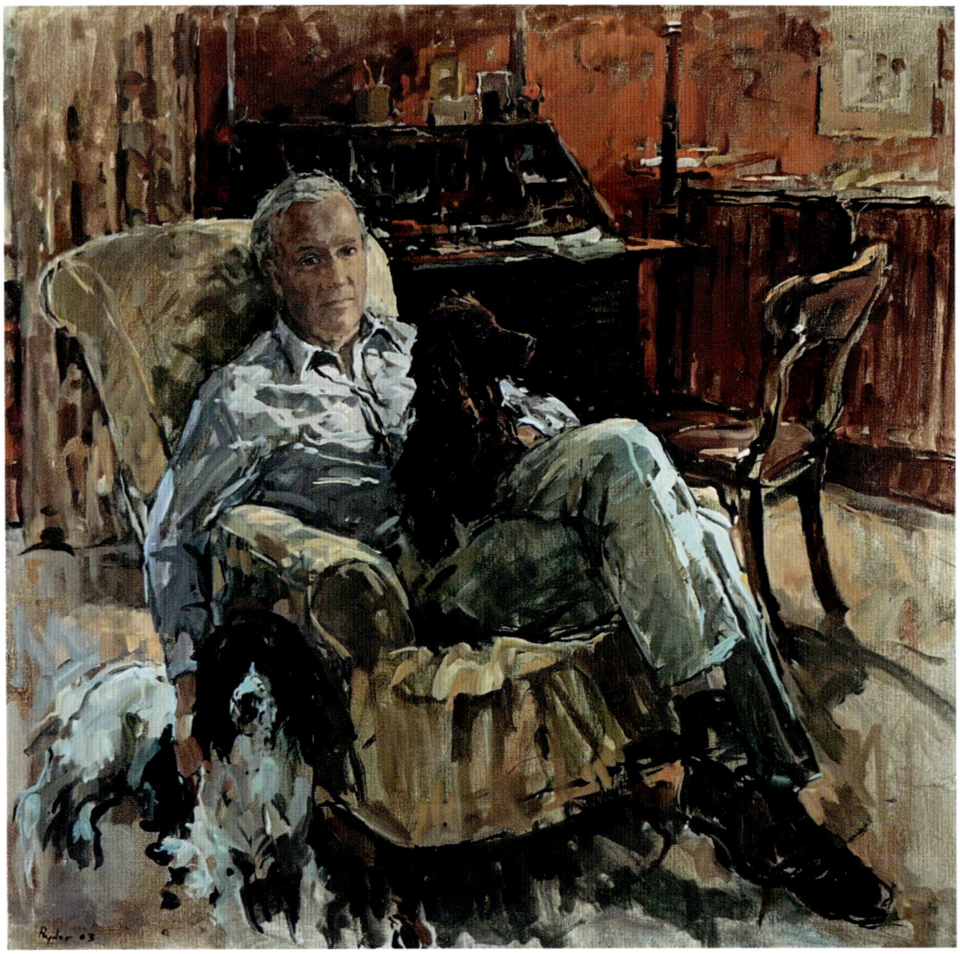

ABOVE

Martin with Pasha and Rocky, 36 × 38

RIGHT

Martin in Lockdown, 22 × 28

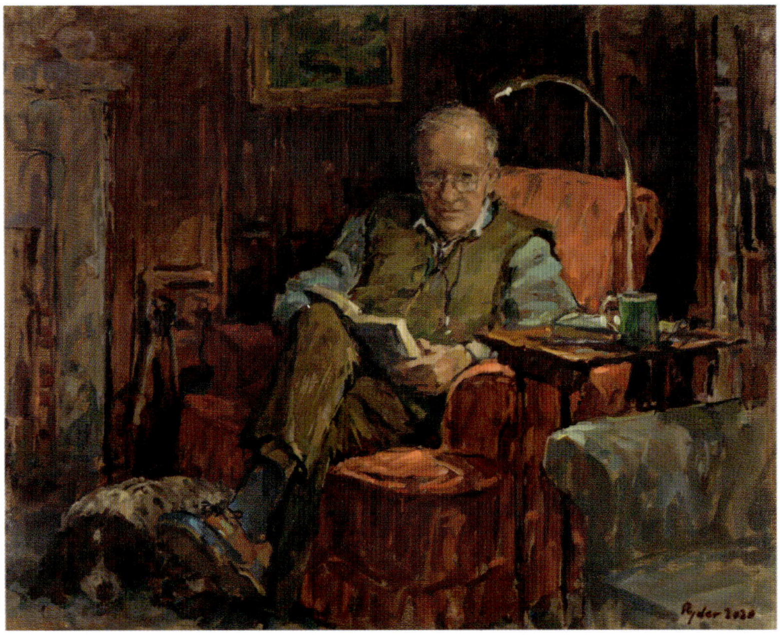

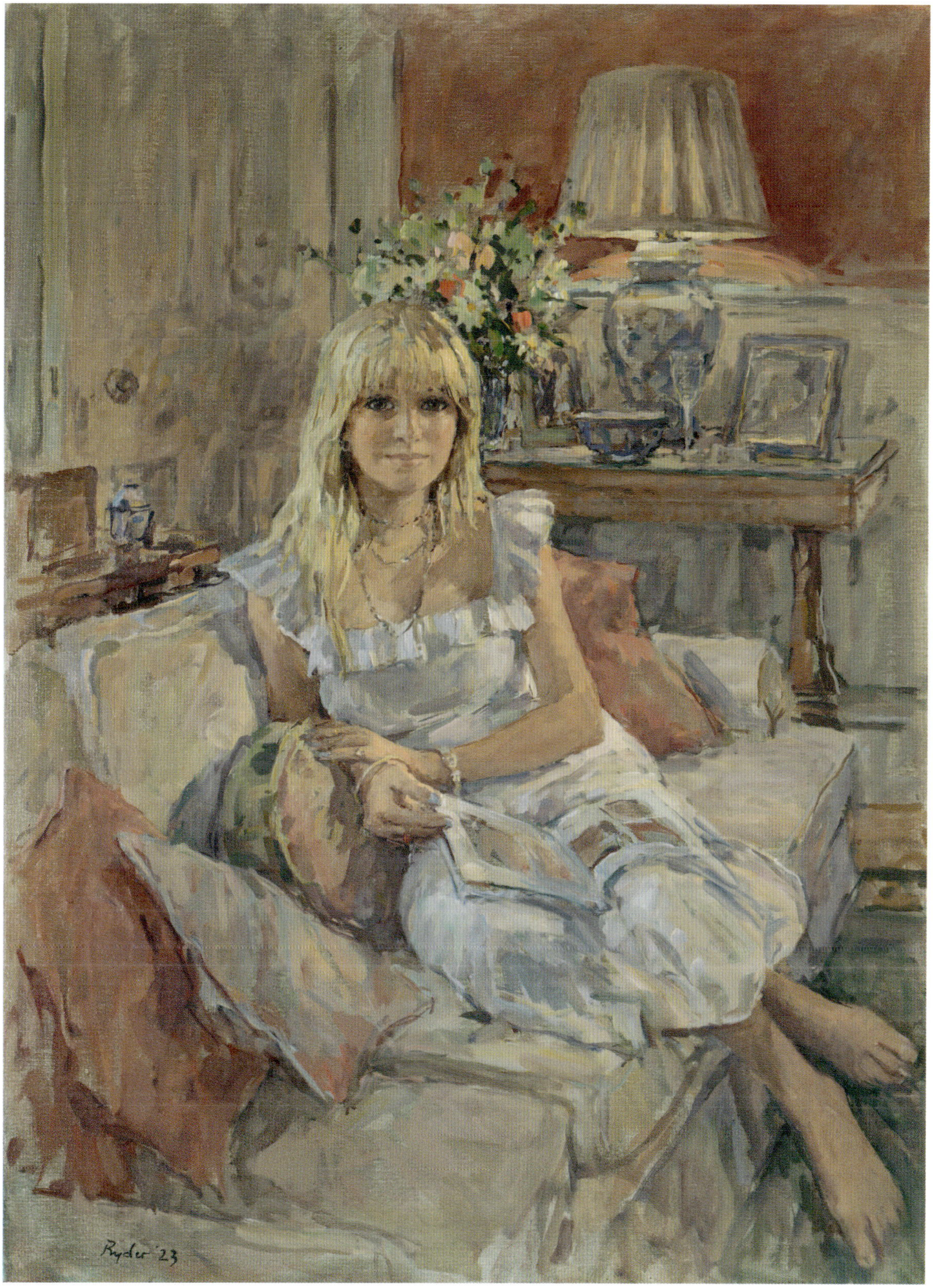

Phoebe in a White Dress, 40 × 30

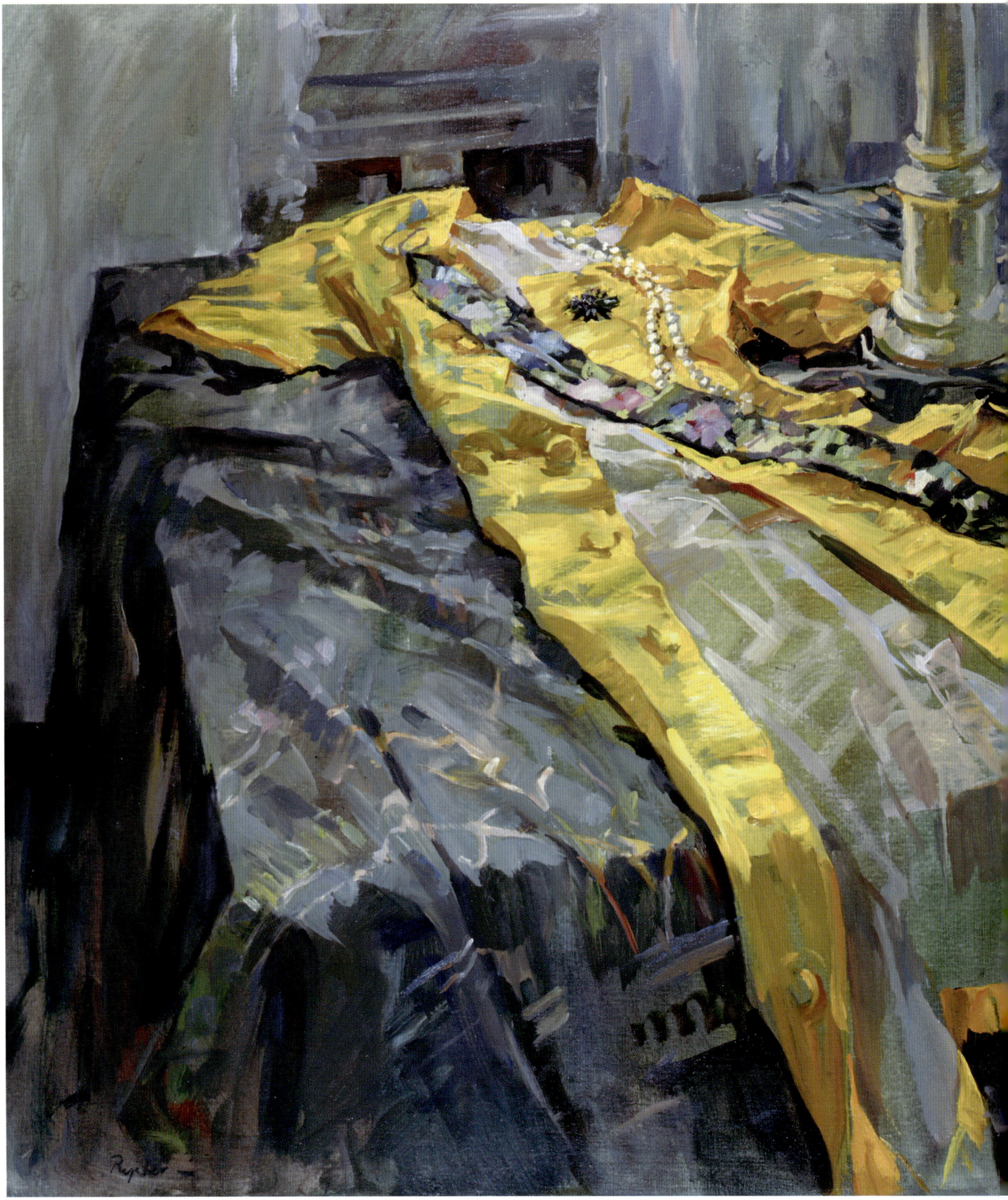

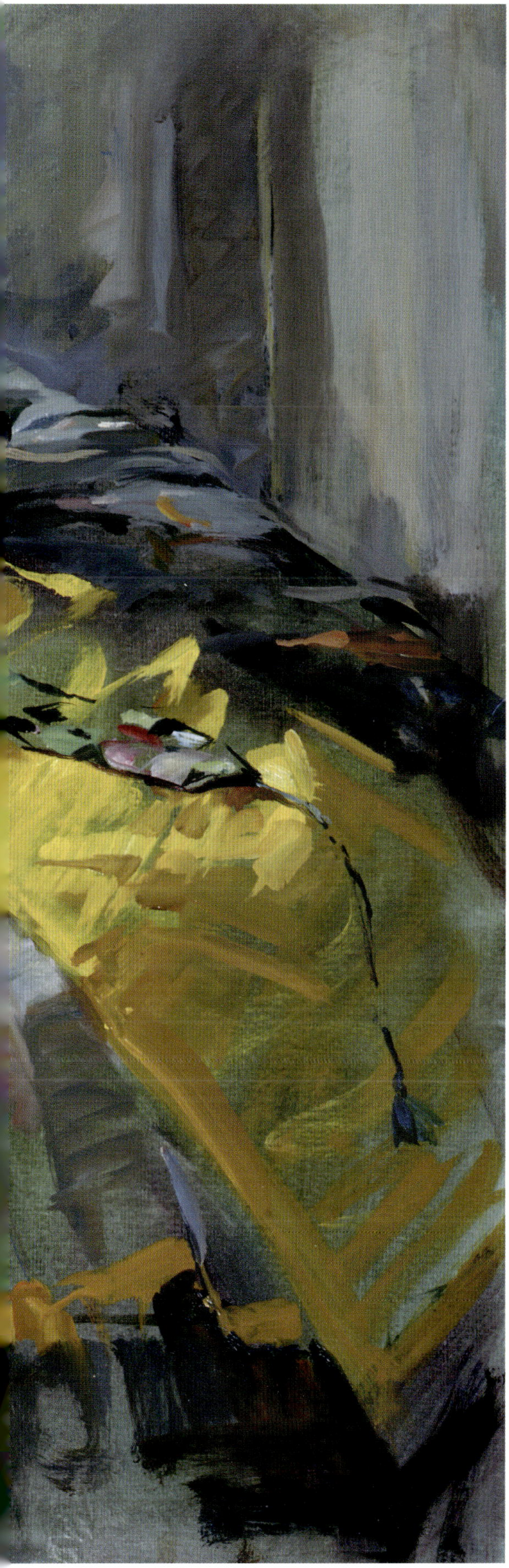

SUSAN RYDER'S PAINTING TECHNIQUES

Equipment and materials

Ryder always arranges the same oil paints on her palette, always in the same order, so she can 'dab and grab' at will, knowing where they'll be without looking, almost like touch-typing.

She'll use the same colours whatever she's painting, whether that's a lady in a red dress, or a snow scene. Her go-to paints, squeezed straight from the tube on to her palette, rather than self-mixed, are (moving from warm to cold): alizarin crimson, cadmium red, cadmium yellow, lemon yellow, flake white (or titanium white), viridian, cerulean blue, Prussian blue and French ultramarine. From making combinations of these pigments, she can create any shade of any colour she wants.

Ryder has a bundle of different-sized round-headed hogs-hair brushes. Sometimes, if she is on a roll, she can use one largish brush for most of a morning. She can stay with a favourite for up to six months, until it loses its shape or bounce. She doesn't need to use larger brushes for thicker strokes: she simply presses harder for a broader mark, and uses the side of the brush if extra thickness is required. She uses two wells to dilute and clean her brushes. Some painters fill one with oil, the other with turps; Ryder puts white spirit in both, with a dribble of oil.

She stretches her own canvases, having progressed from hardboard in the late sixties, buying Bird & Davis dressed linen by the roll. If she travels away from home, as she usually does to paint, she takes a variety of different shapes and sizes of

The Yellow Dress, 24 × 30

pre-stretched canvas, as she won't know until the sketching stage the exact composition of the painting.

At home in her studio in Berwickshire, Ryder has a large H-shaped easel that used to belong to Scottish painter Alberto Morrocco, which was rolled down Pembroke Road from George Bruce's studio when they lived nearby. When she travels to do a painting, she takes with her an old tripod wooden easel; if she's flying, she carries a folding metal one she can fit in her suitcase. Her oils and brushes are stored in a box made for her for this purpose by her father, when she was eighteen, which she cherishes.

Preparation

At the Byam Shaw, Ryder was taught that the canvas should be grounded with a hue which contrasts with the colours used in the actual painting. She has chosen to break this rule, and to use a colour which is quite close to her final scheme. She applies a ground made principally from viridian mixed with cadmium red, and perhaps a little yellow ochre (not included in her palette colours) and Prussian blue, according to the predominant colour of the subject. This, she finds, removes the need to fill the whole canvas, and adds unity to the look of the final painting.

The first stage of any painting is a series of sketches, done in pencil or charcoal on paper. This is a necessary part of the painting, to help her decide on the eventual composition of the piece. People are amazed at how quickly she completes these sketches. When working on a portrait, she is not, at this stage, looking to achieve any likeness. She is more interested in the relationship of the shapes, including the sitters, and the furniture and fittings around them.

Nowadays she also takes photographs of her subject or subjects on her mobile phone. These can come in very handy later in the process, when she's finding a detail – perhaps the turn of a mouth or the curl of a lock – tricky to perfect. This is quite a recent development in her working process; she wonders, now, how she ever did without it.

The **Magor Family**, 36 × 42

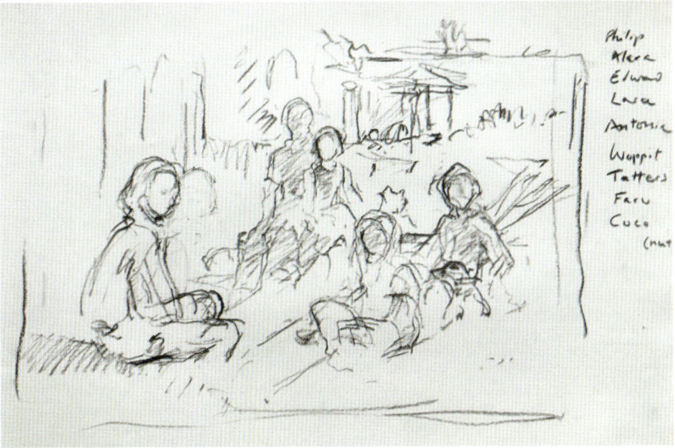

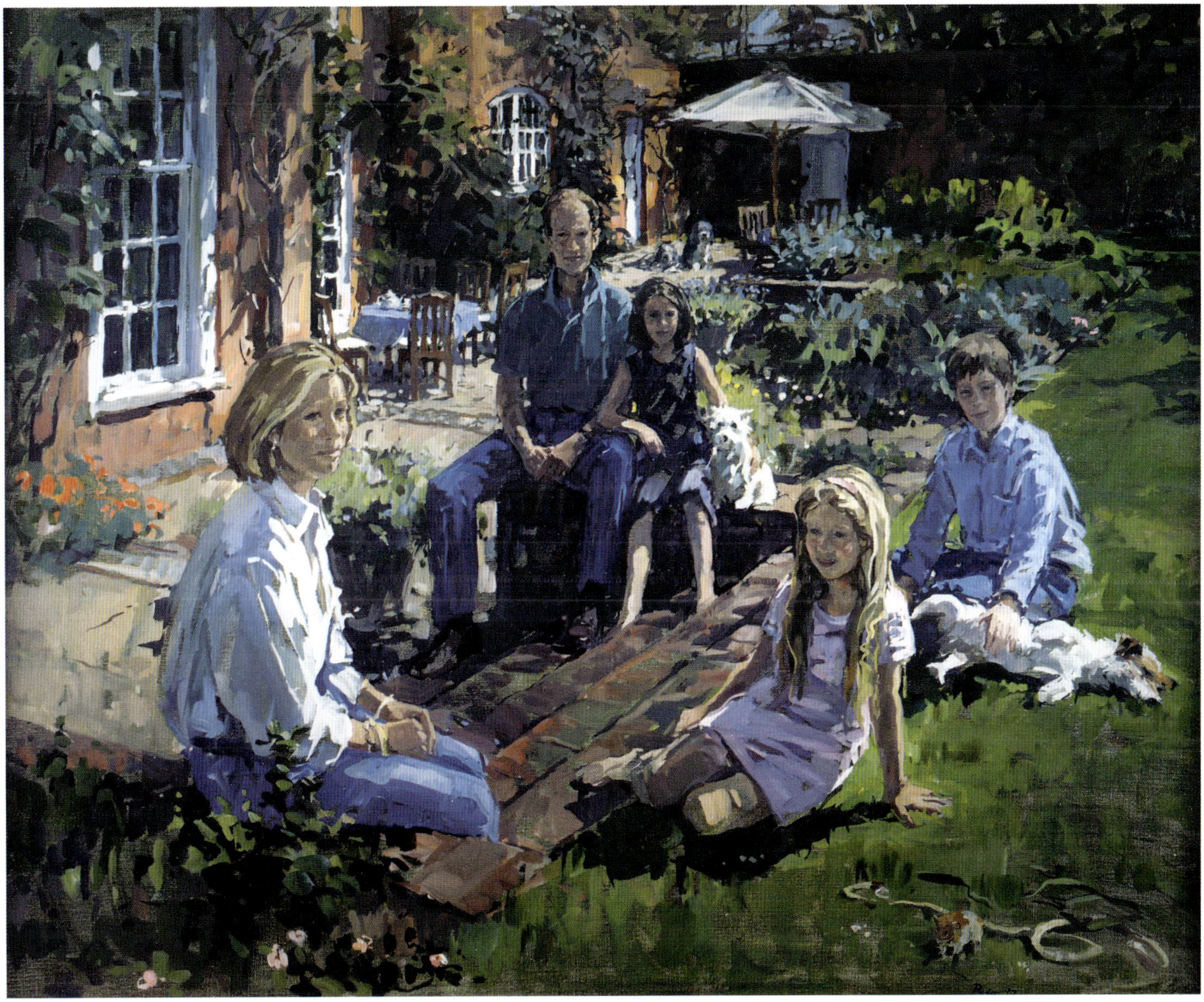

Mark making

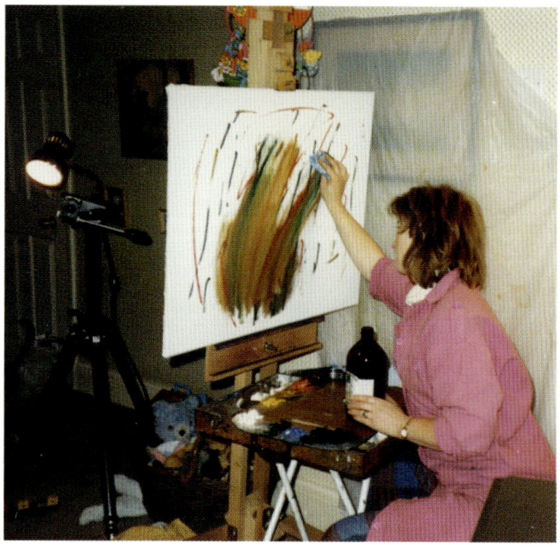

When Ryder has decided on the composition, and thus the size and shape of the canvas, it is time to start painting. She begins by shaping an outline of her main subject, executed in viridian. Then she draws over this with cadmium red. And then again with yellow ochre (which she doesn't use for painting, just for rubbing in, hence it not being on the palette).

Once she's applied this paint, she takes a turpsy oil rag and rubs it all in: all the drawing disappears, but the outline remains fixed in her memory.

She then uses a clean rag to rub out the light shapes: at this point the ghost of a composition is appearing. After this, she starts drawing in the lines, with her large, round hogs-hair brush. She holds the brush at the far end of its stem, unlike how you might hold a pen. The lines are quite dark, in viridian or alizarin. She makes sure not to 'illustrate': she's not attempting to *draw* a nose, rather to capture its abstract quality. Some advice she was given by her friend Jane Corsellis, many years ago, has never been forgotten: 'Take care of the darks, and the lights will look after themselves.'

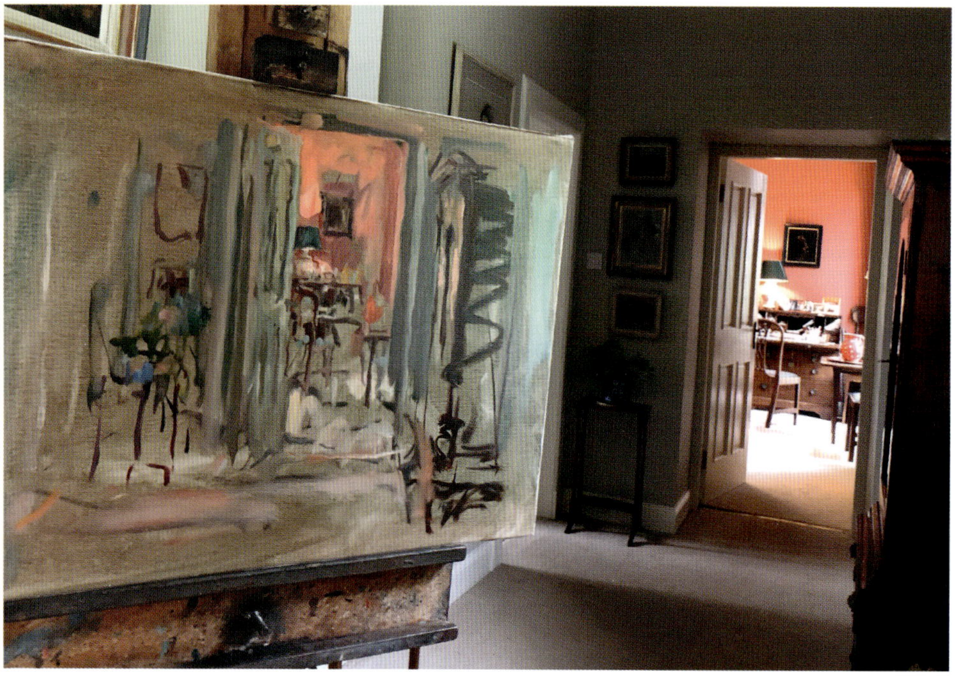

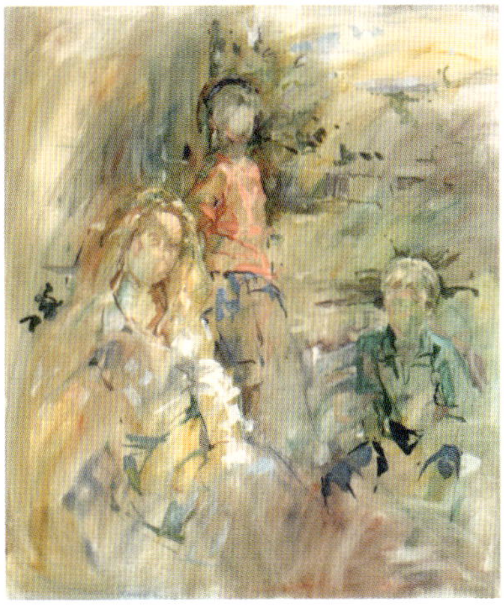

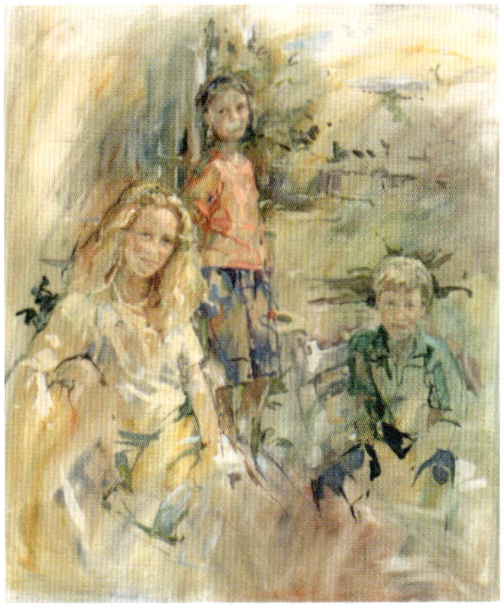

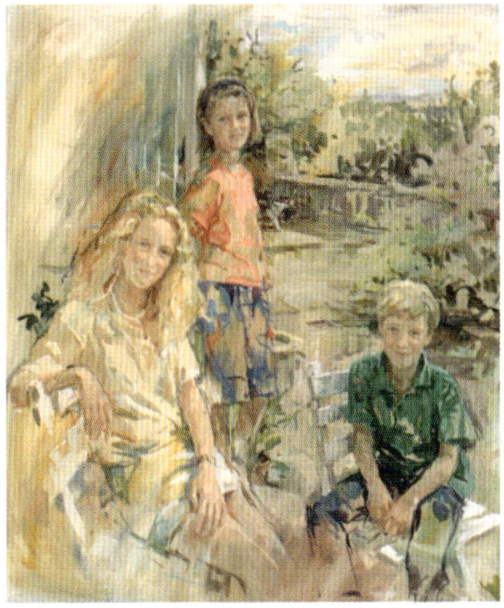

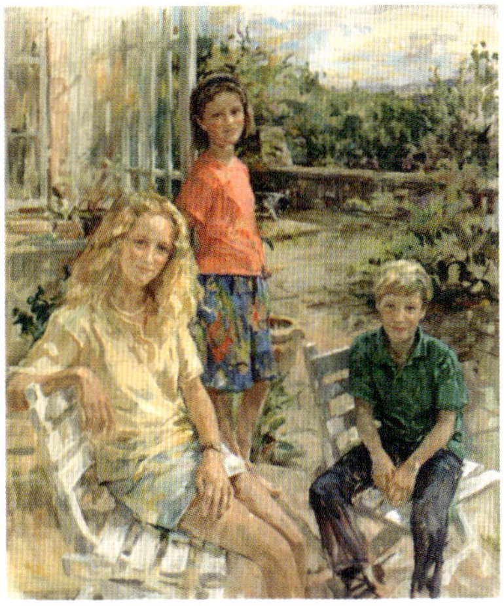

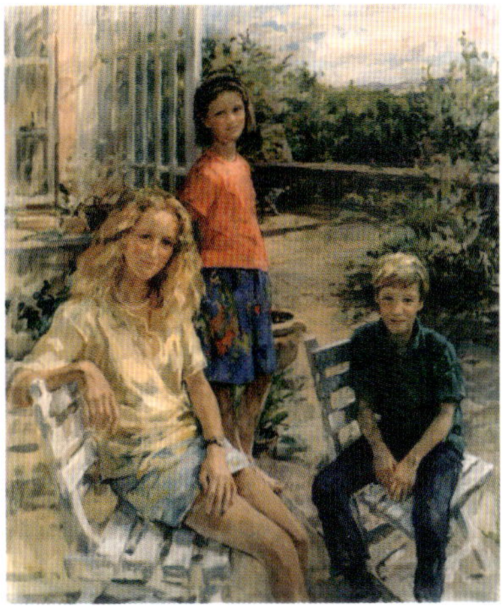

Georgina, Charlotte and Charlens Keyser, 42 × 36

The progression of the painting over five days and finally hanging in the Royal Society of Portrait Painters. Exhibition at the Mall Galleries.

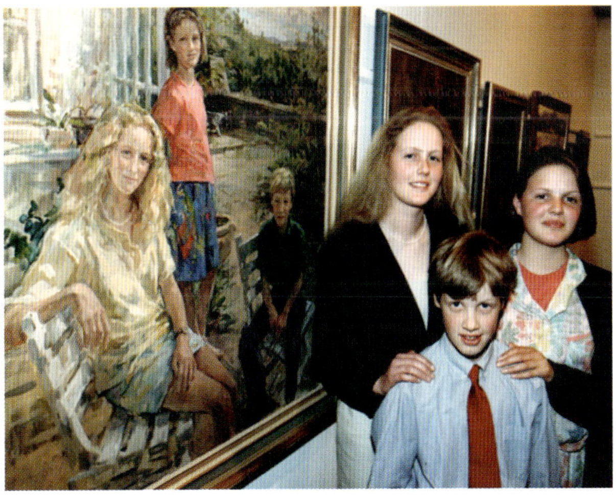

Ryder keeps her whole subject in mind as she makes each mark: while ostensibly painting the line of a pair of glasses, she is simultaneously aware of the angle of her subject's leg. The artist took up golf in her fifties and was fascinated by one similarity with painting: in golf you need to concentrate on the golf ball while simultaneously being aware of the whole fairway. In painting it's the brush mark and the canvas.

Having painted some of the head and skin tones of a portrait, she will 'cut in' behind, filling in the negative space of the background, after creating the positive space of the foreground, thus creating a three-dimensionality with colour and contrast, rather than with perspective. Cutting in the distance after painting the foreground sends the distance back: she views this stage as an act of 'magic'.

She tries not to think about technique, about the marks she makes, while she is painting. Self-consciousness doesn't help her process. One critic has compared her brushstrokes to those of Edward Seago, stating that 'her art pours out of her brush'. On a good day, she feels, this is very true.

Ryder paints very fast, as she has often to depict a fleeting play of light held in her memory, or the shape of a cheek after a momentary smile. Although fast, she isn't a messy painter. Quite the opposite: she only took to wearing a smock in recent years, though she has always put a cloth on the floor, which provides adequate protection for her surroundings. Back in 1981, however, when she was painting Princess Diana, she *was* terrified of flicking oil paint on to her wedding dress. It's difficult to get oil paint stains out of antique lace and taffeta.

About halfway through any painting she starts to use a mirror, and examines areas of the painting back to front. This enables her to see the work afresh: often something jumps out that she wouldn't have otherwise noticed (some artists achieve the same objective by turning the painting upside down). The mirror she has traditionally used is a wing mirror, knocked off her car in Soho many years ago (though the Moormans [see Foreword] have recently given her a new one).

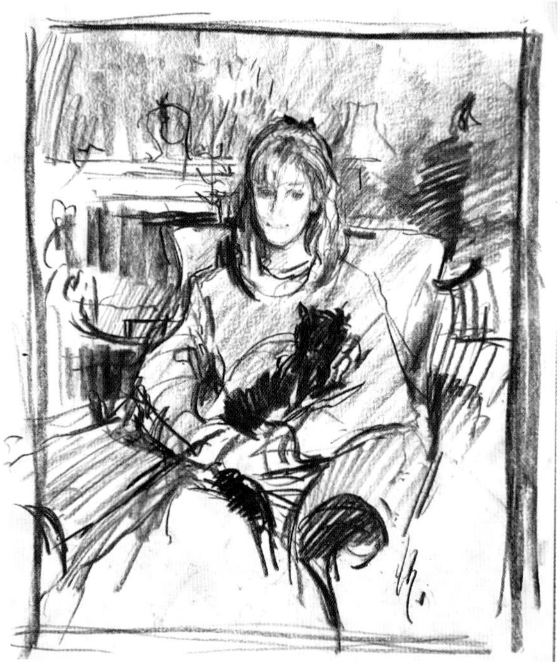

Preliminary sketch for Alice Baker Wilbraham

Sound and light

During the early stages of a painting, when Ryder is concentrating on laying down the foundations of the work, she prefers silence to maintain the requisite concentration. Afterwards, when she's confident about the composition and is adding details – whether in situ or in her studio – she needs something to listen to, to stop her becoming aware of her technique. Radio 4 usually fits the bill, or, of course, chatting with her sitter.

When she is painting al fresco, Ryder needs to be very aware of the direction light is coming from. For outdoor portraits, cloud cover is a positive, bright sunlight can be a negative, as

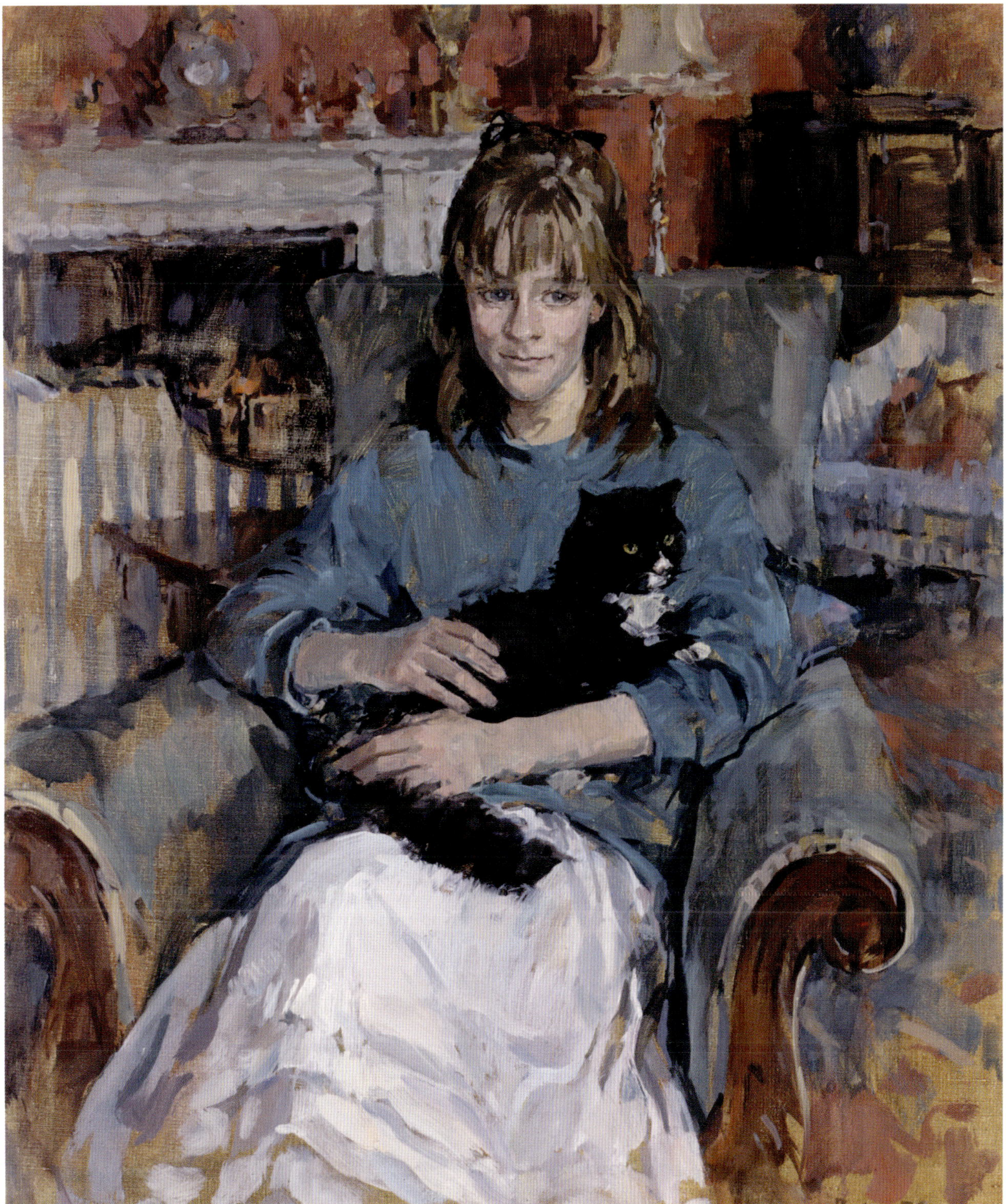

Alice Baker Wilbraham at Rhode, 26 × 20

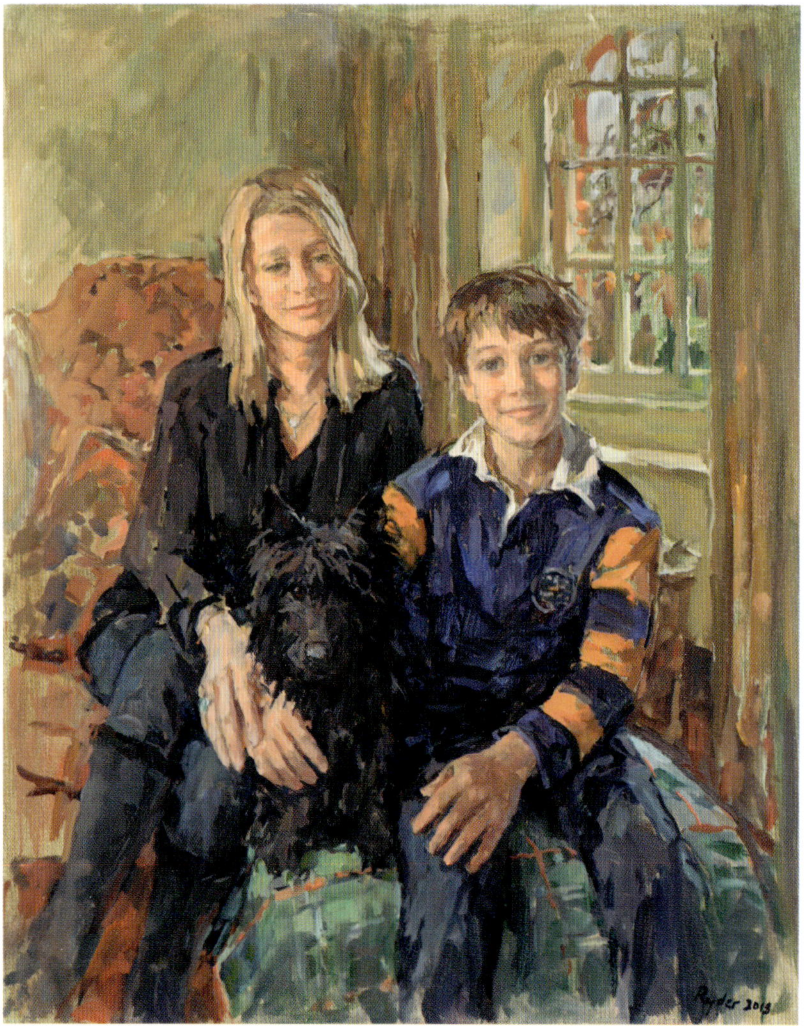

Georgie and Jamie with Ziggy, 30 × 25

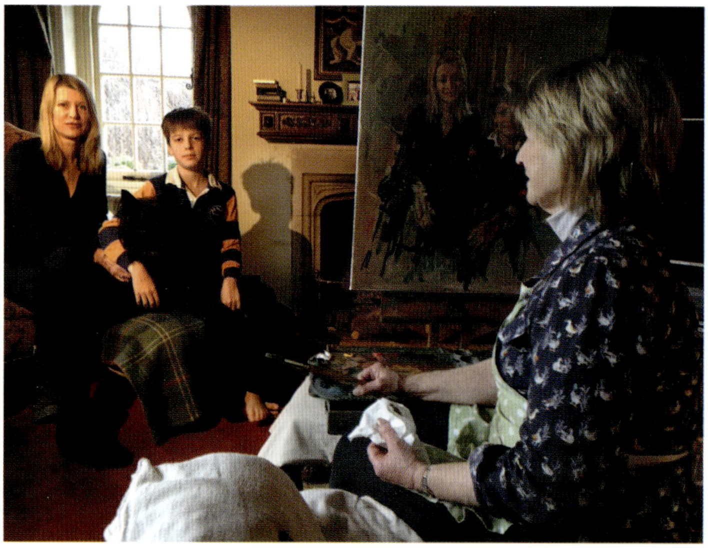

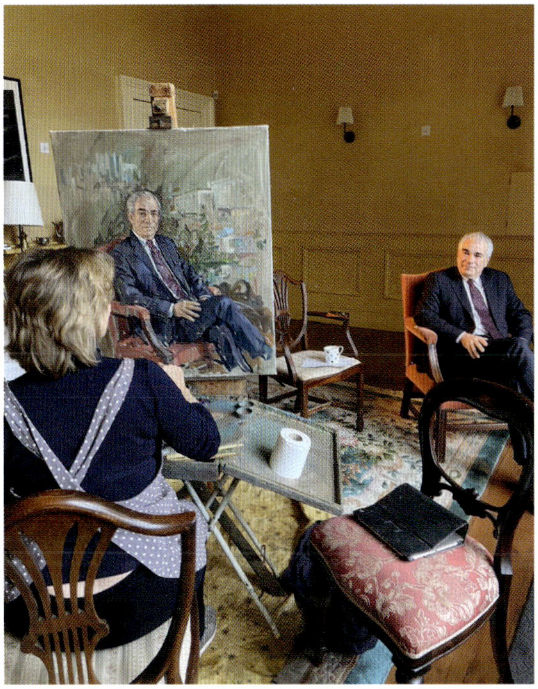

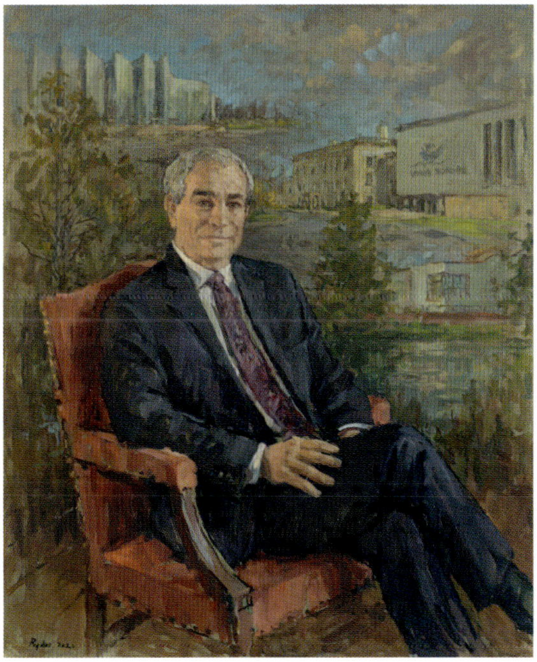

David Dunn – Headmaster of Yarm School, 38 × 30

the shadows change so quickly and sitters tend to screw up their eyes. Torrential rain stops play, obviously, but a strong wind – with the canvas taking off – is more problematic than a light drizzle. When Ryder was painting Bunny Maitland-Carew at Thirlestane Castle, he was happy to keep sitting when it started drizzling, but made sure that an awning was placed over her, to keep the painter – and her painting – dry. His gardener/butler did arrive with a glass of brandy for him.

Capturing the fall of light is key to Ryder's work. Interiors, with the play of the warmth of lamplight and the cool of daylight are her greatest joy. An interior, with sunlight streaming through the window, is an exciting challenge. To augment this play of light-on-light, Ryder sometimes uses a dimmable spotlight, on a tripod.

It was very sunny when she was painting the biologist Dame Angela McLean in 2021, in her office at Oxford University's All Souls College, before she was appointed as the Government Chief Scientific Advisor in 2023. Ryder joked, as they were chatting, that it would be nice to be able to 'stop the sun', so uniform light might shine on her subject throughout the sitting. She mused that 'Stop the Sun' would be a good title for a book about painting. McLean pointed out that this would be rather Pre-Copernican, and that 'Stop the World', while not so catchy, would be more scientifically correct!

Communication

Ryder tends to ask for three to four sittings of two hours each, for a portrait, which generally involves time away from home, so consecutive days are helpful.

Breaks are important, particularly for the sitters, who are not used to staying still for long periods of time. During such pauses, she likes her subjects to inspect the portrait in progress. It is highly important, however, to recall exactly where the subject was sitting or standing before the break. This is done with carefully placed strips of masking tape. These are left in place overnight, between sittings.

Ryder feels comfortable painting her sitters in the clothes they are wearing when she first meets them. So, if she is called upon to paint somebody she doesn't know, before the first sitting takes place, she asks them to wear the clothes they wish to be painted in. They usually don't have to change, though very occasionally a colour clashes with the background, or if patterns are too close together to 'work'. For this reason, she also asks her subjects to have a second choice of clothing to hand.

Composition is very important, especially for group portraits. This is when Ryder is at her most uncompromising, asking people to move closer together, or further apart, moving furniture and arranging animals. The artist must be aware of the spaces in front of her sitters, as well as the spaces behind them. Here, her skill as a painter of interiors and as a portrait painter combine.

Communication with her sitters is key. When Ryder was painting Queen Elizabeth, she politely asked Her Majesty to move her hand, in order to break up the line created by the arm of the chair she was sitting on. The position the Queen was required to take up proved to be uncomfortable, and she wasn't afraid to make this clear, contorting her arm to show her discomfort, and adopting a funny voice: 'I don't think I could manage it!' They shared a good laugh over this, which helped break the ice.

Sometimes, sitters don't want to see the work in progress. When Ryder painted Dame Kiri Te Kanawa's children, the opera singer didn't want to look at the work until it was completed. When she did look at it, she was moved to tears. The artist, touched, responded: 'You know your singing makes *me* cry'.

Sometimes, however, reactions aren't so positive. On occasion a sitter will say 'I'm not sure that quite looks like me!' Ryder usually asks friends or family, in these cases, to give their opinion. More often than not, they'll say: 'You're wrong! That looks *exactly* like you.' This process is important because, she finds, people's idea of how they look is often very different from how they appear to others.

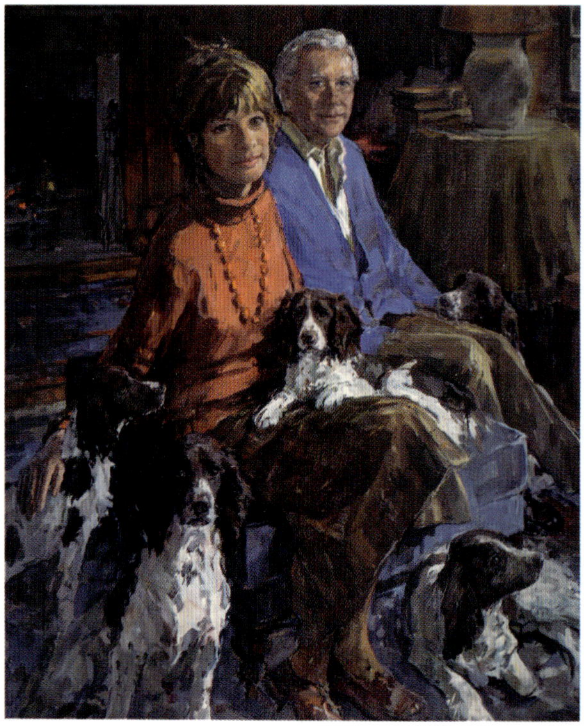

A Love of Spaniels, 30 × 25

On sitters

Some adults are better at sitting still than others. Small children and animals tend to be extremely 'wriggly', but often easier to capture. But it isn't always the children. One recent painting entitled *Elizabeth and her Six Grandsons* was particularly demanding, with the grandmother being the most restless (reproduced on page 94)! Such restlessness makes it important for Ryder to 'nail' the outline of the composition early on in the process, and to ingrain a memory of that outline.

The artist is often called upon to paint group portraits. In this case it may be important to give each member of the group equal status, wherever they are sitting. This can be achieved in different ways. One subject might be told to look directly towards the painter, thus achieving 'eye contact' with the viewer of the painting. Another might be asked to wear a particularly bright item of clothing. One might be in the foreground at the foot of the sofa where the rest of the family is placed; another may be bathed in light.

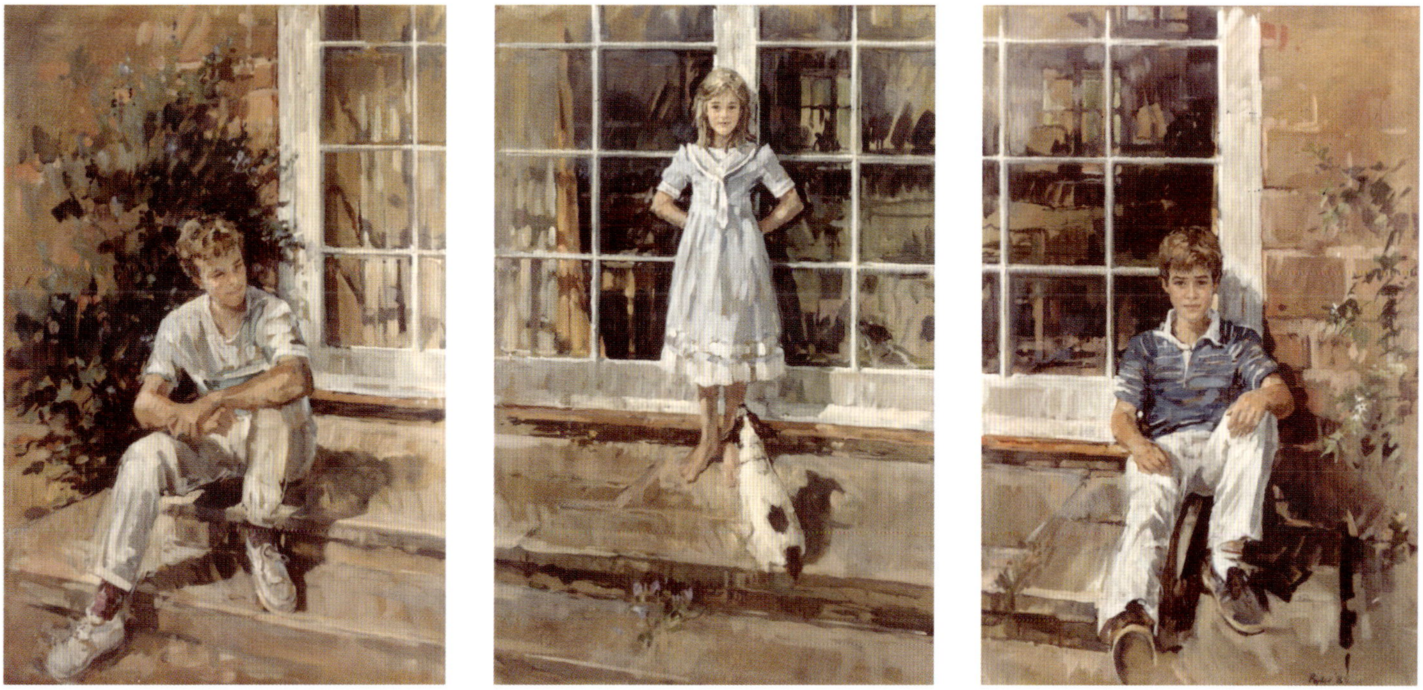

Giles, Rebecca and Matthew Sutcliffe, triptych, each 26 × 20

When Ryder was commissioned to paint portraits of the three Sutcliffe children, it was decided to paint a triptych. It was a terrace scene, framed as one, but with each child painted on a separate canvas. It was important that the composition for each canvas stood up in its own right, as well as being an integral part of the group scene: in that way each child could eventually own their own portrait.

One reason Ryder likes to paint her subjects in their own environment is so that they will feel more at ease and able to open up to her. For this reason, she likes to spend time with them before the painting process, and will chat to them during the sitting. She doesn't just want to capture what her subjects look like, she wants to capture what they *are* like, too. Getting this right requires empathy and intuition, as much as technique. And patience, too. Sometimes she has to wait a long time for a slight smile to emerge, and a cheek to behave the way she wants it to behave. In the meantime, she'll have been getting on with other, less animate details.

On the rare occasion when she is requested to make changes, Ryder is happy to oblige, though usually only once the paint is dry, several weeks later. In this way she can wipe the corrective marks off, if their addition has only made the portrait worse. She has worked out that there are two different patterns to problem paintings: if she's satisfied with the likeness at first glance, but the longer she concentrates on it, the worse the portrait appears, the problem is with detail, and it is easy to correct. If, on the other hand, it looks wrong at first, and the longer she looks at it, the better it appears, the problem is with proportion, which is much more difficult to correct. (If the upper lip is too long, for example, the whole face needs to be altered.)

Of course, nothing is more flattering than when she is asked to paint more members of the same family after a first portrait has been appreciated. Or even, as on one occasion, to paint the same person twice. She was commissioned to paint Richard Morgan as Head of Cheltenham College, and several years later as Head of Radley College.

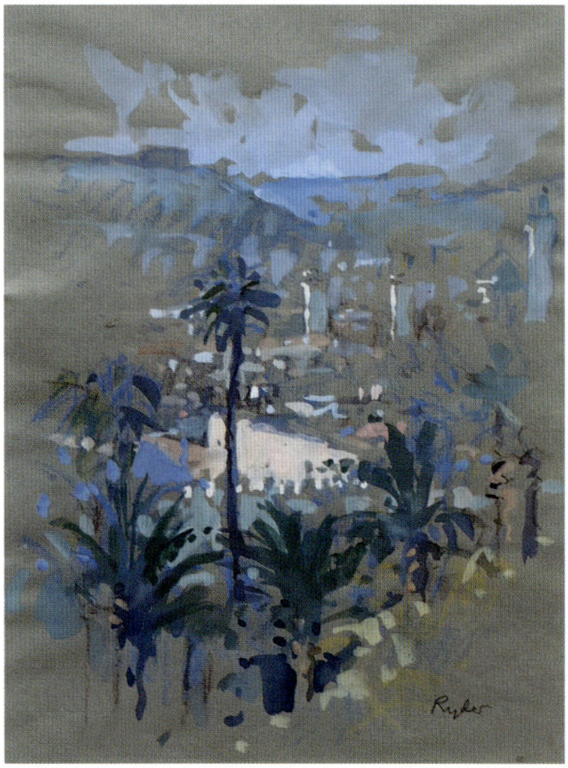

Fez, watercolour on paper

Watercolours

Many of Ryder's admirers have told her that, however skilful an oil painter she might be, they consider her best talent to be as a watercolourist. Which is interesting, as the artist considers this medium a hobby, which she practises for pleasure. Perhaps she will consider selling her watercolours in the future: at present she gives them away to friends or family. Watercolour painting makes her happy: there is no pressure involved.

She likes to work on grey paper, using Chinese white, tinted with watercolour. She starts any watercolour by sketching in the details very lightly, in pencil, whether this is the structure of a building or the outline of a human or canine body. Another thing she likes about the medium is the fact that she can leave the edges untouched, which seems contrived in oil paintings. If she's painting a building, for example, she need only complete the parts that excite her, and leave the rest to the imagination.

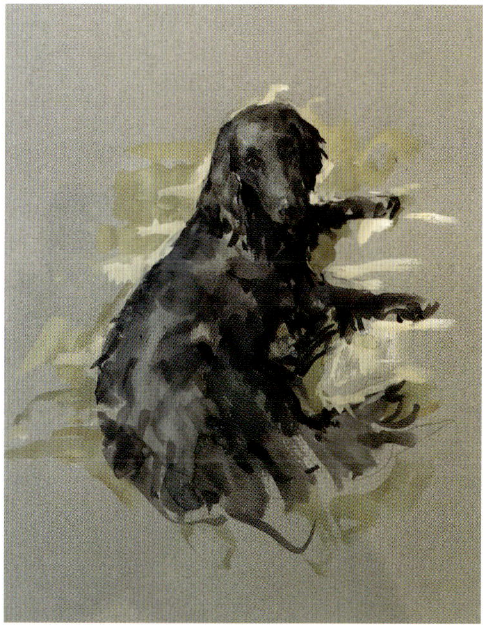

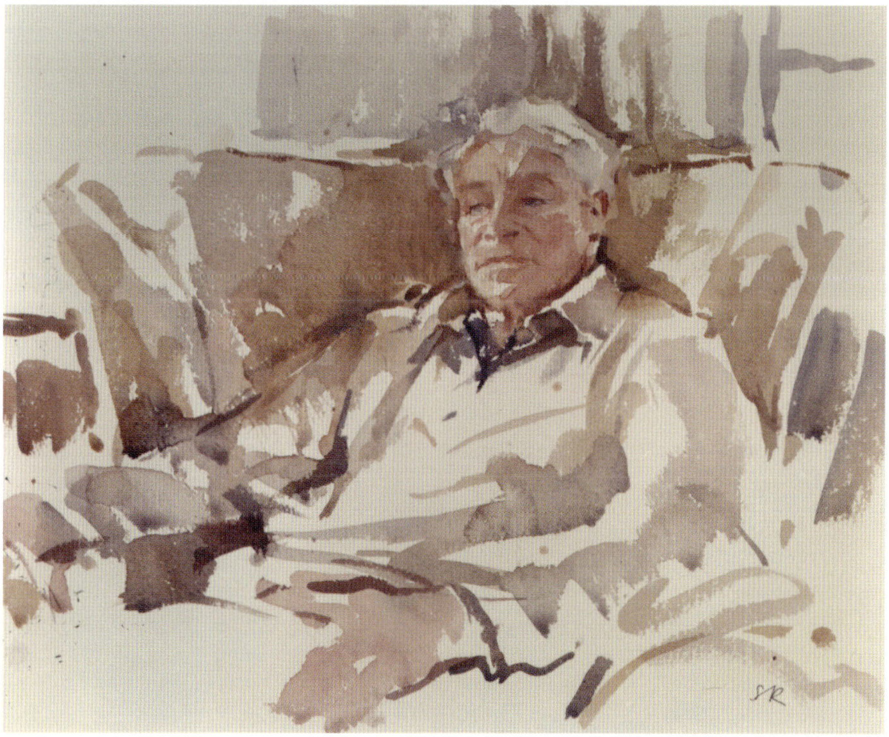

Bryher the Flat Coat, watercolour on paper

Robert Ryder, watercolour on paper

Interiors

When Ryder paints interiors, she doesn't employ 'perspective' to create a sensation of distance: there is no eye-level horizon, there are no lines converging into the distance. She prefers to conjure space and depth using colour and tone. A red jacket on a chair in the distance will draw the eye back; the effect can be accentuated by the representation of light emanating from more than one source (natural light though the window, for example, as well as artificial light from a lamp). Windows, too, are useful: the eye is drawn past the still life that might dominate the canvas, and into the external view.

Ryder enjoys having the freedom to move the furniture around and introduce a few choice props, a process she calls 'setting the scene'. This might include leaving the door the slightest bit ajar, changing a lampshade for something of a more suitable shape or colour, draping a jacket over a chair. A change of tablecloth; a different bunch of flowers in the vase; fallen petals; an opened bottle of red wine on a distant table to draw the eye beyond the foreground.

On the rare occasions Ryder has not been allowed to move things around to her liking – for example when painting a room in the National Trust's Petworth House in West Sussex – she has not enjoyed the experience so much.

Many of her interiors have been painted during her annual working holidays in France – generally in Normandy, the Loire or Provence – with her friends. Having chosen a suitable inspiring rental, Ryder and her friends pack their car with suitable props: deckchairs, tablecloths, lampshades, jugs, vases and candlesticks to supplement the interesting furniture and fittings they are bound to find in situ.

These French properties also give her the opportunity to paint 'outside-inside' paintings, of dining tables set up in the garden or on the terrace, so she can portray – for example – the aftermath of an al fresco summertime lunch. Her interiors are unpeopled, but there is always a '*Marie Celeste*' suggestion that someone has just departed, or is about to return: half-full wine glasses; robes thrown across Edwardian armchairs.

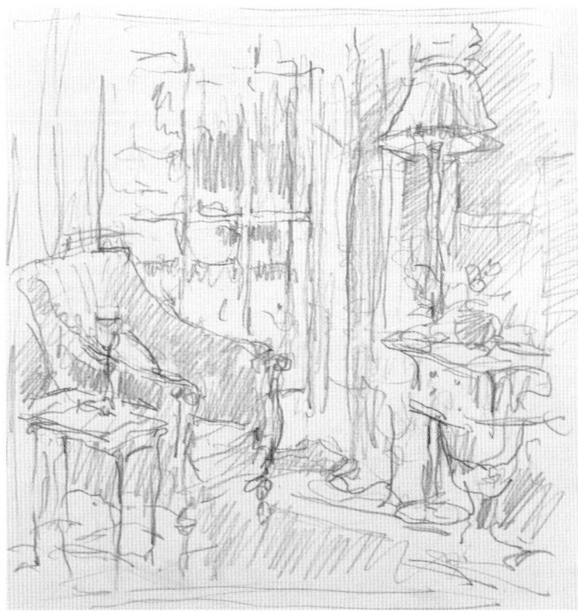

Pencil study for an interior

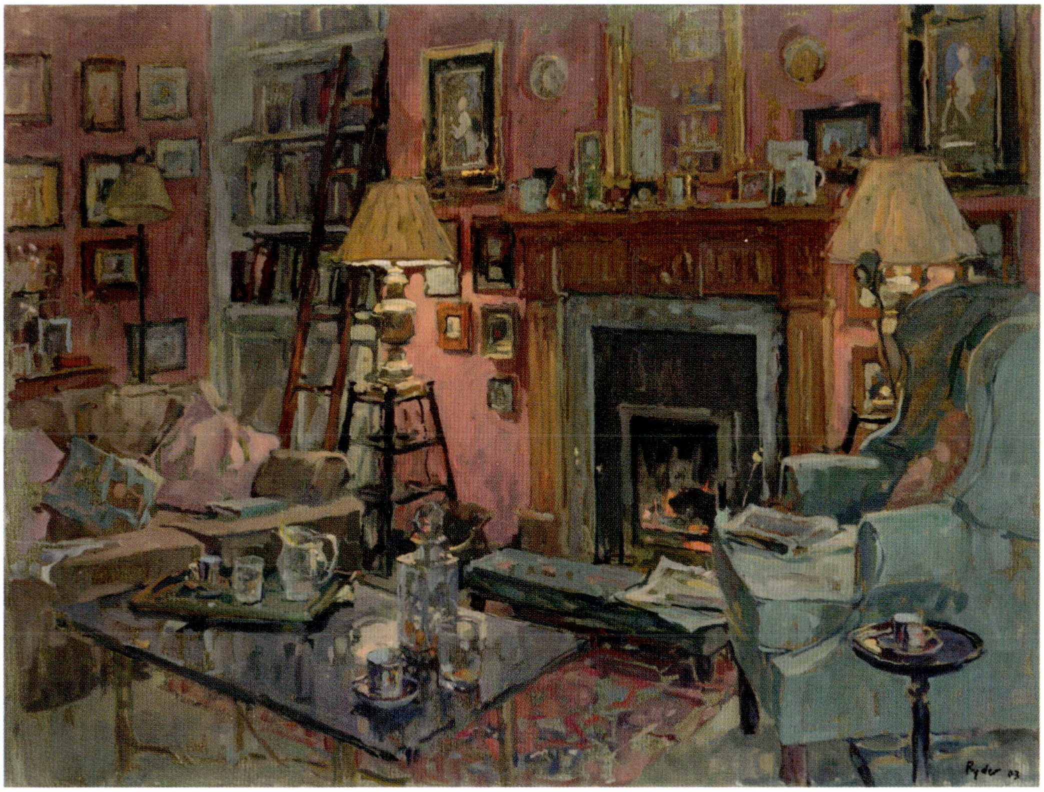

The Library Steps, 30 × 36

Ryder is always on the lookout for subject matter. When she is invited to a dinner party, she will often ask to come back and paint the room in a quieter moment. Other opportunities to discover locations come when she is commissioned to paint a portrait.

Unlike her major influences Edouard Vuillard and Bernard Dunstan RA, Ryder prefers her interiors to be unpeopled: as a portrait artist, she doesn't want human figures to dominate the frame. Indeed, the artist finds the process of painting interiors to be liberating: freed from the need to place a central character in her narratives, she can apply herself to colour and light rather than character and likeness. No wonder these paintings are so popular: every four years or so Ryder is given a solo exhibition at Panter & Hall in Pall Mall in central London, with great success.

That said, when asked if she prefers painting portraits or interiors, she is clear in her response. While she loves the peacefulness of depicting empty rooms, she would, if forced to choose, rather experience the 'adrenalin rush' that accompanies the painting of a portrait.

PORTRAITS

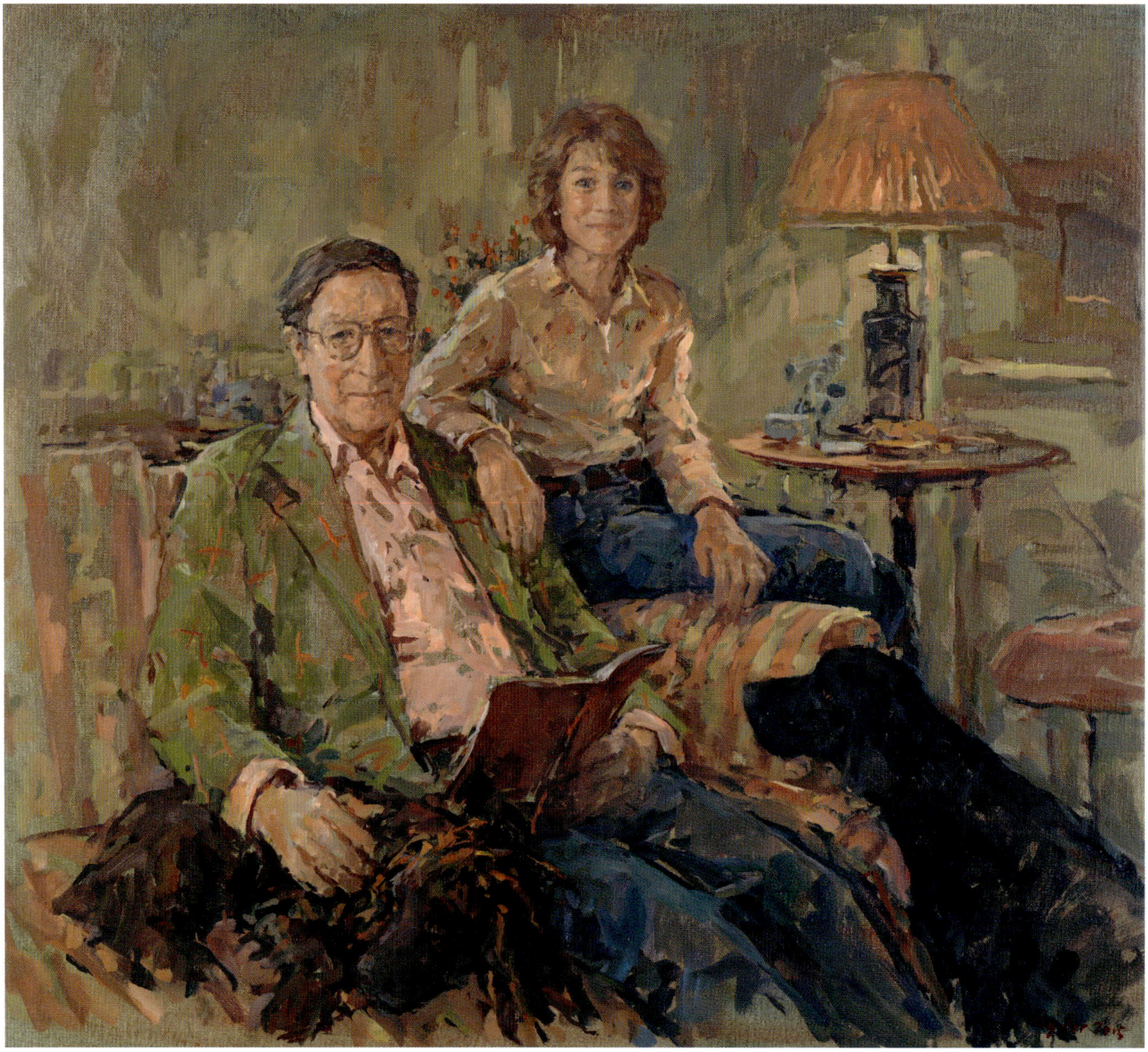

Max and Penny Hastings, 24 × 30

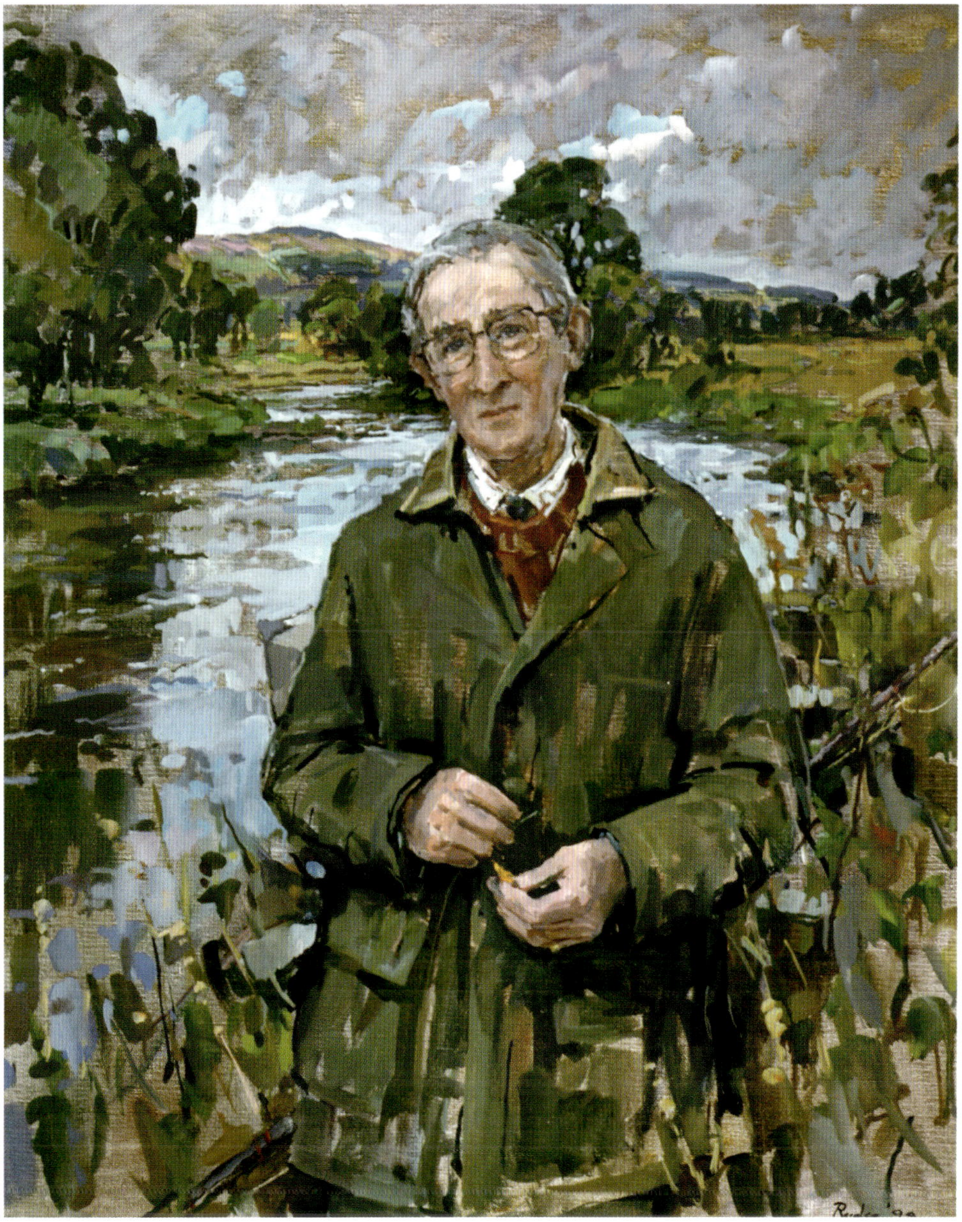

David Ross Stewart on the Tweed, 30 × 25

A keen fisherman, David was happy to pose if he could be seen tying a fly created by his father. We had planned the date sometime in advance not realising that August 10th was to be a total eclipse of the sun – so painting stopped and coffee was had while we waited for the sun to reappear.

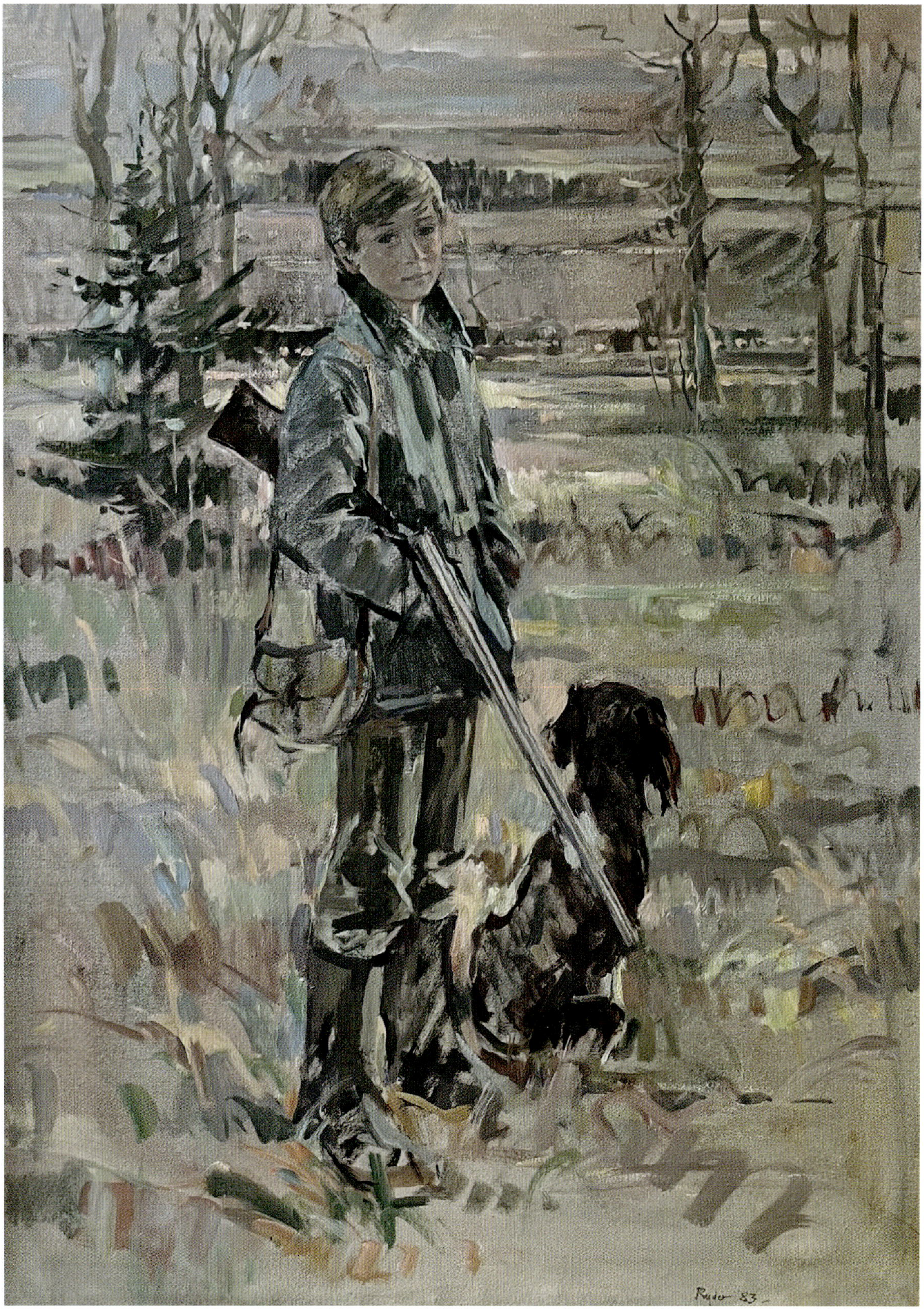

FACING PAGE

Oliver waiting for Pigeons, 40 × 30

It was December, Oliver my son posing with the Cheviot Hills in the distance and plenty of breaks for hot drinks back at the house – his sister Susannah helpfully banging the undergrowth to turn our spaniel's gaze away from stealing the show.

RIGHT

Lars and Iona with Miss Muffet, 30 × 36

BELOW

The Deacon Family, 30 × 42

A family of five adults is a design challenge. It is important to me to in some way give each figure a similar importance. So looking out at the viewer, a red dress or being in the foreground was how I balanced them. Angela in her evening dress suggested holding the dog leads – which captured their humour too.

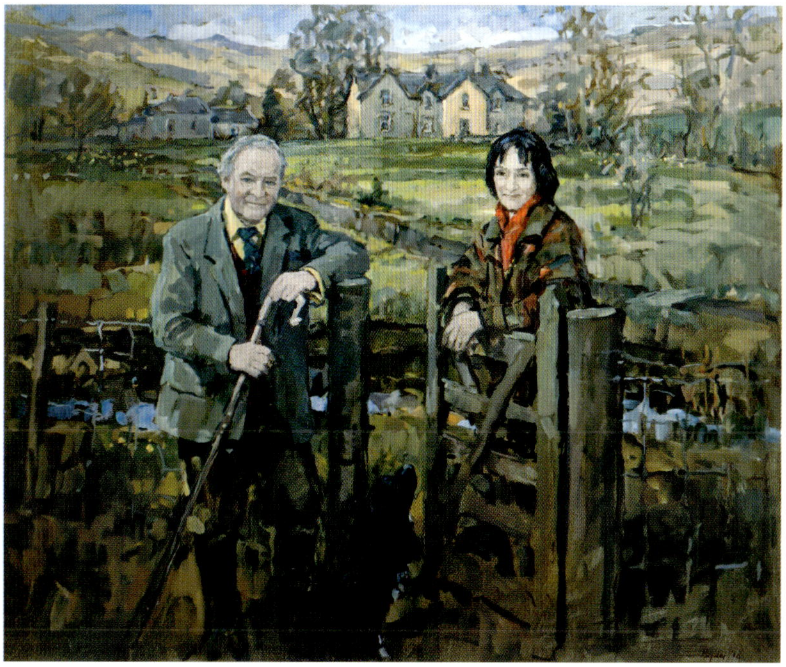

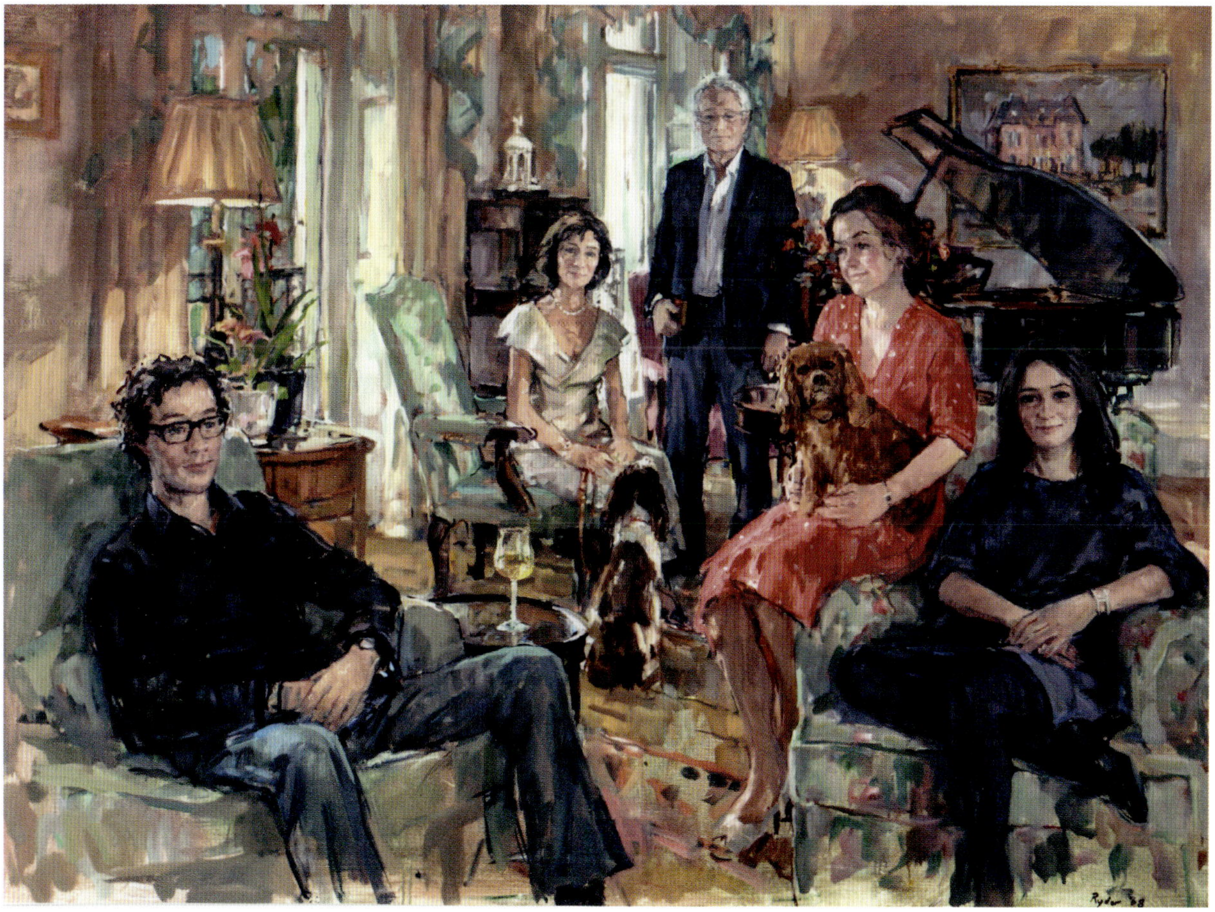

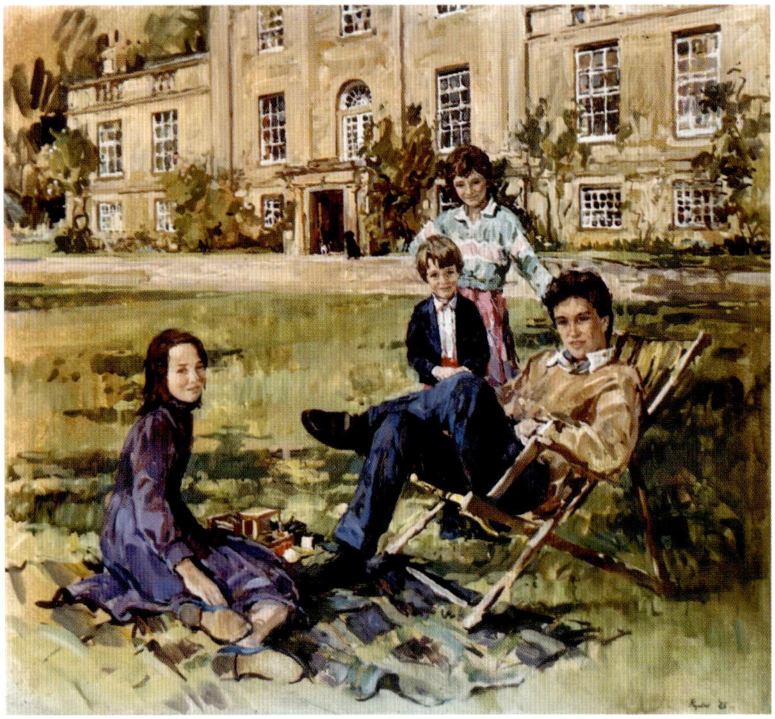

The Ramsay Family, 32 × 40

The Trotter Family, 34 × 40

Edward Trotter, aged nine, asked me 'Do you do the easy bits first?' And at the end of the sittings, 'we will always know each other won't we.' This says so much to me about portrait painting.

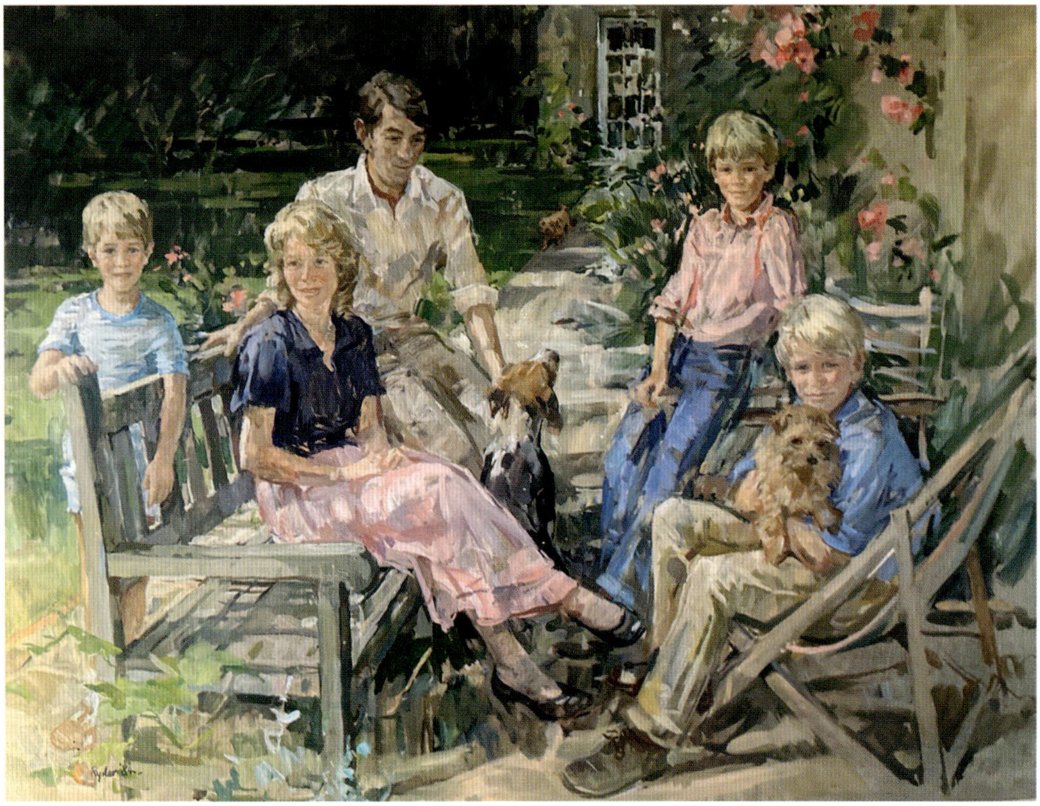

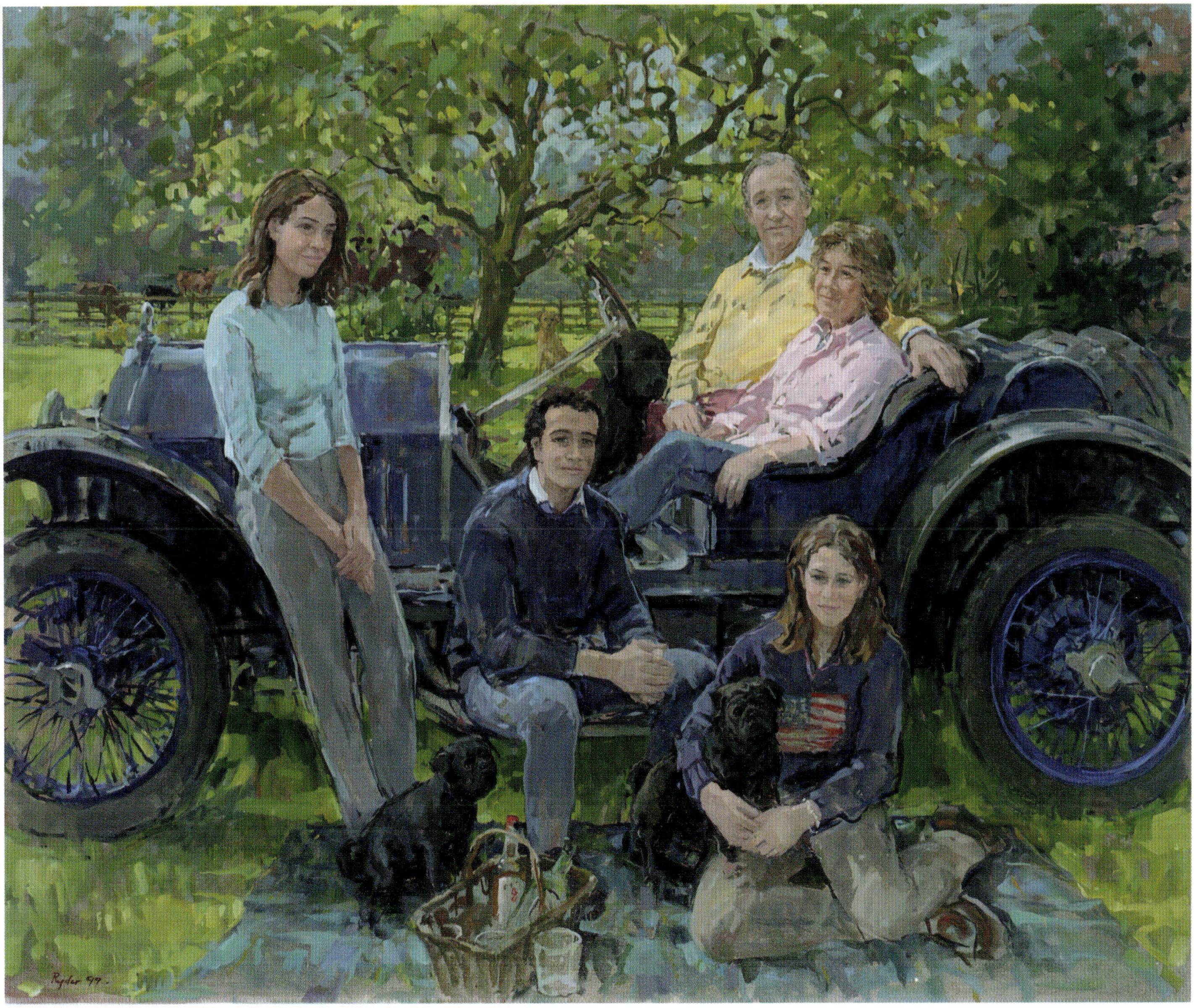

The Crabbe Family, 44 × 52

Colin Crabbe was the vintage car expert at Christie's – so I had a large choice of cars to pose the family round. This Hispana-Suiza was perfect. The family and dogs sat wonderfully all together to start with but by day three they came one at a time. Their youngest daughter sitting on a rug in the foreground got the giggles and turning round I discover the rest of the family with binoculars were watching my every brushstroke from the kitchen window.

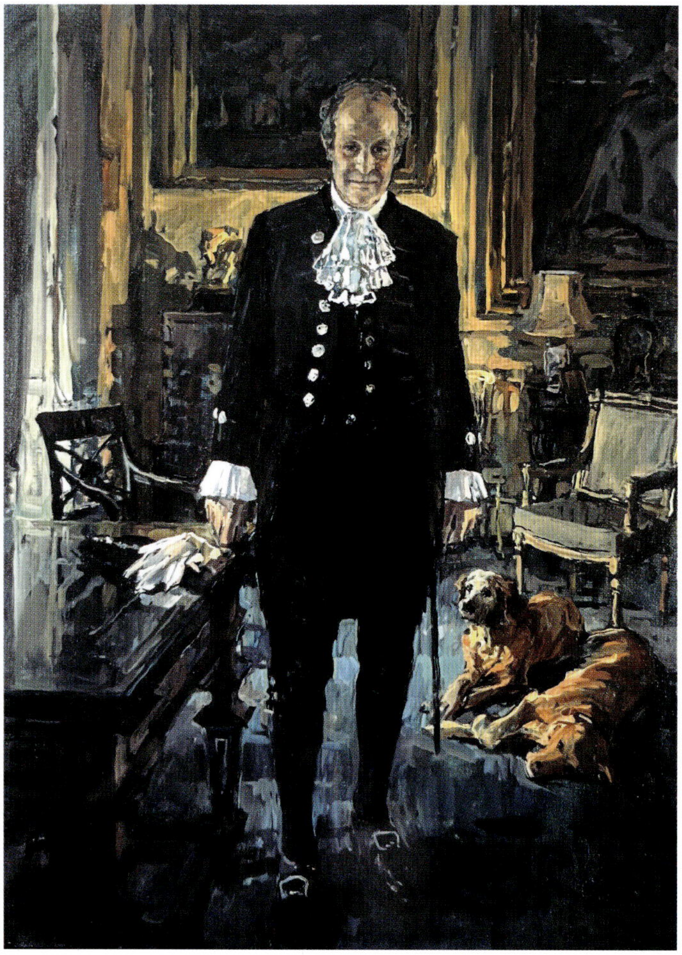

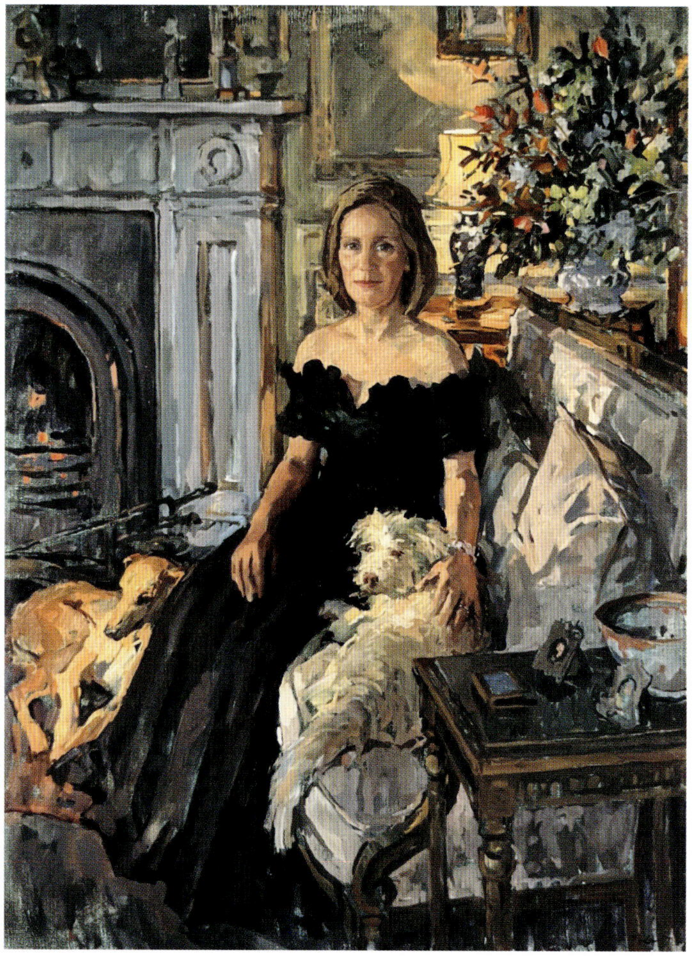

ABOVE LEFT

Roger Graham Palmer, High Sheriff of Clwyd, 40 × 30

ABOVE RIGHT

Vanessa Graham Palmer, 40 × 30

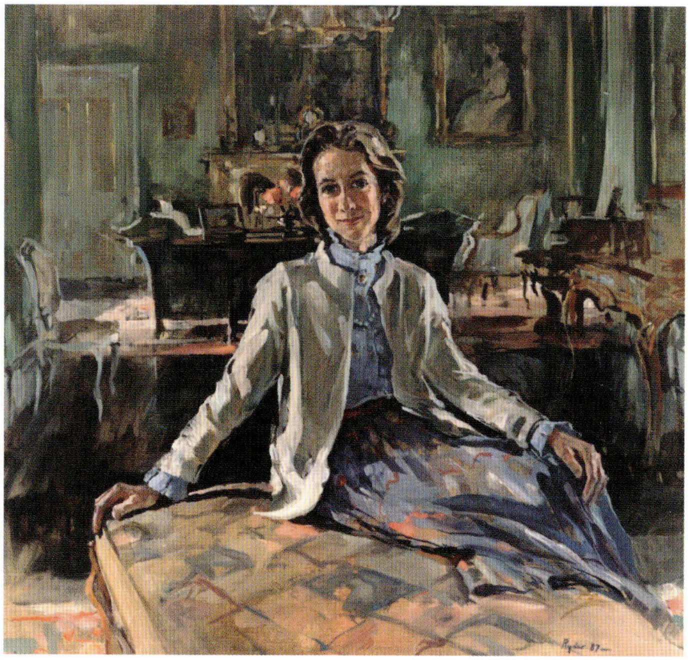

Rossie at Thirlestane, 30 × 36

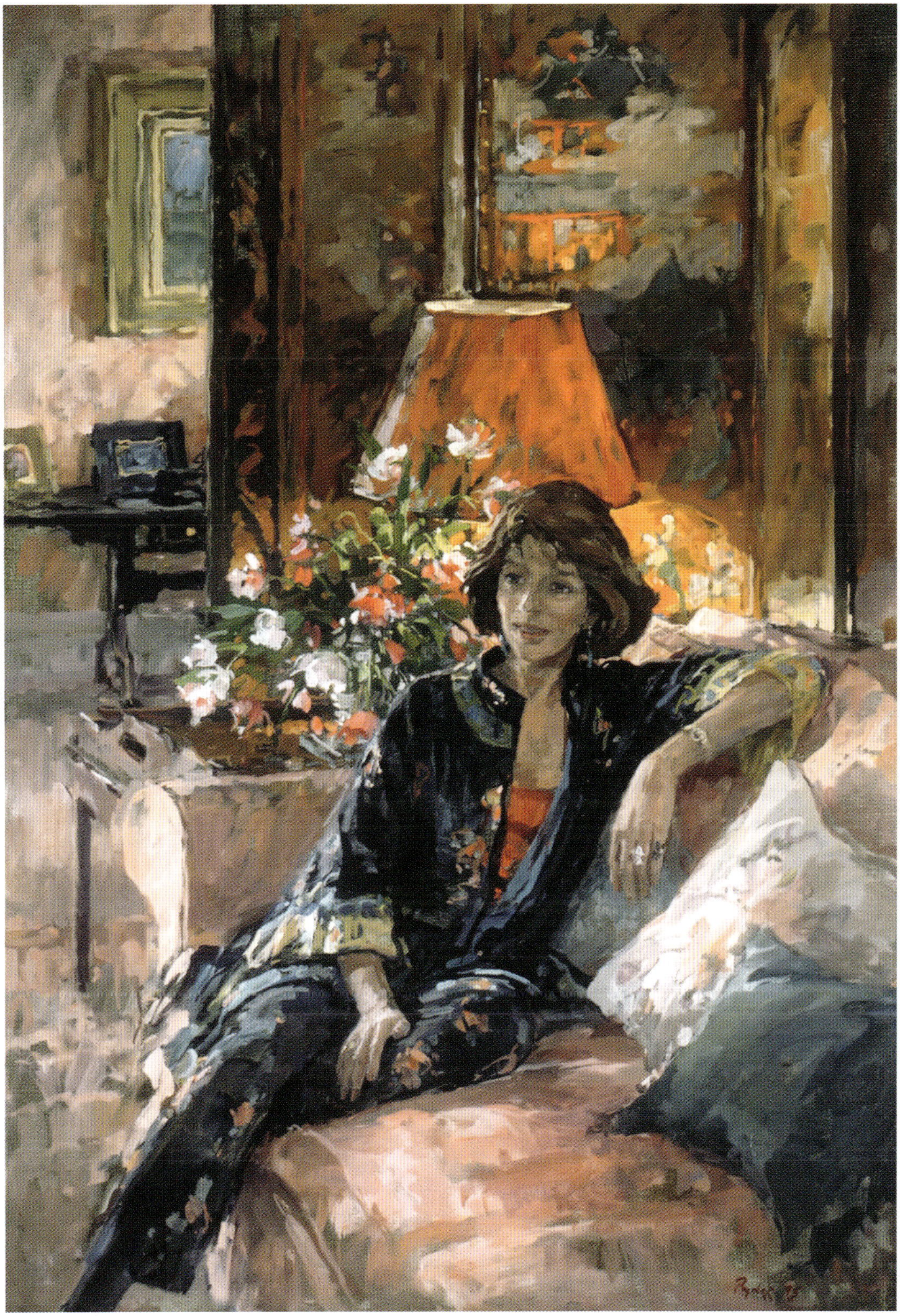

Karen Hambro, 30 × 25

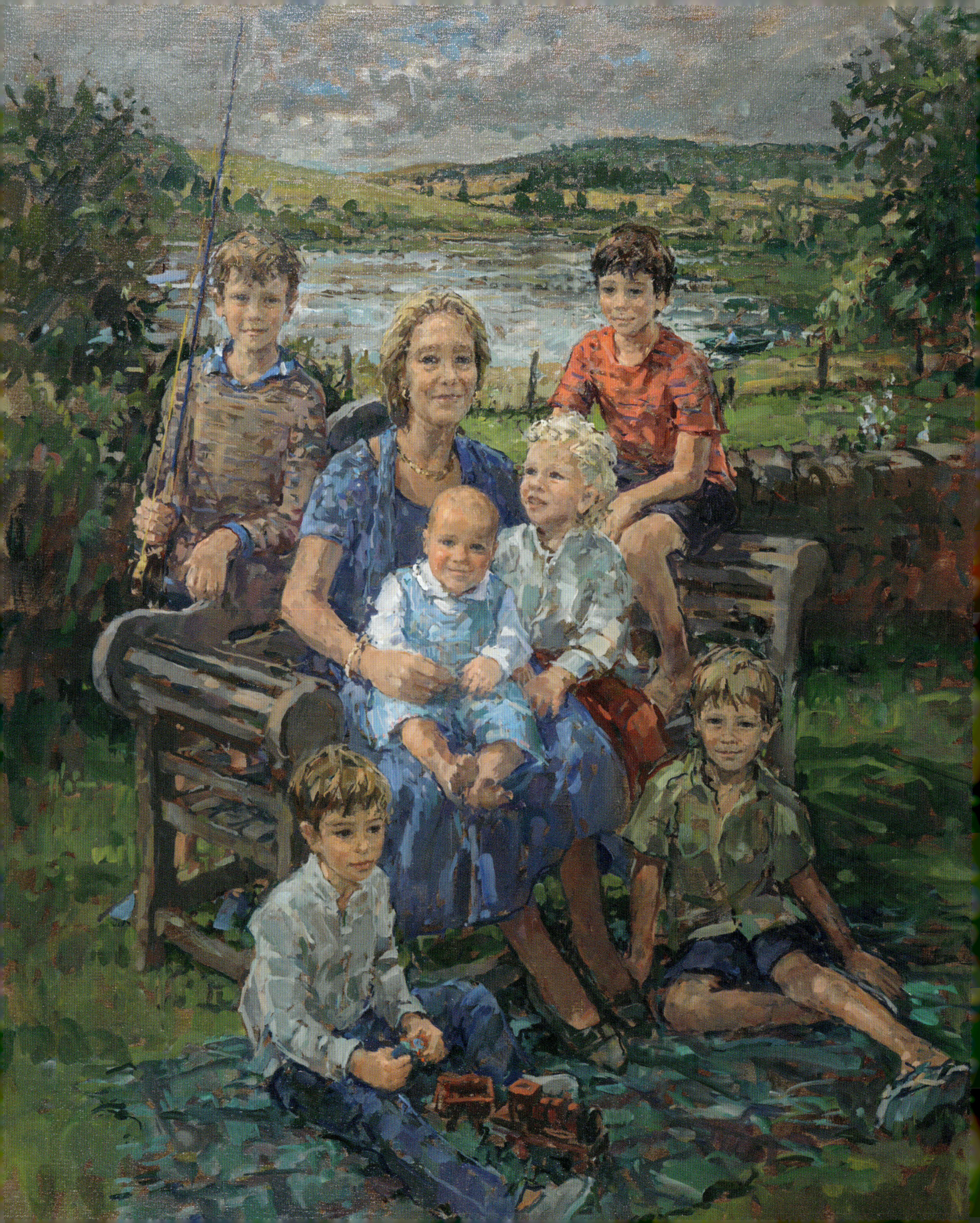

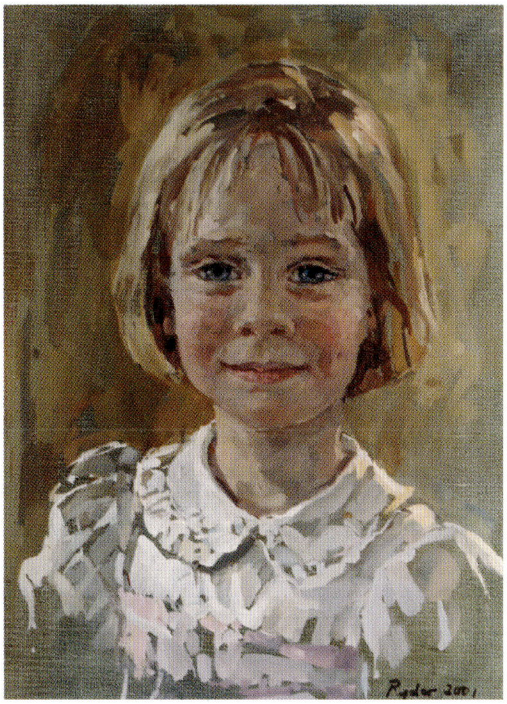

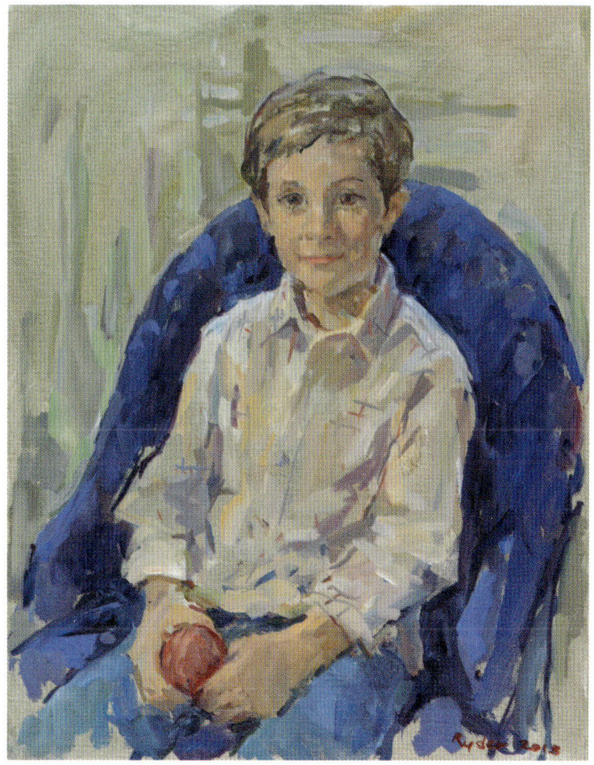

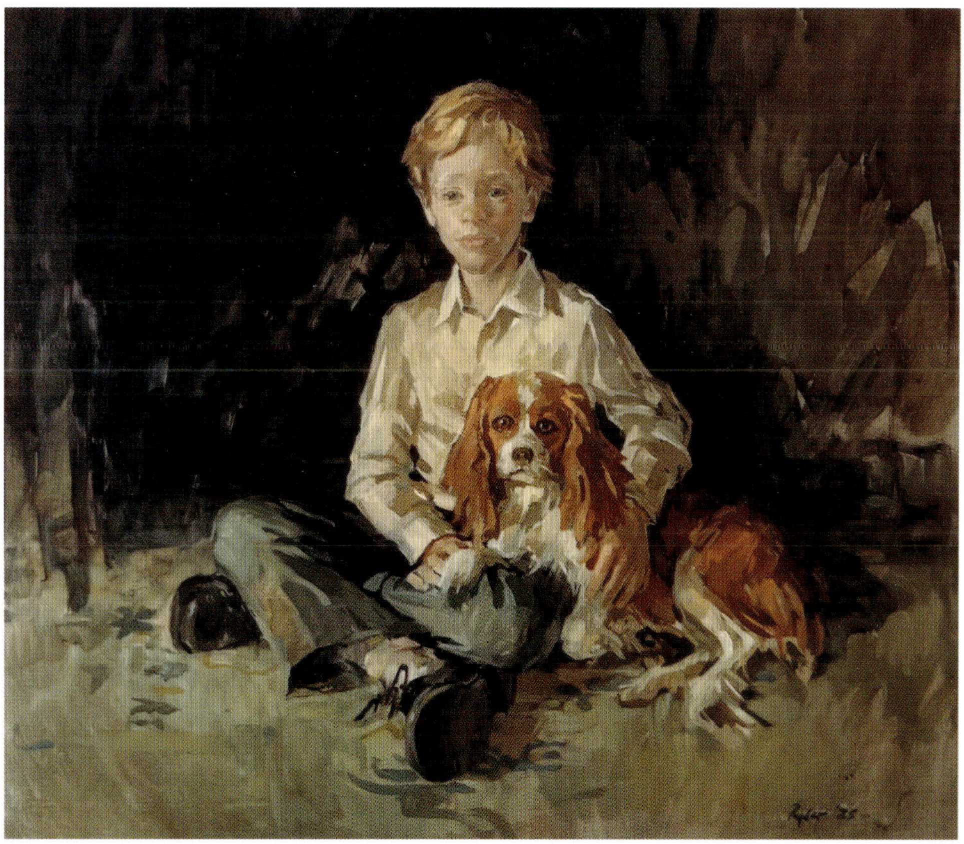

ABOVE LEFT

Sienna Speke, 18 × 12

ABOVE RIGHT

Alexandra Steel, 20 × 16

RIGHT

Benjamin McNair Scott with Daisy, 26 × 32

Benjy is the youngest of four brothers and the last to be painted by me. The McNair Scotts lived just around the corner from us in Kensington. When I would return from walking our spaniel in Holland Park I'd find Benjy and Daisy already posing. I think he was determined to be as good, if not a better sitter than his brothers. Very helpful and touching.

FACING PAGE

Elizabeth and her six grandsons, 48 × 36

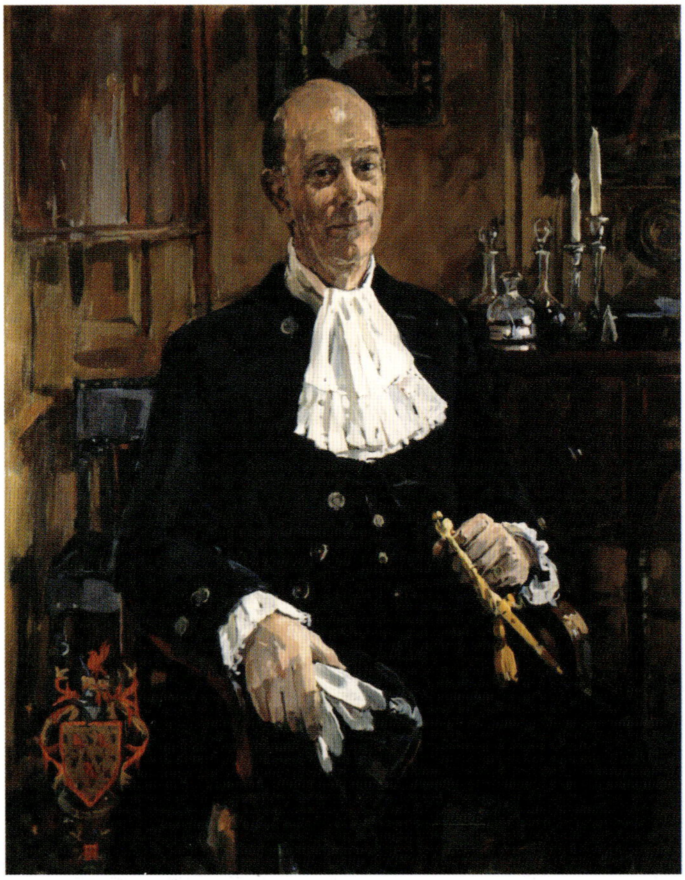

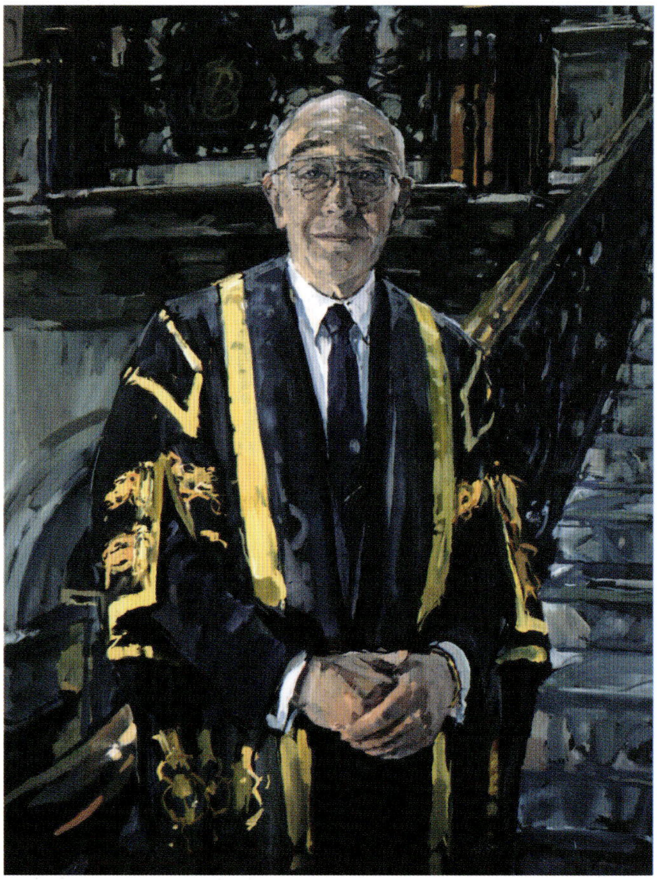

ABOVE LEFT

Robert Erith, High Sheriff of Essex, 1997, 30 × 25

ABOVE RIGHT

Professor Gregory Warden of Goldsmiths College, 1998, 36 × 28

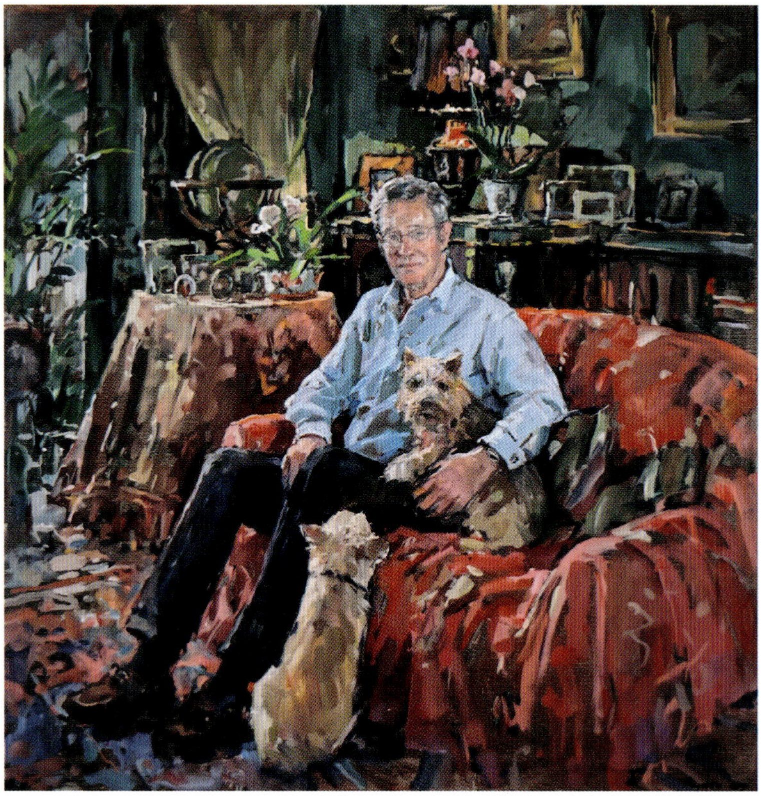

Richard Bernays, 24 × 24

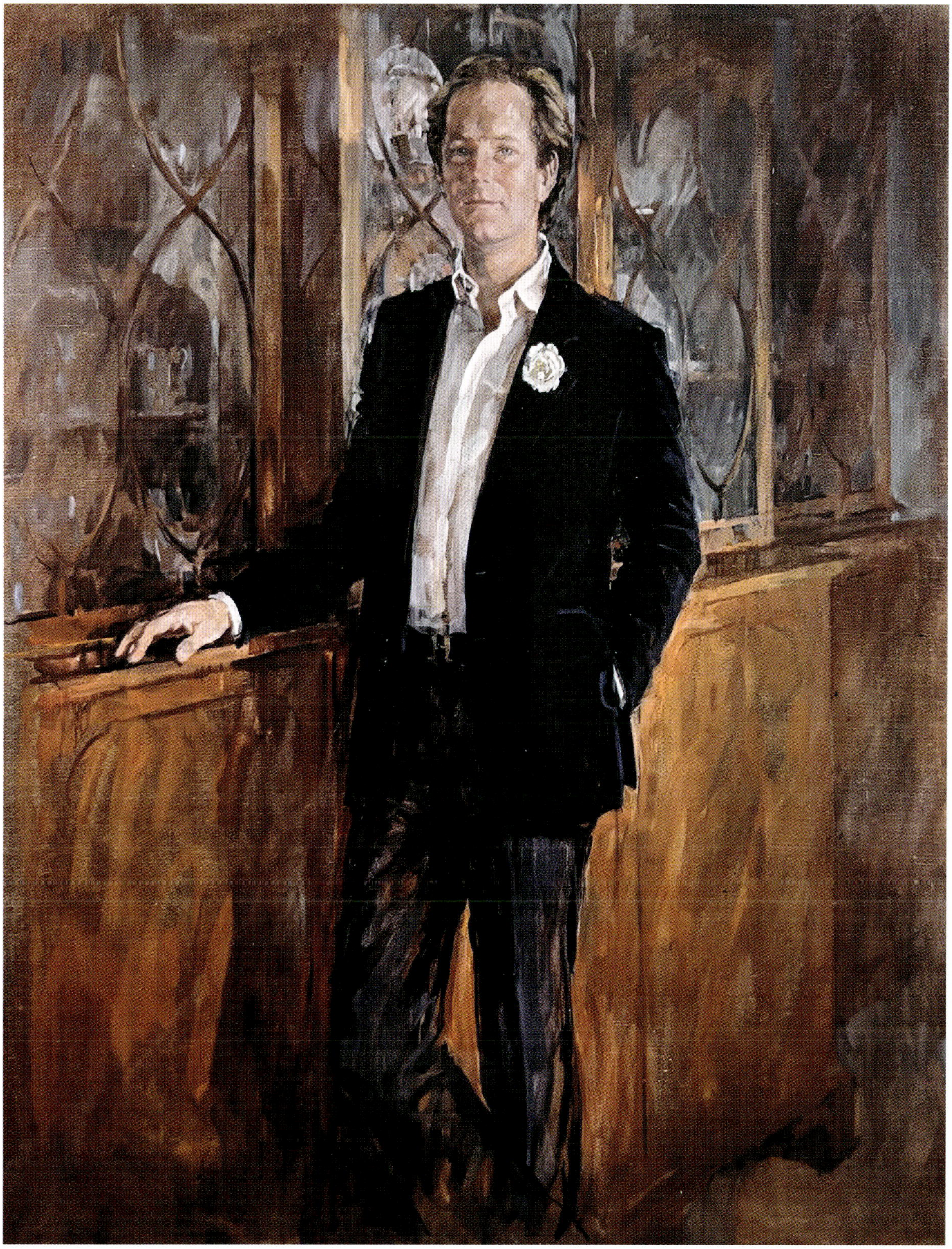

Hugh Poole Warren, 40 × 30

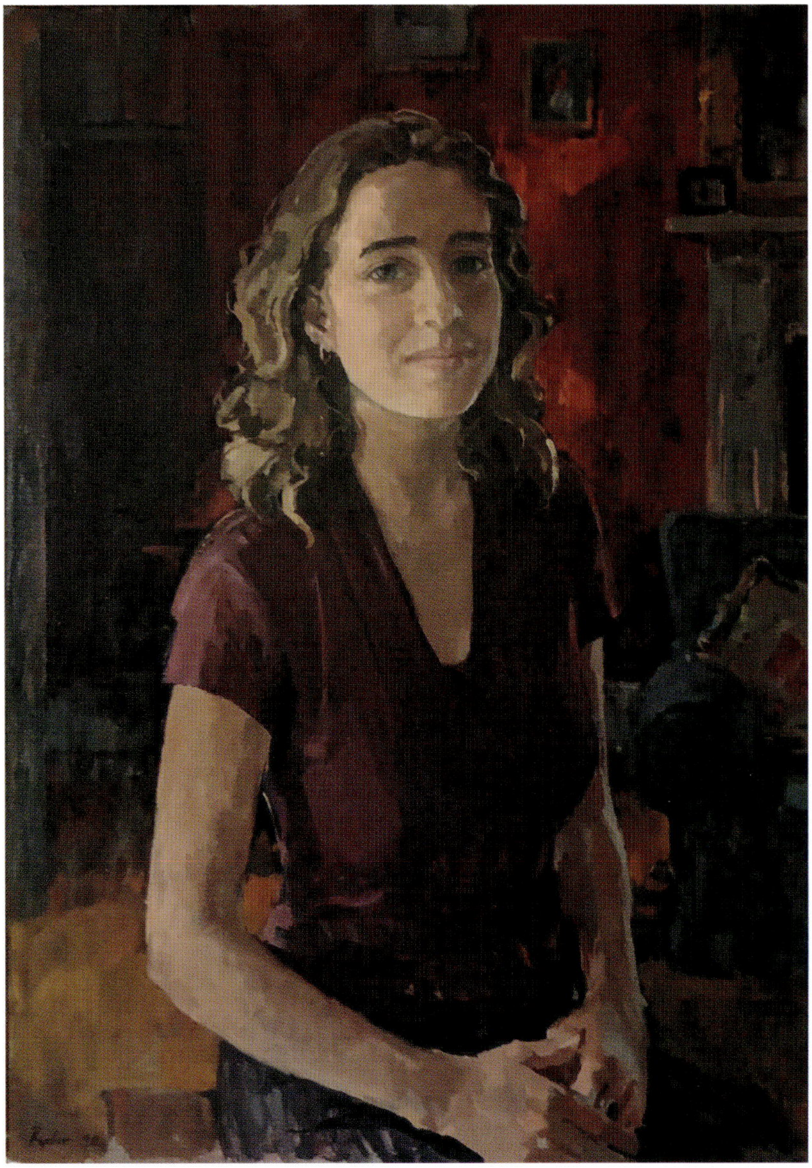

Lucy Anderson, 24 × 30

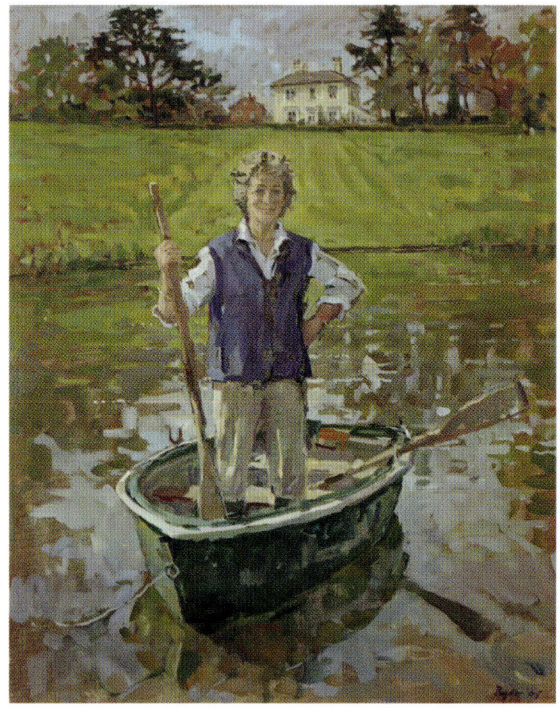

Nicky at Perces, 36 × 30

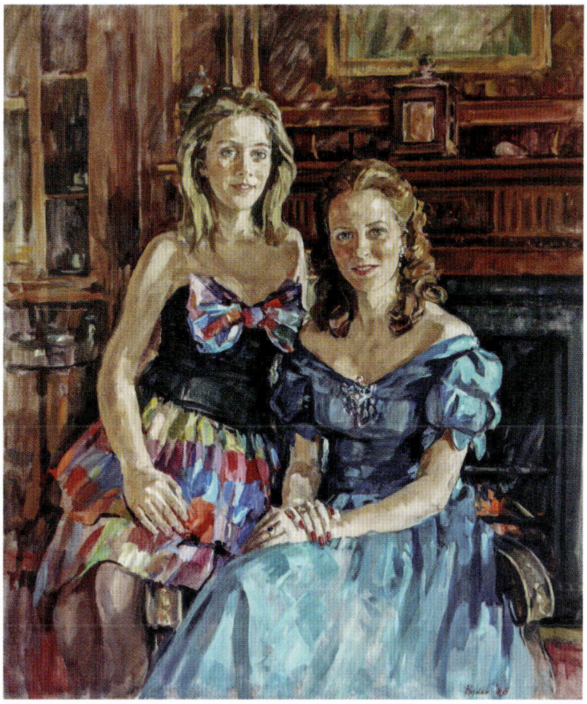

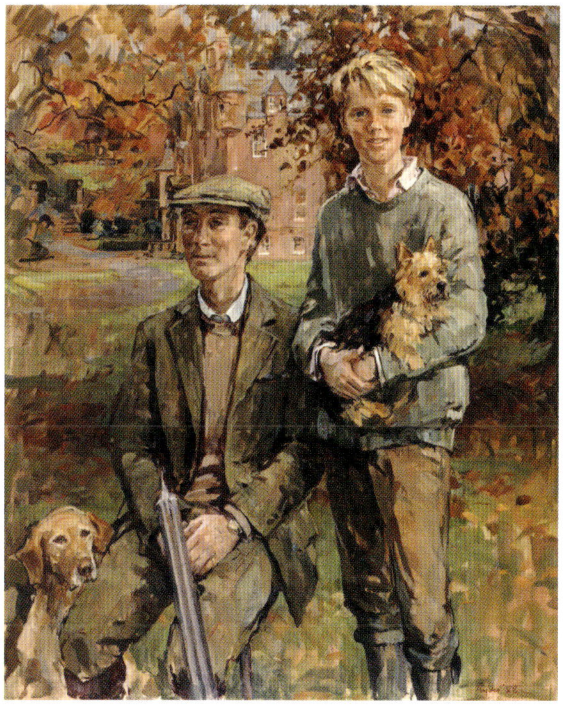

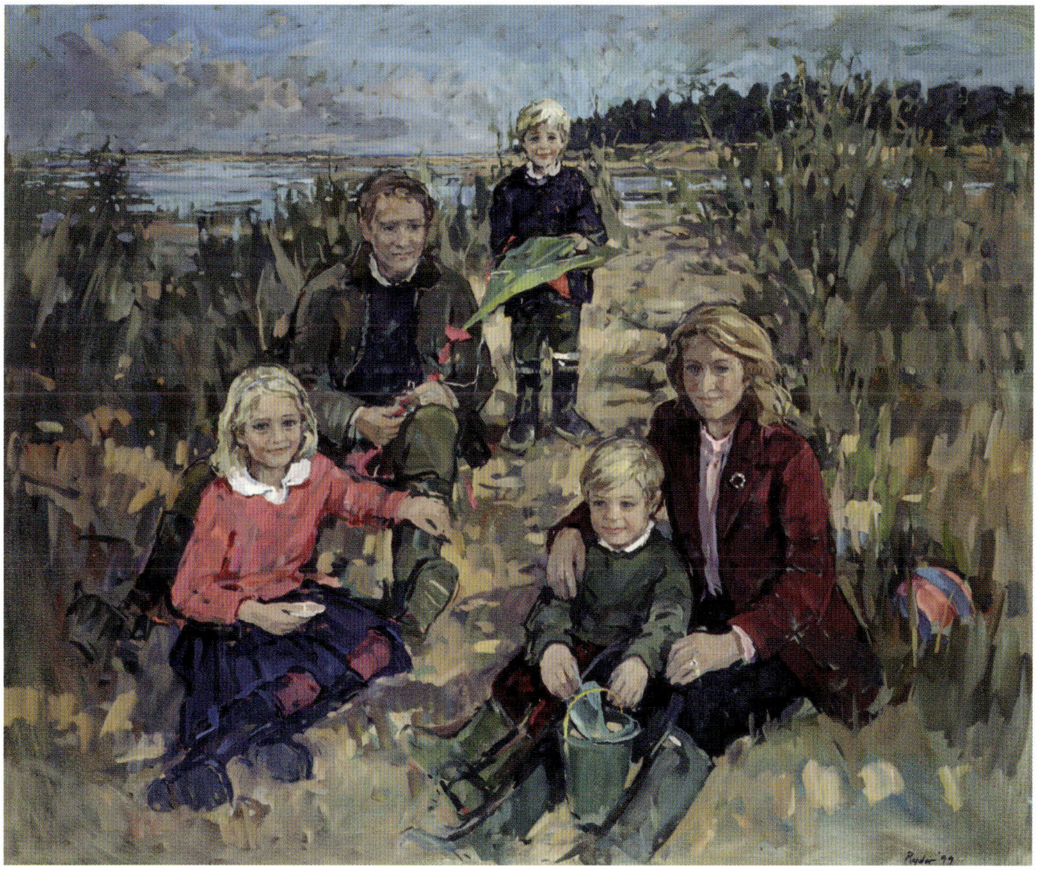

ABOVE LEFT

Miranda and Henrietta Smyly, 36 × 30

ABOVE RIGHT

Robert and Richard Smyly, 36 × 30

On Holkam Beach, 36 × 42

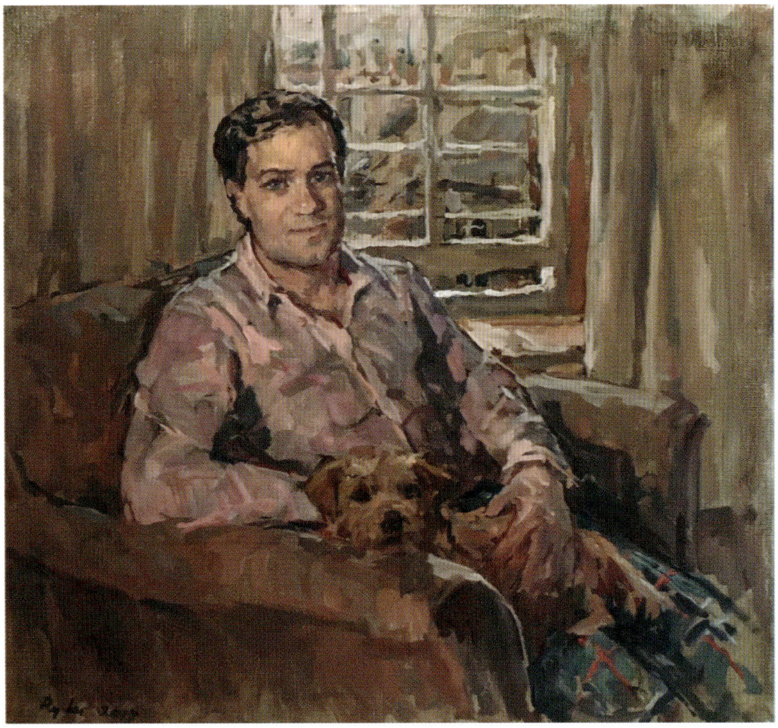

FACING PAGE

Philip, 36 × 30

I told my nephew Philip I would love to paint him on his return from Afghanistan and prayed that he would return safely.

LEFT

Hector with Brodie, 14 × 20

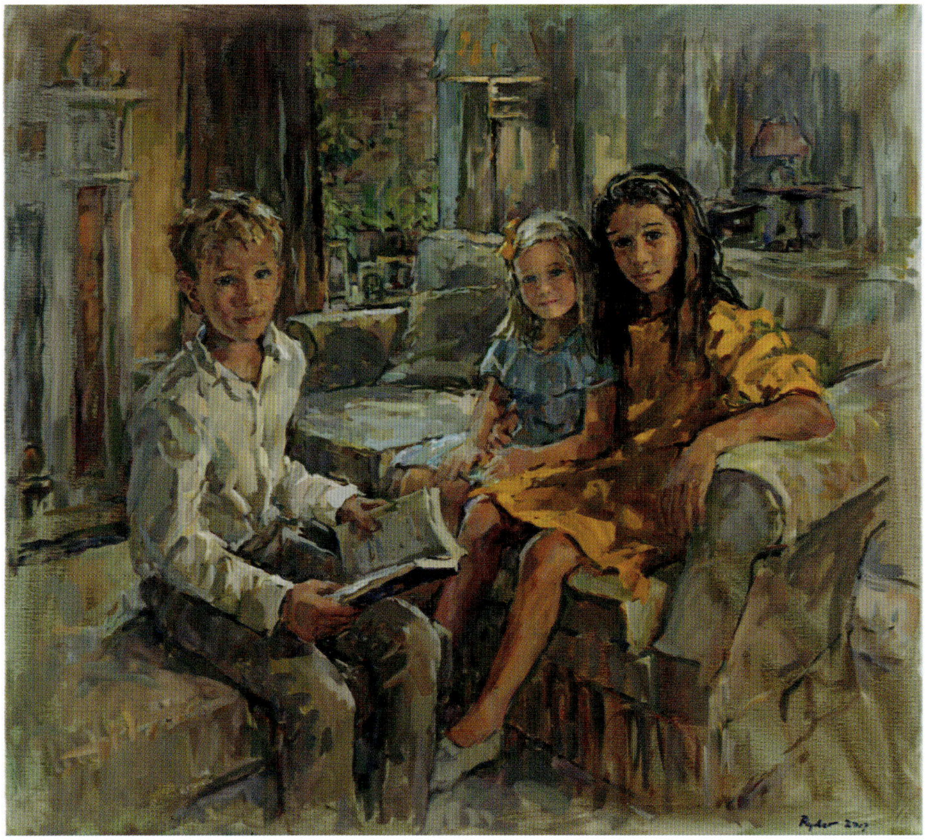

Georgina, Ben and Annabel, 34 × 38

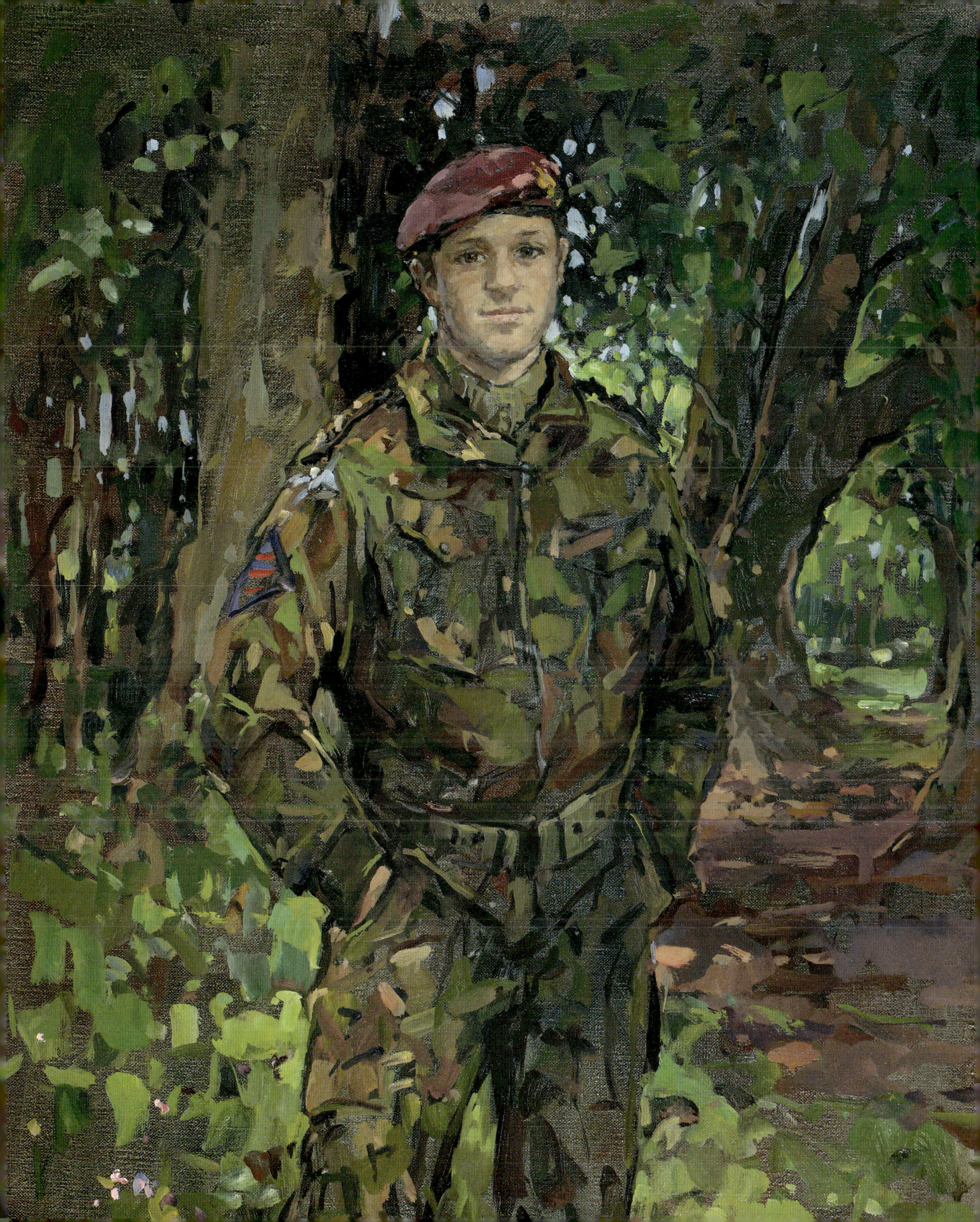

INTERIORS AND EXTERIORS

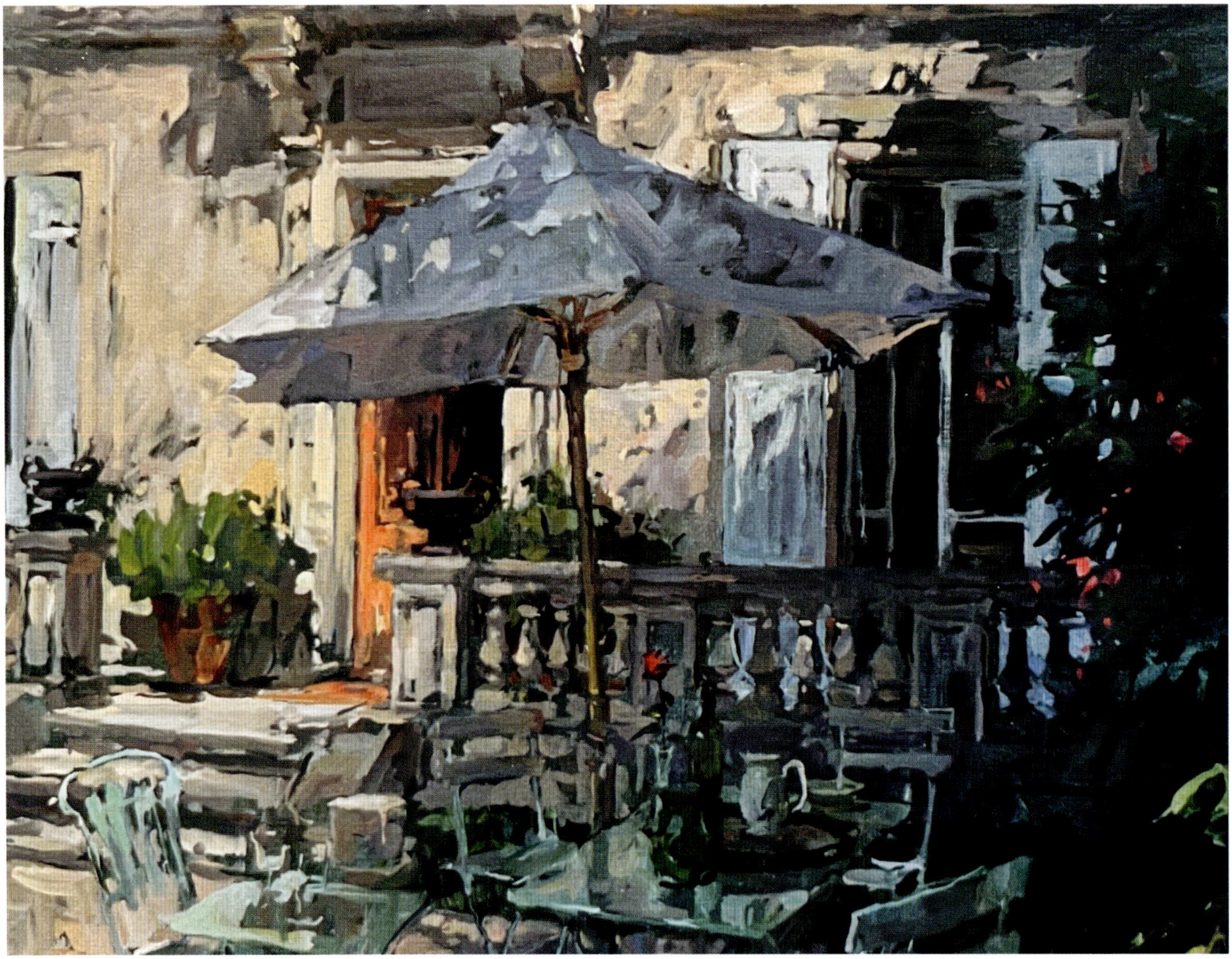

Parasol and Red Rose, 30 × 36

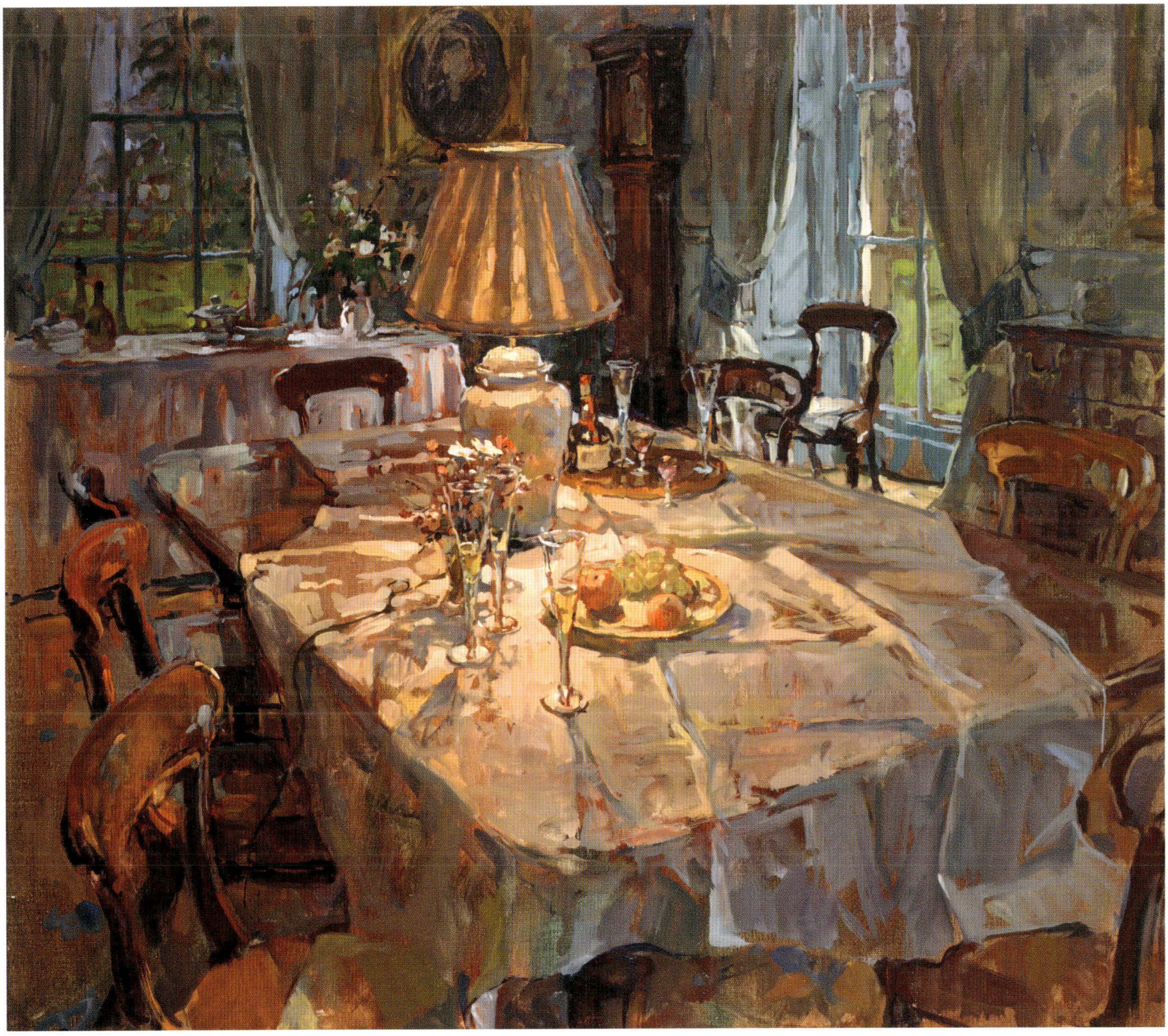

Dining table with Lamp, 38 × 44

FACING PAGE

King James' Room, Chillingham, 36 × 30

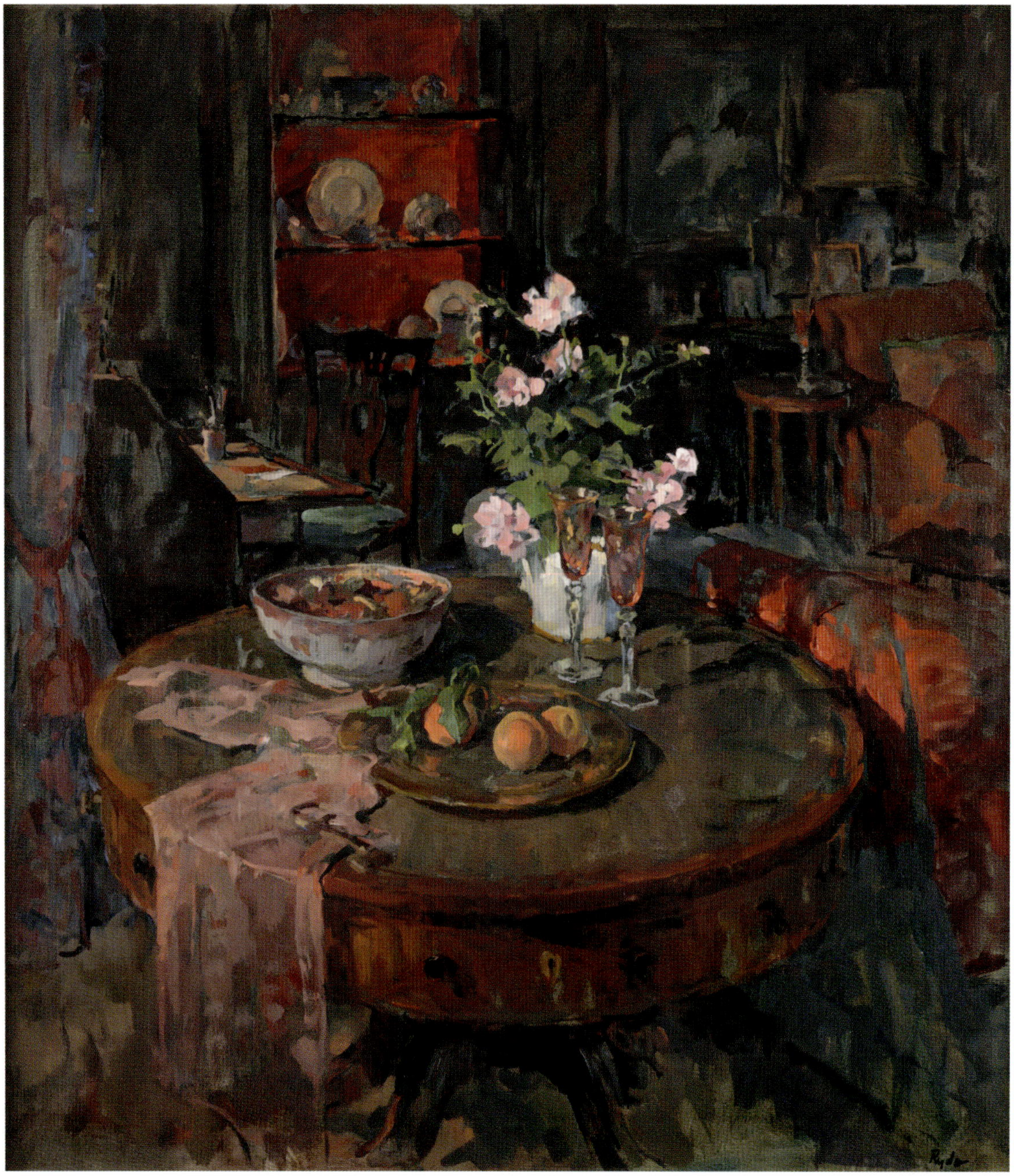

The Drum Table with Geranium, 36 × 30

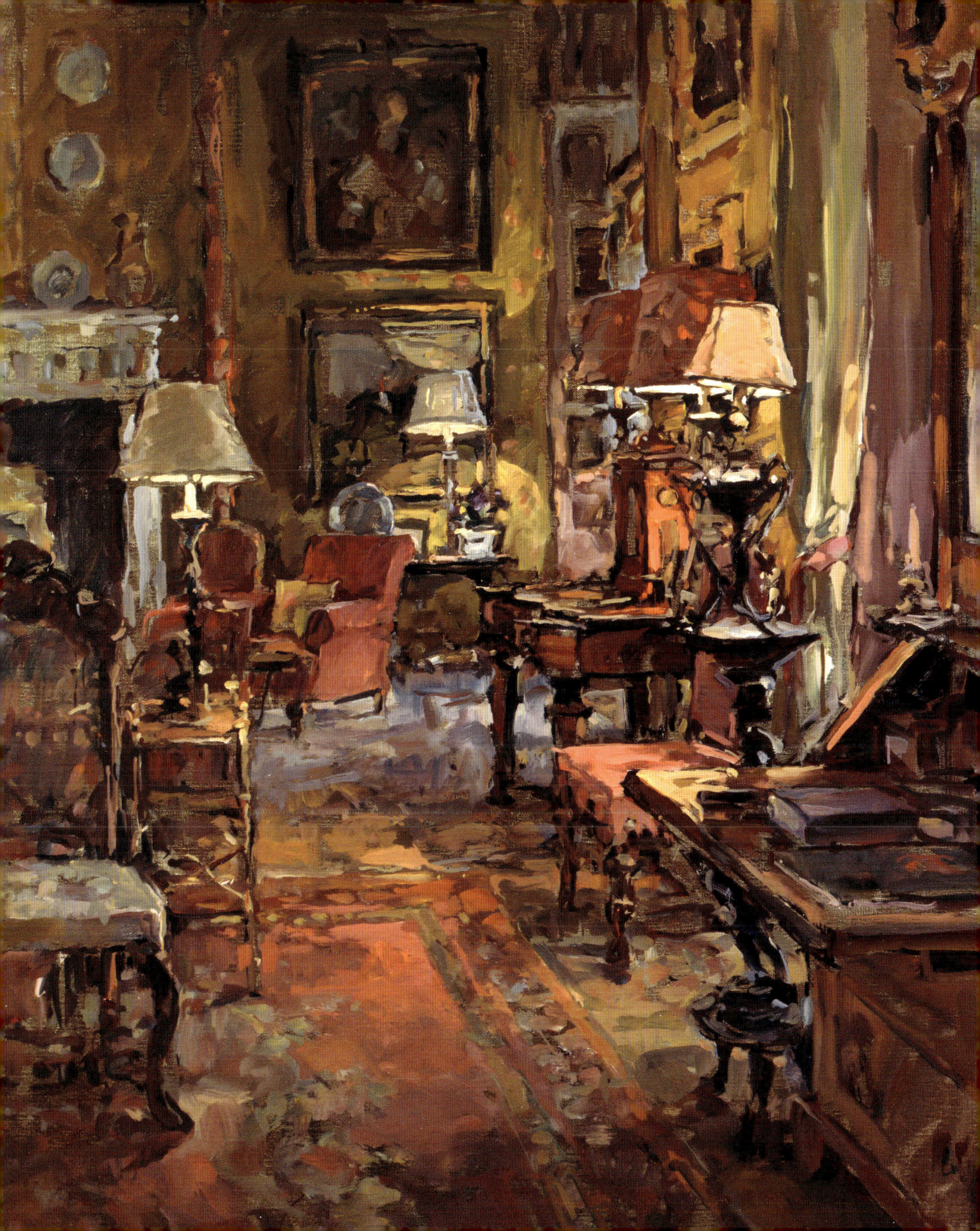

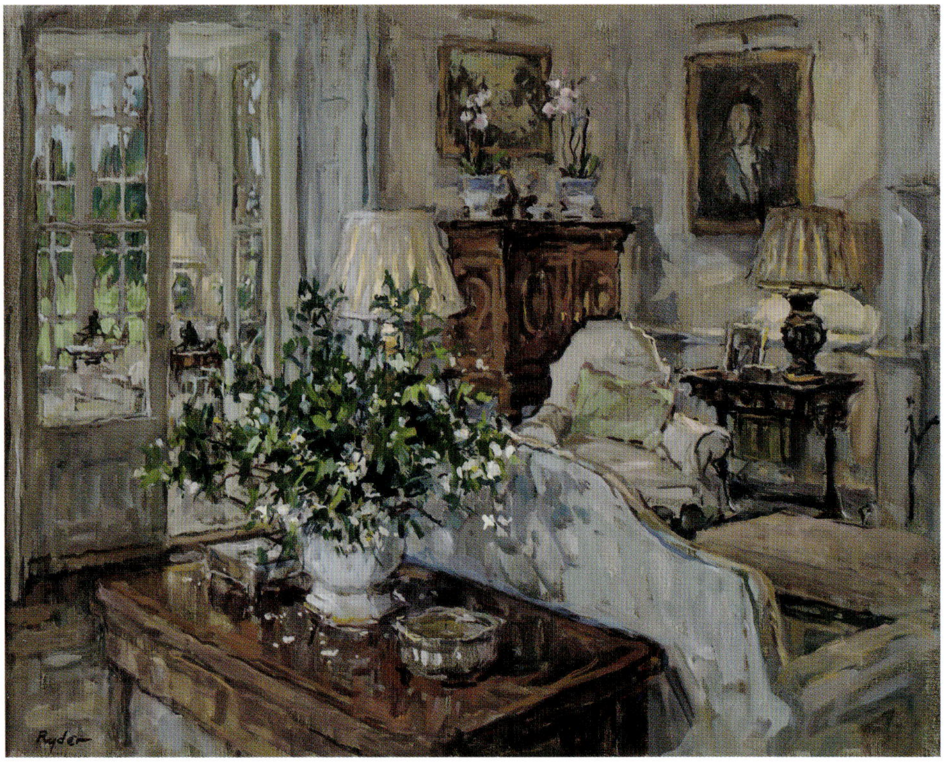

Fallen Petals, 24 × 30

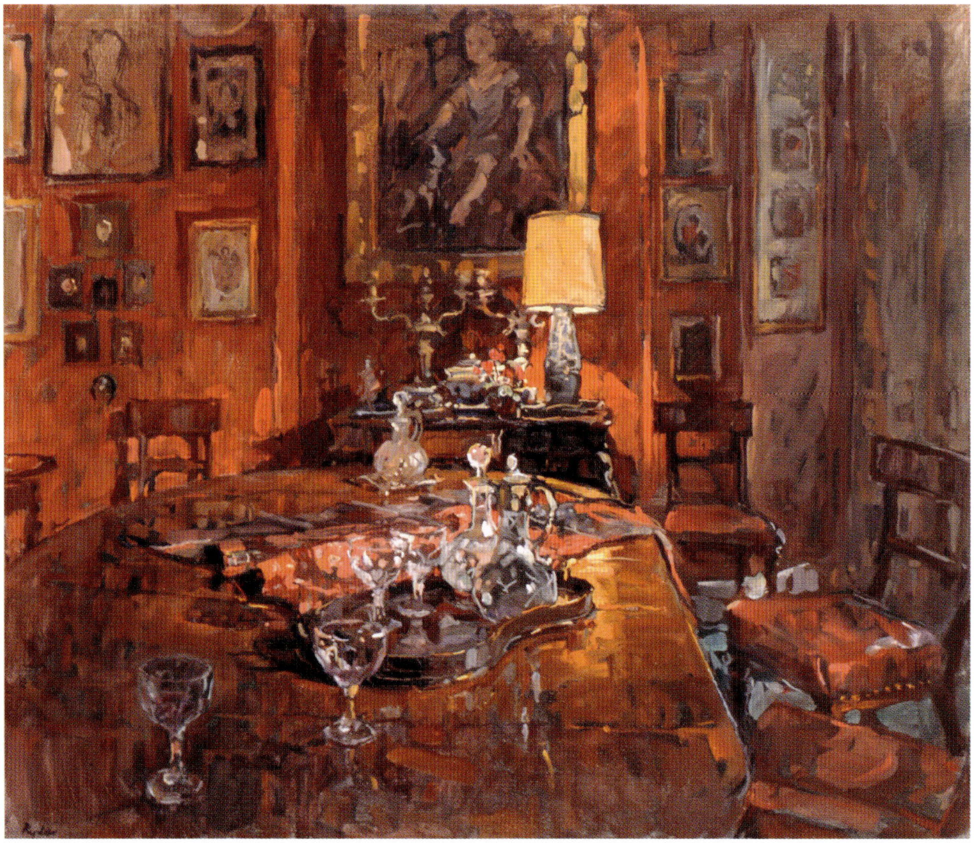

Red Dining Room with Decanter, 30 × 36

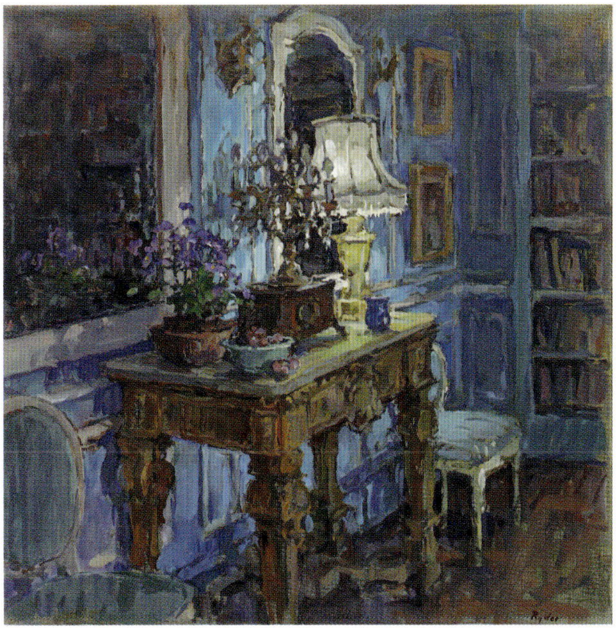

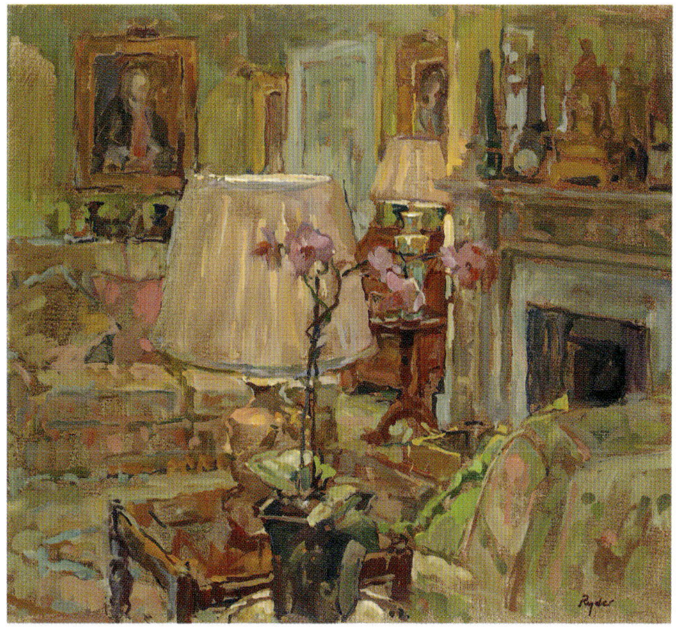

ABOVE LEFT

The Blue Salon, 28 × 28

ABOVE RIGHT

Dower House, Lamps and Orchid, 20 × 22

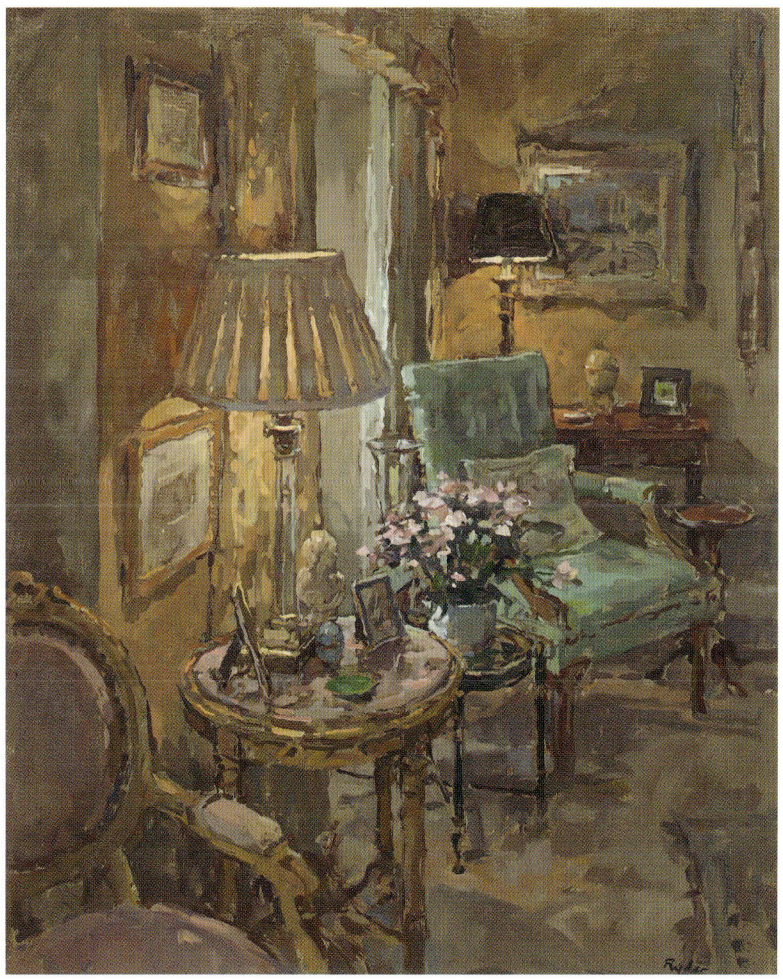

Pink Marble Table, 34 × 28

FACING PAGE
The Sewing Table, 30 × 24

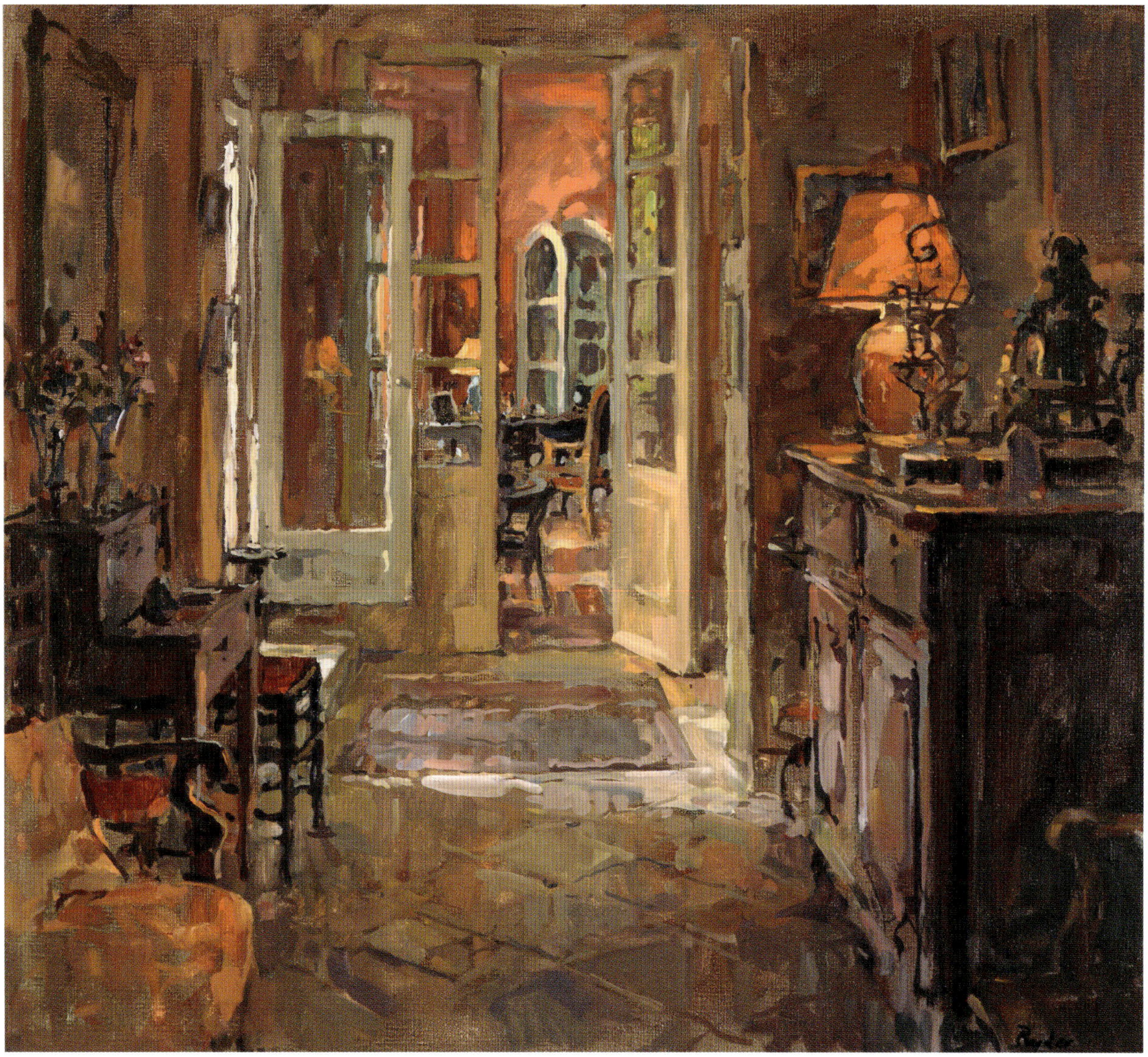

Interior, Rue Emile Zola, 25 × 28

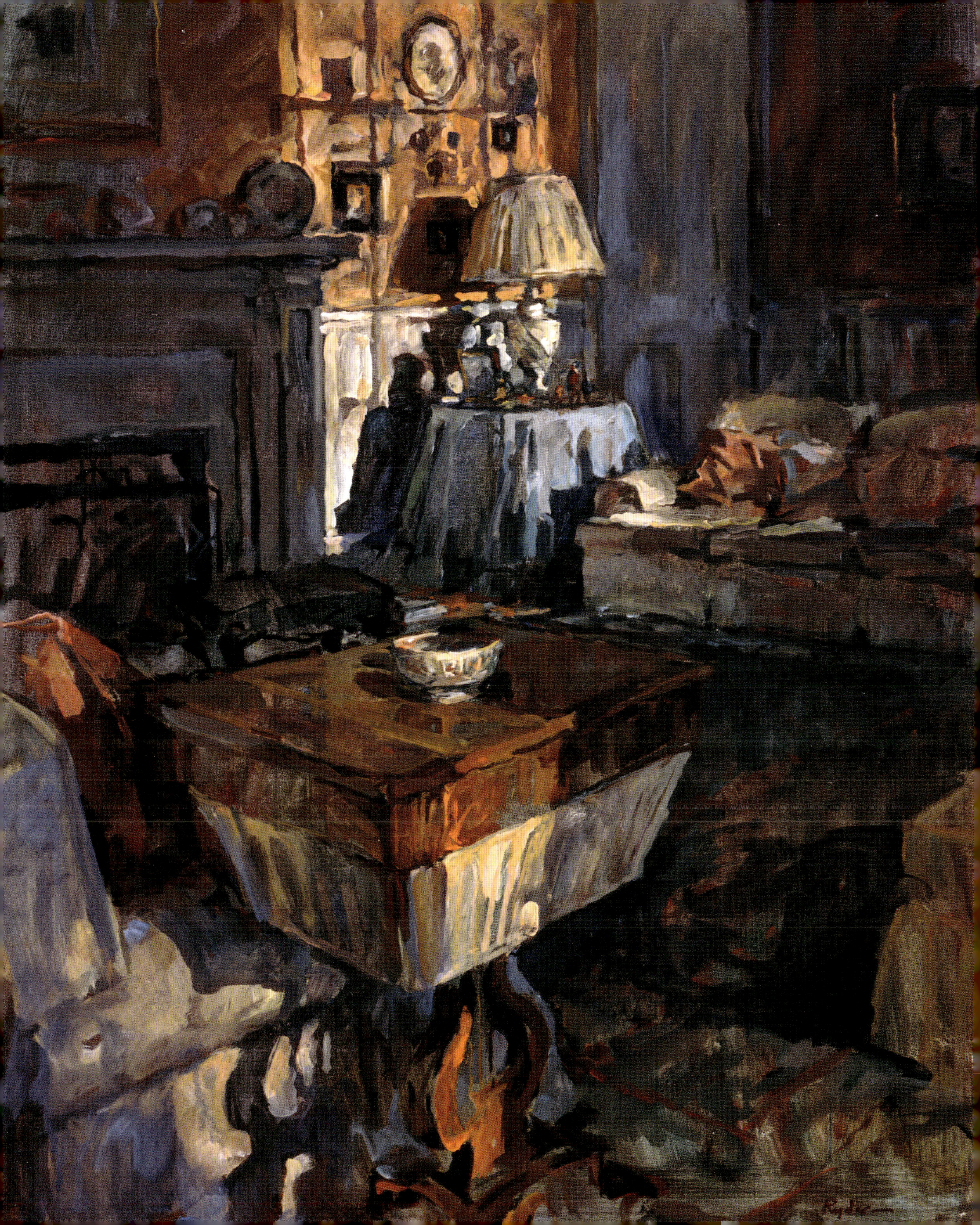

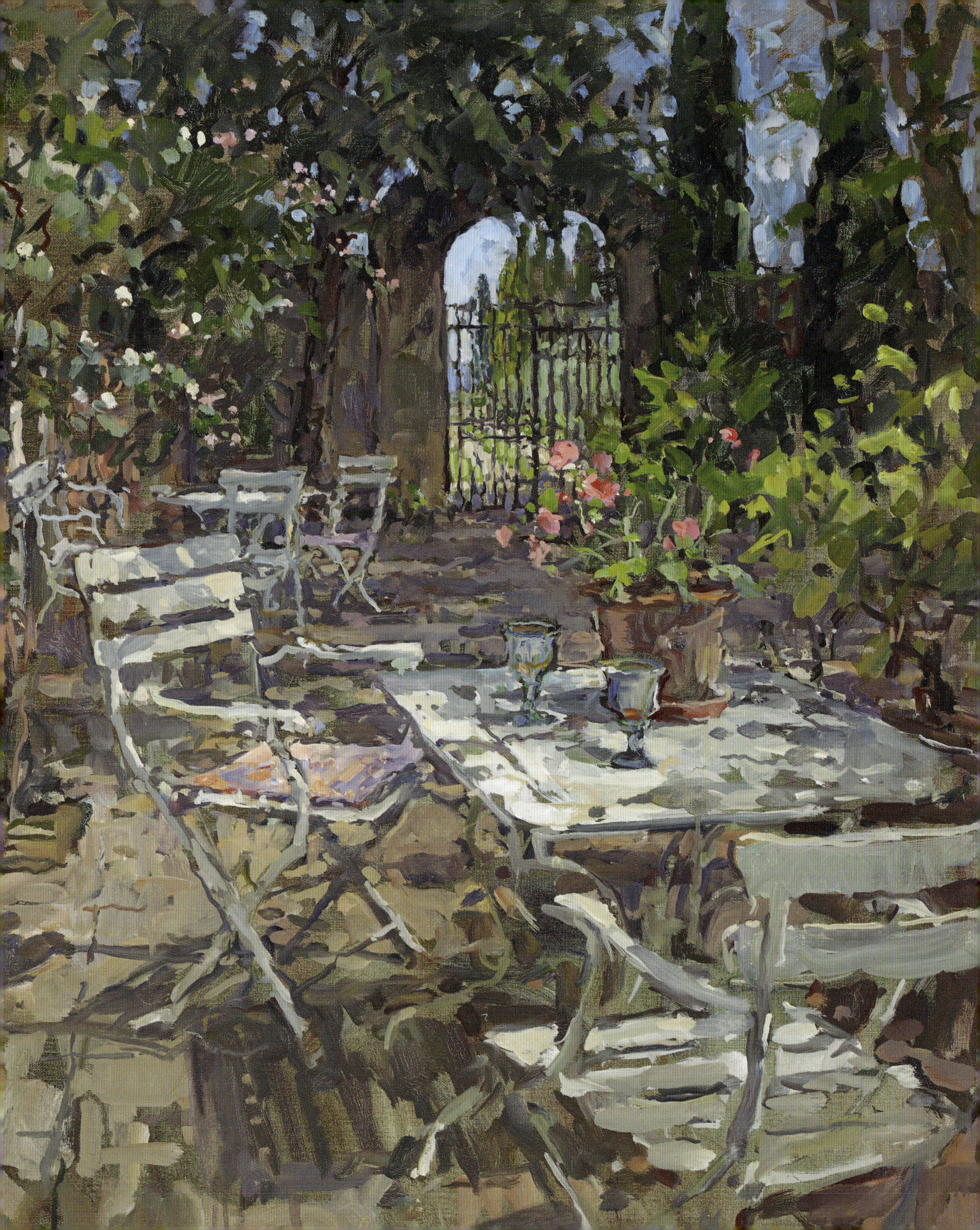

FACING PAGE

Terrace – Mas de la Rose, 30 × 26

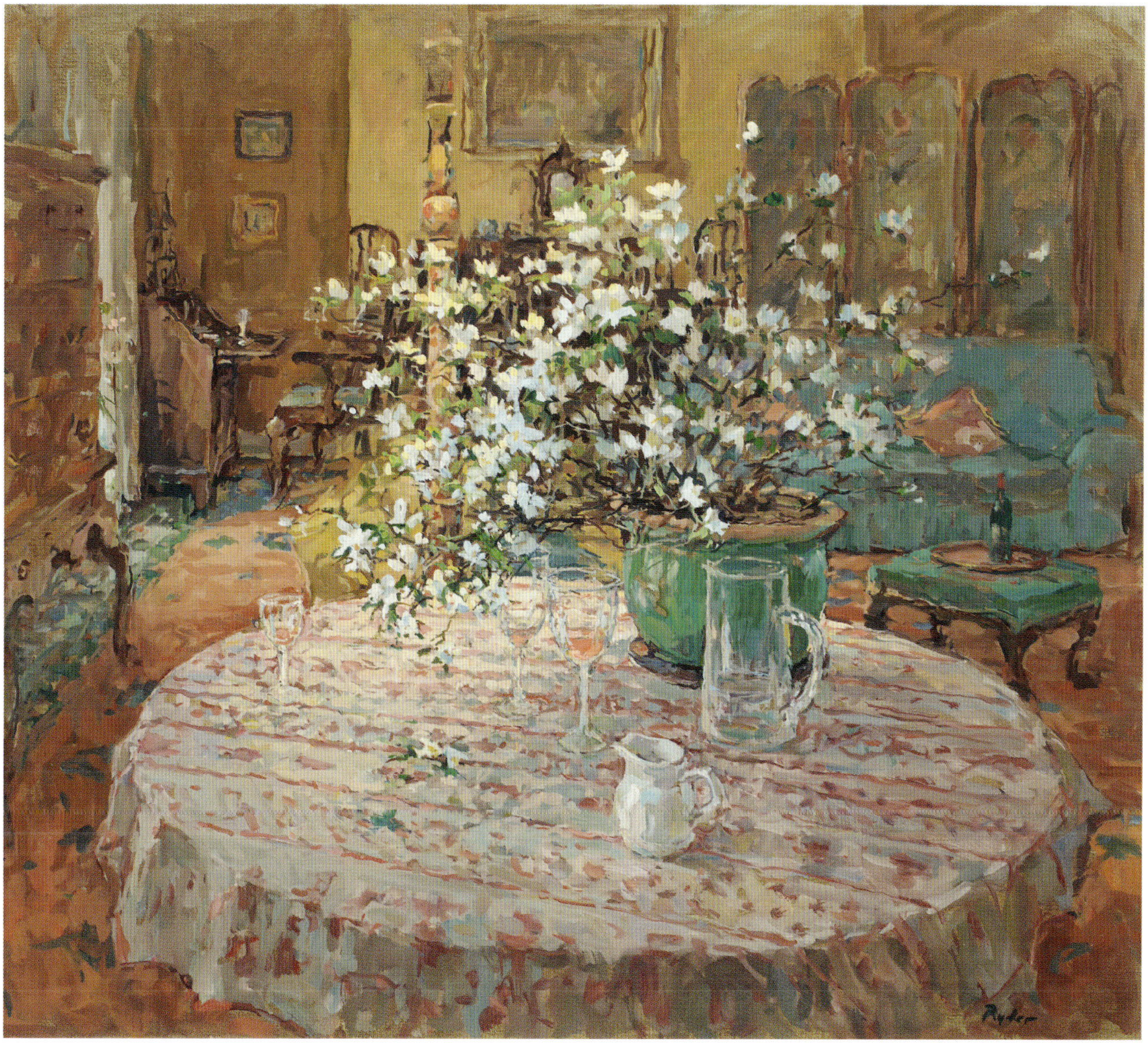

The Little White Jug, 36 × 40

ACKNOWLEDGEMENTS

Firstly, I would like to thank Unicorn Publishers, who contacted me about writing this book and, in particular, Ryan Gearing, Millicent Kenworthy Green and Philip Lewis, the talented designer of this book.

Thank you to Alex Leith who came to visit me several times in the Scottish Borders before writing so accurately about me.

I am grateful to the many galleries that have exhibited my work; the Haste Gallery Ipswich, Peter Keyser, Brian Sinfield, Richard Hagen, Bill Patterson, James Kayll, The Ackermann Gallery, Manya Igel, Sarah Samuels and over many years the incredibly supportive Panter & Hall Gallery who have looked after me through many years and solo shows.

Art Societies include the New English Art Club, with special support from Bernard Dunstan and Tom Coates. The Royal Society of Portrait Painters with thanks to George Bruce and Andrew Festing, and the Society of Women Artists. These societies, all exhibiting at the Mall Galleries with Annabel Elton, John Destin and Alistair Redgrift being hugely helpful.

On the technical side, photographers Kelvin Freeman and Alastair Innes; Steve and Clare Lester, web designers at elimelight; Daryl Laidlaw, my IT guru; Kelvin Lawrence, my accountant; Bird and Davis, art supplies; Picture Post for such safe delivery of my paintings, and my framers Andy Kinloch and for the last forty years Christina Leder.

A huge thank you to the kind friends who had me to stay and painting their inspiring interiors and exteriors in France, Italy, Spain and Great Britain. These include: Robert and Kyrie Stone, Johnny and Sarah Townsend, Isla and Julian Baring, Neil and Annabel Sebag Montefiore, Rob and Miranda Smyly, Lars and Eva Ahrell, Nick and Ana Livingston, Patrick and Lavinia de Pelet, Richard and Rosamund Bernays, Michael and Joan Blake, Alexander and Julia Trotter, Charles and Mary Ramsay, Humphry and Katherine Wakefield, Adrian Palmer, Rose and Anthony Foyle, Bunny and Rossie Maitland Carew and many others.

I am indebted to the many people who have commissioned portraits and bought my work. These include His Majesty the King, Sir Oliver Millar, The RAC, Anthony and Nicky Clifton-Brown, Peter and Sally Sutcliffe, Peter and Clodagh Bonham Carter, Richard Morgan, Sophie Tulloch, Jeremy and Liz Bates, Lisle and Olivia Ryder, Sandra and Damon de Laszlo, Nigel and Anna McNair Scott, Hugh Poole Warren, Tim and Christina Chamberlain, William and Anne Steele, and of course many more, some sadly no longer with us.

I am grateful for support at home from Betty Dunnett, Mr and Mrs Grey, and for the last thirty years, Sue and Chris Hewiit.

Finally, thank you to my parents Robert and Hilaré Ryder, my son Oliver Bates and his wife Annabel, my daughter Susannah and her husband Robin Gurdon and especially my granddaughter, Phoebe Bates, who persuaded me to let this book be written, and most important of all my husband, Martin Bates, whose encouragement and lack of criticism has kept me going over nearly sixty years.

Published in 2024 by Unicorn
an imprint of Unicorn Publishing Group
Charleston Studio, Meadow Business Centre,
Lewes BN8 5RW
www.unicornpublishing.org

ISBN 978-1-916846-23-4

10 9 8 7 6 5 4 3 2 1

Book design by Philip Lewis

Printed in Latvia by FineTone Ltd